COMMUNITY WATER, COMMUNITY MANAGEMENT

From System to Service in Rural Areas

TON SCHOUTEN and PATRICK MORIARTY

ITDG
PUBLISHING

Published by ITDG Publishing
103–105 Southampton Row, London WC1B 4HL, UK
www.itdgpublishing.org.uk

© IRC International Water and Sanitation Centre 2003

First published in 2003

ISBN 1 85339 564 1

A catalogue record for this book is available from the British Library.

ITDG Publishing is the publishing arm of the Intermediate Technology
Development Group. Our mission is to build the skills and capacity of
people in developing countries through the dissemination of information in
all forms, enabling them to improve the quality of their lives and that of
future generations.

Cover photograph: People gathered round an open well
in the north of Ouagadougou, Burkina Faso. Drs J.M.G. van Damme.
Copyright IRC International Water and Sanitation Centre.

Typeset by FiSH Books, London
Printed in Great Britain by Antony Rowe Limited, Wiltshire

COMMUNITY WATER,
COMMUNITY MANAGEMENT

Books are to be re
the

Contents

Contents

Contents

Preface

THIS IS A BOOK about community management of rural water supply. It is about people in rural communities struggling to make their taps and pumps deliver the safe water that is so crucial for healthy and productive lives. Through their eyes we look at the daily realities of managing a water supply system. Their stories concern not only problems with pumps, pipes and taps, but, most importantly, the social problems that have wrung so many systems dry: the struggle to find shared solutions, the problems of enforcing rules, overcoming conflict or just plain fraud. This book emerges from a clear sympathy for the people in these communities who try their best to manage their water supplies, and from a respect for their struggle. The stories are not only about the problems – they are also about the creative solutions that people can find, and how they can overcome problems when they get the right support at the right time. In fact, although the stories are about communities, the lessons are about the way in which support agencies and institutions need to change their approaches to become more relevant to the challenges.

Rural communities play the key role in water provision. That is why this book says that governments, donors and 'experts' have a responsibility to support communities, beyond helping them to install a system and then leaving them with the sole responsibly for managing it.

It will take a long time to settle sustainable and effective water management into rural communities, to secure water supply not for the lifetime of a system but for the lifetime of a community; and not for a happy few but for all. It can be done only if every stakeholder takes up his or her responsibility and the tasks for which each is best equipped. But it can be done and it must be done. We propose changes and a way forward. We do not present blueprints, because our examination of community management has taught us that appropriate models for rural water supply must be found in national and local contexts, with the involvement of all stakeholders. We do identify a number of critical factors that need to be taken into account, regardless of local specificities, and provide a framework for looking at these factors in a structured manner.

The International Water and Sanitation Centre (IRC) has been working and reporting on the community management concept since the early 1980s. One of IRC's biggest projects was the Participatory Action Research (PAR) project, which started in 1994 and entailed work in 22 communities in six different countries. The major aim was to improve methods of strengthening the capacities of rural communities to manage their own water supply systems. The research phase of the project ended in 1998 and yielded a wide range of experiences and stories about the reality of community management. These experiences are at the heart of this book as people from 22 different communities in different geographical, socio-economic and cultural settings report on their efforts to operate and maintain their water supply systems. Their stories are supplemented with reports from the PAR research teams in the six countries, who implemented the PAR approach in the communities and worked closely with those communities for more than four years.

The central message is founded on real-life experience across a number of different countries in different parts of the world, reflecting a variety of cultural and political settings. These experiences suggest that changes have to be made in the way that national and local government relates to community management issues, in the way that external support agencies (ESAs) and non-governmental organizations (NGOs) think and act, and in the way that engineers and social scientists set about their work.

These then are our audiences: anyone who intervenes, or plans to intervene, or wants to learn about intervening in the interface between communities and support organizations. The detailed case studies should be of interest to academics and practitioners alike, since they combine the flavour of genuine human interaction with the necessary analysis and distance to gain a deeper understanding of the issues, problems and solutions. The book should, of course, be read by those who will manage water schemes or agencies connected with water schemes. They will find much about what can go wrong with choosing technology, pricing a water system, planning for future expansion and dealing with conflict. They will also learn how others have overcome some of these problems. The book will be useful to all those who are studying in this area, since it will walk them through the many aspects of community-managed rural water supplies that do not usually get a mention. It will also be of use to sector professionals who are looking for a framework for discussion about the difficult issues they encounter in their work.

It should be required reading for staff in funding agencies, NGOs and bilateral organizations, since they are going to step into these situations and should know where many predecessors fell off the track and disappeared, and how others made it safely to the other side. For these and others we hope that this book is a reality check. We hope that it will be read by policy makers and that, having read it, they will cease to regard capacity building as a one-off activity, and community support as a time-bound project. Engineers will not find within these pages anything new about how to lay pipes or sink wells. They will, however, find a wealth of information about how the people interact with their pipes and wells, and this is information that is useful for them to know. They, like us, might wonder how anyone can install a water system for which spares are not available, or which is too complex for those who live with the system to maintain, let alone repair. This book should also hit the mark with those who are interested in general management since it deals with issues like leadership, gender differences and conflict that can arise in many different circumstances.

Finally, we hope that the book will be read and used as a tool by those who believe that people across the world, in rural areas as well as in cities, should be able to access clean water.

Many people contributed to this book. First of all we want to thank the people in the 22 communities who participated in the PAR research project on which this book is built. Then, of course, the research teams of IRC's partner organizations that executed the PAR project: Ms Pauline Ikumi, Mr Isaack Oenga, Mr Vincent Njuguna and Mr Stephen Ngingi of NETWAS in Kenya; the late Mr Amouye Nguettakan, Mr Andrew Tayong and Ms Christine Poubom of PAID-WA and WSMC in Cameroon; Mr Raju Khadka, Ms Hari Subba, Mr Rajan Thappa, Ms Renuka Rai and Ms Laxmi Paudyal of NEWAH in Nepal; Ms Dilferoze, Mr Altaf Hussain, Mr Muhammed Saleem, Ms Nahida Aziz, Dr Tameez Ahmad and Mr Haider Raza of WASEP in Pakistan; Ms Cecilia Gomez, Mr Alfonso Rojas, Ms Ana Ariztizabál, Mr Mario Pérez, Ms Mariela Garcia, Mr Johnny Rojas and Mr Jairo Benavides of CINARA in Colombia; and Mr Jaime Pacajoj Cifuentes, Mr Fabián Gonón Ortiz, Mr Carlos Simón Perén, Mr Oscar Nimatuj and Ms Milagro Escobar of Agua del Pueblo and SER in Guatemala. They made intimate bonds with the people in the communities and worked with them to improve the management of their water supplies, and they documented these experiences. A large part of this book is based on their documents and reports. Without their observations, investigations and reporting this book could never have been written.

IRC research associate Carolien van der Voorden spent a year collecting relevant information on the subject of community management of rural water supply. This provided us with a detailed overview of how community management is made operational in policies and projects worldwide. This overview helped us to strengthen the messages of this book.

We also want to thank the IRC staff members who participated in the PAR project over the seven years of its duration. In the first place Eveline Bolt, who remained loyal to the project for the full seven years and gave us the resources and confidence to enjoy writing this book. Catarina Fonseca and Peter Bury were project team members in the last phase of the PAR project, while former IRC staff members Nora Espejo and Marc Lammerink provided major inputs in the first years of the project. We gratefully used their documents, reports and articles to write this book.

Jon Lane and Sue Coates reviewed the book, Jon at a very early and virtually unreadable stage. Their valuable comments helped us to improve the book. Peter McIntyre, from Oxford, edited the text and guided us through the final stages.

The government of the Netherlands financed the PAR project and we thank it for its continued support.

Figures, tables and maps

Figures

Tables

Maps

Boxes

Acronyms

ADB	Asian Development Bank
Approtech Asia	Asian Alliance of Appropriate Technology Practitioners
CARE	Cooperative for Assistance and Relief Everywhere, Inc.
CBO	Community-based organization
CIUDAD	CIUDAD Centro de investigaciones
CRT	Community Research Team
DED	Deutsche Entwicklungsdienst
DFID	Department for International Development (UK)
DGIS	Directorate-General for International Co-operation (Netherlands)
DRA	Demand Responsive Approach
ESA	External Support Agency
Finnida	Department for International Cooperation Finnida
GWP	Global Water Partnership
Helvetas	Swiss Development Agency
HIPC	Highly Indebted Poor Country
IAG	International Advisory Group
IAP	Iguaçu Action Programme
IDWSSD	International Drinking Water Supply and Sanitation Decade
IMF	International Monetary Fund
IRC	International Water and Sanitation Centre
ISW	International Secretariat for Water
KfW	Kreditanstalt für Wiederaufbau
MANAGE	MANAGE Dissemination Project of IRC
NGO	Non-governmental organization
NRG	National Reference Group
O & M	Operation and Maintenance
PAR	Participatory Action Research
PRA	Participatory Rapid Appraisal
UNCHS-Habitat	United Nations Centre for Human Settlements
UNICEF	United Nations Children's Fund
UNDP	United Nations Development Program
WASH	Water, Sanitation and Hygiene Programme of the WSSCC
WASHE	Water, Sanitation and Hygiene Education
WHO	World Health Organization
WSP	Water and Sanitation Program
WSSCC	Water Supply and Sanitation Collaborative Council

Kenya

KFWWSP	Kenya Finland Western Water Supply Programme
NETWAS	Network for Water and Sanitation
RDWSP	Rural Domestic Water Supply Program

Guatemala

ADP	*Agua del Pueblo*
APAGUA	*Asociación de Proyectos de Agua para Aguacatán*
INFOM	*Instituto de Fomento Municipal* – Institute of Municipal Public Works
SER	*Servicios para el Desarrollo*
UNEPAR	*Unidad Ejecutora del Programa de Agua Rural*
URNG	*Unidad Revolucionaria Nacional Guatemalteca*

Pakistan

AKF	Aga Khan Foundation
AKPBS	Aga Khan Planning and Building Service
AKRSP	Aga Khan Rural Support Programme
LBRDD	Local Bodies and Rural Development Department
SAP	Social Action Programme
VO	Village Organization
WASEP	Water and Sanitation Extension Programme
WO	Women's Organization
WSHHSP	Water, Sanitation, Hygiene and Health Studies Project

Cameroon

CD	Community Development, Department of the Ministry of Agriculture
MINMEE	*Ministère des Mines de l'Eau et de l'Energie* – Ministry of Mines, Water and Energy
PAID – WA	Pan African Institute for Development – West Africa
SATA	Swiss Association for Technical Assistance
VDA	Village Development Association
WSMC	Water and Sanitation Management Consultants

Colombia

CINARA	*Instituto de Investigación y Desarrollo en Agua Potable Saneamiento Básico y Conservación del Recurso Hídrico*
JAC	*Junta de Acción Comunal*

Nepal

DDC	District Development Committee
DWSO	District Water Supply Office
DWSS	Department of Water Supply and Sewerage

LRWSSP	Lumbani Rural Water Supply and Sanitation Project
MHPP	Ministry of Housing and Physical Planning
NEWAH	Nepal Water for Health
NRCS	Nepal Red Cross Society
PMC	Project Management and Maintenance Committee
VDC	Village Development Committee
WUC	Water User Committee

South Africa

DWAF	Department of Water Affairs and Forestry SA
EDC	Eastern District Council
PSC	Project Steering Committee
RDP	Reconstruction and Development Programme
TLC	Transitional Local Council
VWC	Village Water Committee

Introduction

COMMUNITY MANAGEMENT has become the leading concept for implementing water supply systems in rural areas in developing countries. It is seen as an answer to the large-scale break down of water supply systems and the failure of governments either to provide clean water themselves, or to devise a system where other agencies supply it reliably and consistently. The idea that communities should operate and maintain their own water supply systems came partly from an erosion of belief in the ability of central governments to supply services for their populations, and partly from the belief that communities have the skills and motivation to meet their own essential needs. Many different methods have been used, and are still being used, to strengthen the capacities of communities to manage their own water supply systems. Demand-responsive approaches, different participatory methods, training and capacity building all aim at increasing responsibility and capacities in the community. It has been assumed that, once a new water system had been installed in a rural community, success or failure in sustaining it would be determined by factors within the community, such as the level of skills, the quality of the leadership and the willingness of community members to pay for water.

Now, after more than two decades of applying the concept, it is time to look back and consider the opportunities and constraints of community management in bringing water to the millions of people in need of it. Is community management the right way to increase both the sustainability of water supply systems and the coverage of safe and reliable water supply in rural areas? There is increasing evidence that community management has been no more successful in delivering a sustainable water supply than any other approach.

Since the early 1980s IRC has followed the application of community management in the field. It has been involved in advisory work, programmes, training and workshops in many different countries. One of the main projects in the field of community management was the Participatory Action Research (PAR) project. It involved research in 22 communities in six different countries and has collected an unprecedented wealth of material about what happens in a community when it tries to improve its water supply. The major part of this book is built on that material. The material is mainly presented in the words of the community people themselves. We believe that others who have been involved in work to strengthen community management will recognize the truthfulness of these accounts. They are written with a clear sympathy for the people in the communities and the project staff working with them.

A few crucial issues of understanding and definition need to be clarified, including what we mean by community management, by sustainable water supply and by a community.

1

When we started working with these experiences we took the straightforward view that community management meant that communities took on the full range of management tasks related to maintaining (and in some cases developing) a domestic water supply. These tasks include setting tariffs and collecting payments, carrying out routine maintenance, and making decisions about system extension. By the end of our work, based on the range of models practised in the PAR project, we had developed a narrower, but we believe a more precise view.

We think that, for the further development of community management as a valid management option for rural water supply, it is crucial to distinguish between strategic decisions about how a service is developed, and the nuts and bolts of day-to-day operational issues. We believe that the core of community management is the former. It is about communities making strategic decisions: what level of service they want, how they want to pay for it, where they want it. The community may also be involved in the day-to-day operation and maintenance, in collecting money from users and in buying spare parts – but they do not have to be. They may choose to hire a professional to do this for them. Community management is about power and control. Supporting community management is about empowering and giving control.

In this book we talk a lot about sustainable water supply, so let us identify what we believe this to be:

- that the 'water supply system' is sustainable, technically and institutionally and indefinitely – most importantly that eventual replacement or expansion of the system can be delivered within the existing framework, and that the system can adjust to changing demand
- that a successful community water supply carries with it an implicit assumption of equity. A system that reliably and sustainably meets the needs of 80 per cent of the population while leaving the poorest 20 per cent unserved cannot be counted a success
- that the resource is sustainable – that is, that the system does not fail at any time due to failure of the water resource – e.g. due to drought, excessive water table draw-down, streams drying up, etc.

We realize that in most situations 'indefinite sustainability' seems like a tall order. Yet that is what we demand for ourselves (assuming we are part of the happy group of people for whom water is a utility – something we don't notice until it stops working). We do not expect our water supply to work well for five years, then intermittently for five years, then sporadically for five years, and then not at all while we try to identify a new donor to come up with the capital investment to renew or expand the system.

Systems inevitably get to a stage where major renovation is necessary. With many 'appropriate' technologies such as handpumps this can happen in five to ten years. A system that a community maintains by carrying out minor repairs over a five-year period, but that fails when it is time to replace the entire pump rather than a few nuts, is not sustainable. We do not say that the community must take responsibility for eventual replacement, but someone must. We do not believe that it is acceptable to talk about a sustainable water supply if it is not clear where the responsibility for eventual replacement of the system lies. If a village grows rapidly then it may need a new system. We do not expect the old system to continue if it cannot cope with the demand, but we do expect the over-all management system to continue to deliver a service as it evolves to meet the new demand. As such, we set sustainability as an exacting benchmark rather than as a 'feel good' adjective.

In this book we also look closely at what we mean by a community. As soon as we begin to look, it becomes apparent that people who live in close proximity to each other do not necessarily have the same interests, the same levels of power and control, or the same obligations. Men and women have different levels of responsibility and different tasks. They may have very different attitudes as to the value of a water source close to home. They probably also have different degrees of influence over decisions. Gender differences are one major fault line through many communities. There are also differences in wealth, different interests in water between those who want their cattle to drink, those who want to water their crops, and those who simply want water for the home. Within communities there are powerful people and powerless people. There may be differences in the quality of leadership, and different kinds of leaders. Some communities have forms of democratic control over those who take decisions. Others have traditional power structures. The power relationships may be very subtle and not obvious to outsiders. Sometimes it even appears as if the people living in one place constitute two communities rather than one. Clearly this makes questions about community management especially complex, and the answers must take account of differences in power and influence.

The demand for community management of water supply did not emerge out of nowhere. The phrase has been around for more than 30 years, and in the mid-1980s was identified as one of six prerequisites for improved water and sanitation. The 1980s – the International Drinking Water Supply and Sanitation Decade – expanded services but ended with the job half done, and sustainability still a distant dream. After such a huge effort, there seemed to be little point in just agitating for more of the same. A series of landmark meetings following the end of the Decade brought forward a number of new ideas which were rapidly adopted and became a kind of new orthodoxy. In New Delhi in 1990 community management was endorsed for the first time in a set of guiding principles (UNDP 1990). The Dublin Statement on Water and Sustainable Development (ICWE 1992), put forward a set of principles that included a participatory approach, the central role of women, and the need to recognize water in all its competing uses as an economic good.

Out of this movement grew the idea of management at the lowest appropriate level – the community – a gender approach based on a recognition that women use water differently to men, and a movement towards seeing cost recovery and willingness to pay for water as a benchmark for measuring demand. These approaches led to creative thinking about how they should be applied. And, of course, they were also hijacked and used in an unthinking way. To some extent 'community management' became a mantra for those who were dispensing with their own responsibilities. Such a major change should have involved a focus on the structural, organizational and institutional implications. This did not happen, although much attention was paid to 'capacity building' in the community. It is this approach that this book seeks to expose and reverse.

Indeed, the experiences of communities in the PAR project made us realize that, to increase the sustainability of rural water supplies and increase coverage, we have to look beyond the community and throw out a challenge about the institutional support. Our conclusion is that communities cannot alone bear the full responsibility for managing their water supplies. Community management cannot mean that, following the installation of a system, outside agencies drive off into the sunset and everyone lives happily ever after. Indeed, a comprehensive and effective framework for institutional support is needed if we want to keep the systems working after 'handing over'. That is the theme of this book.

We call this theme our 'red thread'. It is a thread because it is woven through the stories of the communities, highlighting where and what institutional support is needed. The thread connects the lessons that communities have learned across the world and, although at times it may seem to disappear beneath the focus on community responsibility, it will emerge as both a warning and a guide. The thread is a guide because if we follow it carefully we shall reach the end of our journey and some inescapable conclusions. It is red because it is a warning. The warning is that if we continue to pursue 'community management' without addressing the support needs of communities this will become another muddy pool, another false trail in the story of global failure to resolve the problem of millions of people who lack access to clean water.

This is a wake-up call for decision makers, donors and external support agencies to take their share of responsibility, and to support communities in their efforts to maintain the systems that have been handed over to them. They cannot do it alone. Community efforts and skills are indeed crucial, but their capacities and motivation need to be supplemented with the capacities and mandates of governments, agencies, NGOs and the private sector. Together, they can create a rural water supply service in which each stakeholder takes its share of responsibility, in an institutional framework that addresses all the functions needed to provide water to rural people, including policy making, regulation, legislation, financing, support, operation and maintenance.

This book gives limited answers as to how to create such a support structure but in the last chapter we present some guiding principles. A lot of discussion and research is needed to agree on the most effective models for support. This is a complex matter because it should move beyond community management and address wider issues of sector reform, private sector involvement, donor policies and the role of government. If we can play a role in shifting the focus of the debate to give equal emphasis to continuing support for communities as to building community capacities, then we are confident that the discussion will be better focused and enriched and will lead to better practice and better results.

Our message is also directed to the communities themselves. Because we have respect for their efforts and struggles, they should not be left with a sense of failure because, by themselves, they cannot indefinitely sustain water systems. Our message to communities is that it is not you who have failed, but the support mechanisms that have failed you. This does not mean that communities should give up trying, but that they have a right, and perhaps a duty, to demand support from the institutions that should be there to help them.

Not least, this message applies to those that sponsor a project approach to water issues, whereby the community has to conform to the parameters of the project and the project is 'over' when the sponsor's budget line comes to an end.

Community management stands at an important threshold in its development as a management model. Until recently it was largely confined to pilots, academic research and NGO projects but it is now being taken up by a number of countries as *the* approach for providing rural water services. Ghana, Uganda, Zambia, South Africa and most recently India have all begun large-scale experiments in implementing community management at a national or regional scale.

The urgency of this change in approach is underlined by the ambitions of the water and sanitation sector, which are focused not on executing an interesting pilot project here or there but on making a difference to millions of neglected people. These ambitions are expressed as Vision 21 – a shared vision for hygiene, sanitation and water supply which has won commitment from the sector and which sets out the challenges in uncompromising terms (WSSCC 2000a).

What key messages will help to realize the aims of Vision 21? First, that communities can do a great deal to make water supply systems function. But, second, that communities cannot do it on their own. Sooner or later community management that is left to operate in a vacuum breaks down. The fragile management constructs left in place after implementation break under the strain. Community management requires outside support: troubleshooting, backstopping, facilitating and enabling. This support is essential to ensure sustainability, and is equally necessary to increase coverage.

If this book deals mainly with water supply, rather than with sanitation, that is not because sanitation is less important. Indeed, the two issues are inextricably linked as pressures of population increase the risk of polluting traditional water supplies and shallow wells. However, the PAR project focused mainly on water supply, not on sanitation, and the experiences in the communities were directed at improving water supplies, although, as you will read, there are some experiences described here that include both water and sanitation. It is gratifying that one of the major successes of the World Summit on Sustainable Development in Johannesburg in September 2002 was to give clean water and hygienic sanitation equal status in a commitment to halve the proportion of people without access to both by 2015.

The essence of Vision 21

'... a Vision is offered of a clean and healthy world in which every person has safe and adequate water and sanitation, and lives in a hygienic environment.'

The four decisive components, which determine the VISION 21 approach, are

- **Building on people's energy and creativity at all levels**
  requiring empowerment and building the capacity of people in households and communities to take action, and applying technologies that respond to actual needs
- **Holistic approach**
  acknowledging hygiene, water and sanitation as a human right, and relating it to human development, the elimination of poverty, environmental sustainability and the integrated management of water resources
- **Committed and compassionate leadership and good governance**
  changing long-accustomed roles, leading to new responsibilities of authorities and institutions to support households and communities in the management of their hygiene, water and sanitation and being accountable to users as clients
- **Synergy amongst all partners**
  encouraging shared commitment amongst users, politicians and professionals; requiring professionals within the water and sanitation sector to combine technical expertise with an ability to work with users and politicians and with the health, education, environment, community development and food sectors

WSSCC, 2000a

How this book is structured

THIS BOOK is divided into three parts, each further divided into chapters on a particular theme.

Part 1 describes how community management became the leading paradigm for the implementation of rural water supply systems. It looks at how the major conferences and international declarations and programmes came to promote community management as the way forward to increase water supply coverage. It describes the background and objectives of the PAR project from which the experiences with community management in this book are drawn. Part 1 concludes with some basic information about the 22 communities and the countries in which they are located.

Part 2 reports on the experiences of communities in managing their water supply systems. It addresses the most important aspects of community management and presents community experiences gathered around these topics. Chapters 4–6 deal with community dynamics, social and cultural relationships and with the patterns of power and decision making in communities that impact on community management of water supply systems. Chapters 7 and 8 look at instruments and techniques of management and at management capacities. Chapter 9 addresses cost recovery and transparent decision making. Chapter 10 looks at system design and source protection. Chapter 11 takes a look at the enabling environment, including legislation, policies and the capacity of support agencies. Part 2 concludes by analysing why communities have such difficulties in keeping their systems working. It points to the mismatch between rural communities and the water projects they are offered.

Part 3 addresses the question of how to move forward, once we accept that institutional support is needed, to sustainable rural water supply in which communities have a role. It describes the main elements that such institutional support must address, and broadly identifies which stakeholders should be involved. Chapter 13 maps the key factors in community management, and the need to balance the complexity of a system with management capacities. It looks at the factors within a community. Chapter 14 looks at factors outside the community that make or break the ability to sustain a system over time. It provides the outlines of the design of an institutional support model. It looks into wider trends in development co-operation, the changing role of the state, policies of donors, trends in the water sector and changes in scientific thinking. We conclude this section with an appeal for increased capacity building focused on the levels of institutional support above the level of the community.

The book ends with a call for action from donors, governments of developing countries and, to a lesser extent, NGOs to stop treating community management as the last management option, but rather to accept it as a logical and appropriate model for a given set of circumstances. It calls on key actors systematically to address institutional development and capacity building to create the enabling environment in which community management can take place.

PART 1
SETTING THE SCENE

Community management, the project,

countries and communities

PART 1 LOOKS at the concept of community management, where it comes from, why and by whom it was initiated and how it developed over three to four decades. It shows that community management surfaced in the 1970s and 1980s but came to fruition only recently. It started with a project approach, mostly through international NGOs, but the emergent role of rural communities in managing rural water supply was soon taken up in the policy texts of national governments. Only in the past decade have some governments started to translate their policies into legislation, institutional frameworks and rules and regulations for community-managed water supply systems.

This part also describes the Participatory Action Research (PAR) project on whose outcomes large parts of this book are built. The PAR methodology is briefly presented as well as the way it was applied in the communities that participated in the project. Short descriptions of the organizations that executed the project conclude this section.

Part 1 finally presents the countries and the communities in which the project was implemented. It looks at who the communities are, their main characteristics and the main problems with their water supply at the start of the project. There is a fair amount of detail in this chapter, but it will help to ground the reader for the experiences that are described in Part 2. It is worth noting here the variety of different communities, and the different water problems that they have to overcome. As will be seen later, there is a surprising amount of similarity in the way that these problems manifest themselves in the different communities, and in the ways that people try to overcome problems. The communities are completely independent of each other, but their collective experiences suggest that it is possible to draw common conclusions.

CHAPTER 1

A brief history of community management of rural water supply

COMMUNITY MANAGEMENT of rural[1] water supply and sanitation schemes is now entering its second decade as a key paradigm for water supply development and management. While this book will deal mainly with the current state of community management and the future challenges, it is worth looking briefly at the history of community management and its precursors in the rural water supply sector.

Community management approaches did not appear spontaneously, nor do they exist in a vacuum. They emerged from a long history of trial and error in the rural water supply sector, and are linked to and affected by developments in many other sectors, particularly those related to more general rural development, but also natural resource management and, specifically, water resources management.

The rural water supply and sanitation sector gradually emerged in the two decades prior to the 1980s International Drinking Water Supply and Sanitation Decade (IDWSSD). It developed in reaction to the struggles of post-colonial states to extend the benefits of 'modern' infrastructure to their rapidly expanding populations. In the view of many of these states, rural water supply was the responsibility of the national state.

If a single starting point for the more recent development of the sector is sought, it should be the 1977 Mar del Plata conference which set the groundwork for the IDWSSD. The Decade put the emphasis on community *involvement* in rural water and sanitation programmes. Community *management* came into being only during the IDWSSD, when the problems with existing, state and supply-driven management paradigms came to the surface. One of the main arguments of this book is that it is only now, at the start of the twenty-first century, that community management is ready to grow up from being an interesting pilot approach to become a paradigm for rural water supply throughout the world.

Pre-1980s – early days – the first steps towards involving communities

The earliest documented experiences of community involvement in water supply projects date from the late 1960s. The first use of the 'community participation'

---

1 While community management approaches are not limited exclusively to rural areas, this is where they are most commonly used, and represent the main focus of this book.

keyword in IRC's library database (IRCDOC[2]) dates from 1967, and concerns an introduction to evaluative research (Suchman 1967). The first books in the IRC collection on community involvement in water supply projects came from Taiwan (1969) and Colombia (1975) (Chang 1969; Inpes-Bogotá 1975). The IRC was an early champion of community involvement, and in the late 1970s it produced the first of its many books on the subject. The first bibliography and literature review on participation and education in community water supply and sanitation were published in 1979 and 1981 (Wijk-Sijbesma 1979, 1981).

1980s – the International Drinking Water Supply and Sanitation Decade – community involvement

The community involvement paradigm was officially adopted by the international community during the 1977 World Water conference in Mar del Plata, Argentina. The conference adopted a declaration in which it announced the IDWSSD, the slogan of which was to be *Water and Sanitation for All*. The conference recognized that to come close to accomplishing this goal, a 'radical overhaul of precepts and investment strategies governing the proliferation of taps, pumps and pipes in the developing world' was required (Black 1998:4).

Such an overhaul was long overdue. The conventional water and sewerage systems, the only ones the international donors had to offer, were complex and affordable only to an elite minority, leaving a large majority of people without services of any kind. Public health experts and engineers had learnt from experience that poor people could only expect exclusion and marginalization from existing models of service delivery (Black 1998). 'The vast majority of those without water and sanitation services were poor, and the countries in which they lived were frequently water short and had little to spend on public infrastructure' (Black 1998:4). Therefore, if there was to be any substance to the Decade's slogan, entirely different, lower-cost approaches would have to be found, capable of extending services to poorer urban and rural areas; and governments and donors had to be persuaded to invest in them.

The new approach was found in concepts of self-reliance and community action that had begun to be popularized using the phrase 'small is beautiful' (Schumacher 1973). Small is beautiful was to become one of the key slogans of the water and sanitation sector. It came with a shift in focus to small NGO-led projects, in which users were encouraged to take an active role in terms of providing inputs, labour or cash for the development of simple, low-cost systems. This was the basis of the 'community participation' model that was to remain accepted practice for much of the rest of the Decade. The Decade also saw a massive expansion of donor investments in water supply and sanitation. These investments were mostly harnessed in projects and programmes. Both the community

---

2 IRCDOC is IRC's online documentation centre:
   www.irc.nl/products/documentation/ircdoc/search.html

participation model and the project approach meant a drive away from the supply-driven models that were the territory of the post-colonial states. However, these models of the IDWSSD remained small and scattered and did not begin to approach the scale necessary to address the Decade's ambitious goals.

In parallel with the water sector activities of the IDWSSD, awareness grew throughout the various fields of development co-operation of the need to involve communities or users at all stages of the project cycle. An important chronicler of this process was Robert Chambers. In a number of publications, he stressed the importance of 'putting the last first', and highlighted the dangers of allowing outsiders with their characteristic 'biases' to drive the development process. Rather he suggested a 'bottom up' development model in which the subjects of development themselves defined their needs, priorities and preferred developmental pathways (Chambers 1983).

By the early 1980s there were therefore three main drivers to community participation-based approaches.

- First, a new paradigm for development rooted in the concept that development should come from the roots of a society, instead of from the top.
- Second, there was a widely shared perception that many conventional water supply policies and programmes were failing to achieve their goals.
- Third, a vision that community participation could replace some of the loss of the state's implementation capacity brought about by the implementation of IMF-promoted Structural Adjustment Programmes (Brikké 2000).

Halfway through the IDWSSD, in 1987, the donor community assembled in the External Support Agency Collaborative Council, which officially identified community participation as one of the six basic prerequisites for improved performance of the water and sanitation sector (Appleton 1994). As a result, many projects started involving women and men in trench digging, system maintenance and water committees. However, it soon turned out that sustainable water and sanitation could not be achieved without involving people not just in the manual work, but also in the planning of programmes and the selection of technology.

It is perhaps not surprising, therefore, that it is around this time that the first references to 'community management' start to appear. Early examples include David Korten's monograph on community management in Asia (Korten 1986) and Parwoto's model for community-based management in Indonesia (Parwoto 1986). Later, in 1988, field studies in which community management played a major role emerged from Chile (Razeto 1988), Guatemala (Barrientos 1988), and Malawi (IRC 1988), while a year later experience emerged from Cameroon (Knecht 1989), sub-Saharan Africa (Andersen 1989), Ghana (GWSC 1989), Indonesia (Narayan-Parker 1989), and a WASH study (Roark et al. 1989). Experiences such as these were brought together in New Delhi in 1990 to mark the official birth of the community management paradigm.

The IDWSSD – a case of limited success

By the end of the Decade a total of US$73 891 million had been spent on expanding water supply, and by 1990 no region had achieved less than 73 per cent coverage of the population in urban areas (South East Asia) and less than 32 per cent coverage of the population in rural areas (Africa). Overall, this represented a significant increase in water supply service coverage: from 75 per cent in 1980 to 85 per cent in 1990. This was an enormous achievement; however, it also fell far short of attaining 'water and sanitation for all'. During the Decade it also became clear that many of the constructed water and sanitation systems broke down soon after implementation as a result of poor maintenance and management. Although coverage was increased, the sustainability was often questionable.

While missing by a wide margin its objective of water and sanitation for all, the Decade did trigger a number of activities and initiatives, which resulted in 1.2 billion more people worldwide having access to adequate and safe drinking water supply facilities, and 770 million more having access to sanitary facilities. In addition to this, a clear success of the Decade was in putting 'appropriate technology' firmly at the centre of rural water supply.

1990s – New Delhi – community management – Dublin and Rio

As the IDWSSD came to an end in 1990, a flurry of regional and global meetings sought to draw together the lessons of the Decade and to map out new directions for the water and sanitation sector in the 1990s. The resulting New Delhi Statement promoted the principle of 'Some for all rather than more for some', which set out the guiding principles as the basis of future sector work. For the first time at a global water conference, community management was endorsed in the guiding principles (UNDP 1990).

This was in part a reaction to the failures in upkeep and maintenance of the community participation schemes of the 1980s, and was supported intellectually on the 'last first' paradigm championed by Chambers et al. Put simply, the new paradigm said that communities should not just be involved in system inception, but should accept ultimate responsibility for and ownership of the entire life cycle of the system.

Other guiding principles adopted in New Delhi also have a bearing on community management. On institutional reforms, the New Delhi Statement promotes an integrated approach, including changes in procedures, attitudes and behaviour and the full participation of women at all levels in sector institutions. It also urges adoption of sound financial practices, where community management can also play an important role.

The emphasis on community management was strengthened in the Nordic Fresh Water Initiative in 1991, which called for water management responsibility to be devolved to the lowest possible level (Earth Summit 2002). The subject was further stressed in the Dublin Statement on Water and Sustainable Development in 1992 (ICWE 1992). The 500 participants at that meeting agreed that water development and management should be based on a partici-patory approach, involving users, planners and policy makers at all levels. They underlined that women play a central part in the provision, management and safeguarding of water, and suggested that in principle water should be recog-nized as an economic good.

At the Earth Summit[3] in Rio de Janeiro in June 1992, world leaders commit-ted themselves to a comprehensive programme to provide sustainable water supply and sanitation services to the hundreds of millions of the world's popu-lation who currently lack them. At the summit, all states and support agencies were urged to implement activities aiming for universal coverage outlined in Agenda 21, a strategy for sustainable development in the twenty-first century.

A guiding principle of Agenda 21 is: 'Community management of services, backed by measures to strengthen local institutions in implementing and sustain-ing water and sanitation programmes'. The activity list includes numerous measures to bring about effective community management – see box (Evans and Appleton 1993:7).

Agenda 21 activities linked to community management

- encouragement of water development and management based on a participatory approach, involving users, planners and policy makers at all levels
- application of the principle that decisions are to be taken at the lowest appropriate level, with public consultation and involvement of users in the planning and implementation of water projects
- support and assistance to communities in managing their own systems on a sustainable basis
- encouragement of the local population, especially women, youth, indigenous people and local communities in water management
- linkages between national plans and community management of local waters
- integration of community management within the context of overall planning

Evans and Appleton, 1993:7

To consolidate desk research and field studies, and to provide guidance in community management, IRC in collaboration with UNDP, UNICEF, WHO, the UNDP/World Bank Water and Sanitation Program and the Netherlands Directorate General for International Co-operation (DGIS) organized an inter-national workshop in November 1992 in The Hague, the Netherlands, with the theme 'The Role of Communities in the Management of Improved Water Supply Systems'. The workshop brought together experiences in community water

---

3 The United Nations Conference on Environment and Development (UNCED), Rio de Janeiro, Brazil, June 1992.

management from seven developing countries: Cameroon, Guatemala, Honduras, Indonesia, Pakistan, Uganda and Yemen. Participants from these countries presented case studies, which were reviewed together with a background paper and a review of experiences from 122 completed water supply projects prepared by the Water and Sanitation Program (WSP) (Evans and Appleton, 1993). This workshop was the prelude to the PAR project: participatory research to strengthen the capacities of communities to manage their water supplies. Some of the organizations taking part in the workshop would become IRC's partners in the PAR project.

The Third Global Forum of the Water Supply and Sanitation Collaborative Council (WSSCC) held in Barbados (November 1995) endorsed the creation of a WSSCC-sponsored Working Group on Community Management and Partnerships with Civil Society, led by the International Secretariat for Water (ISW). Regional co-ordinators were selected in Africa (NETWAS), Asia (Approtech Asia and NEWAH) and Latin America (CIUDAD). The aims of the working group were:

- to facilitate more harmonious interaction among governments and the various actors of civil society – private sector, non-governmental organizations (NGOs), community-based organizations (CBOs)
- to identify best practices of community management approaches
- to influence governments and external support agencies (ESAs[4]) to adopt these approaches, including involving the actors of civil societies in their planning processes (WSSCC 1996).

The working group presented a Code of Ethics on Community Management in Manila in 1997 (WSSCC 1997).

Members of this group also became involved in developing the Water for People Vision 21 that fed into the overall World Water Vision endorsed by the ministers at the ministerial conference in The Hague in March 2000. Vision 21 sets out the approaches that are needed to reach the goal of hygiene, sanitation and water for all by 2025. Vision 21 focuses on mobilizing people's own creativity and energy in developing solutions to improve their health and welfare. This people-centred approach builds on community management as its main vehicle (WSSCC 2000a).

During the 1980s and 1990s a variety of different actors, with very different agendas, signed up to the concepts of community management. Governments saw community involvement as a way of reducing demands on over-stretched resources. Donors saw an opportunity to focus and stretch development budgets towards effective implementation of water supply and sanitation facilities, and to

---

4 ESAs are organizations other than government or local NGOs that become directly involved in implementing water projects, or that support government or local NGOs in implementation. Working directly with communities, or at one step removed, they are often multilateral organizations, bilateral organizations or international NGOs.

bypass the problems posed by corrupt and inefficient governments. NGOs became the voice of the community and happily seized an opportunity to increase their role, becoming in many countries a parallel provider of services and, in that respect, a kind of parallel government. Finally, multilateral donors such as the World Bank saw community management as an ideal vehicle for their messages about reduced government involvement, and increased private sector and civil society roles. The World Bank, and later the Water and Sanitation Program (WSP) developed the Demand Responsive Approach (DRA), which is heavily geared towards putting community management approaches into effect (Sara and Katz 1997; World Bank 2002).

Community management had, therefore, clearly been accepted – albeit for a variety of different reasons – as a management concept. More and more examples of community management could be found around the world, and Uganda, Ghana, South Africa, India and Tanzania had all made community management a key concept in their national water policies and laws. However, as was highlighted in the Vision 21 report, the problems of lack of sustainability, inappropriate technologies, and failure to increase water and sanitation coverage all continued to be serious.

2000 and beyond

As we have seen, the first stirrings of what was to become community management can be seen as far back as the 1960s, yet, in 2001 'a supply-side approach, in combination with weak and fragmented institutional structures, still prevails in many countries, as water-related services are extended to promote public health and food production', (United Nations 2001:2). Community management may be at the heart of donor policies and even national policies and legislation; it is often not in the hearts of government officials and politicians who still see public services as something that should be supplied by the state.

In November 2000 the Fifth Global Forum of the WSSCC in Brazil reached consensus on the way forward for the water supply and sanitation sector: the Iguaçu Action Programme (IAP). The IAP's mainspring is Vision 21 (WSSCC 2000b). It translates that Vision, which has caught the imagination of the world and is shared by all WSSCC members, into practical activities to improve hygiene, sanitation and water for poor people. Vision 21 covers many subjects, and it is important, for impact and consistency, to concentrate mainly on a small number of them. The WSSCC therefore suggested four main advocacy subjects for its work at all levels over the next few years. Two of these deal with community management issues:

• *Institutional management options, public–private partnerships and the adoption of a code of sector ethics and rights*

The IAP states that the main task is now to promote institutional reform and good governance, to raise the capacity of public sector agencies and to promote engagement of all sector stakeholders. This engagement includes partnerships with the private sector and implementing institutional arrangements to support sanitation.

The Code of Ethics developed by the Working Group on Community Management and Partnerships with Civil Society should facilitate adoption of people-centred approaches. 'Now we must promote the Code of Ethics and appreciate the rights and responsibilities of consumers in development of sustainable water supply and sanitation services' (WSSCC 2000b). Moving to these 'people-centred empowerment approaches' will present additional institutional challenges.

• *Community-based approaches*

'At the heart of Vision 21 and the IAP is a commitment to building on people's energy and creativity. This implies the development of community-based approaches to water supply and sanitation in both urban and rural areas, in which householders and communities take the important decisions and actions' (WSSCC 2000b). And the IAP states that such community-based approaches should be incorporated into work programmes and implemented on a larger scale.

Summary

Over the past decades community management has become the leading concept in rural water supply. It started with community involvement in system construction and developed into community participation and community management. In the process, the responsibility for service provision gradually moved from national government to local people. The theoretical frameworks that underpin community management differ widely, from neo-liberal perceptions about reduced state involvement, to water as a basic human right, to water as an economic good, to people first and empowerment approaches. For most water supply and sanitation projects community management is now the guiding principle.

Two of the four main goals of the Vision 21 Water for People relate to community management, and we feel that the lessons in this book come at the right time. They are useful not only for planners and decision makers in water supply and sanitation, but in other water sectors and outside the sector as well.

However, we want to go further than simply producing a 'how to' guide for community management. As has been shown in the brief history of community management, it is an approach that arises as a result of real needs. However it can also be seen as arising from failure – most notably that of governments to provide services to large portions of their populations. A key argument of this book will be that, while community management can indeed help to address the huge unmet needs, it cannot do so as a kind of 'least worst option'. Community management too needs action by non-community players, it needs an enabling framework in which to be implemented, and it needs policies and laws to allow it to work efficiently.

CHAPTER 2

Participatory Action Research on community management of rural water supply

THIS CHAPTER DESCRIBES the background and history of the PAR project and sets the scene for each of the participating countries, communities and research partners. There are significant differences between the countries and between the communities, which on the one hand inhibit the extent to which we can draw generic lessons from the research work, but on the other, show the power of the community management approach and its capacity for application in widely differing situations.

Map 2.1 The countries where the PAR project was executed

Background and history

Research on 'the role of communities in the management of improved rural water supplies in developing countries' (the PAR project) started in 1994 and ran in its research phase for four years. During this time, participatory action research (PAR) was used as a methodology to work with communities with a number of interrelated aims.

- To improve the current state of understanding community management of rural water supply.
- To analyse and identify support requirements for building capacity for community management.
- To develop and test approaches, methods and tools to enhance the capacity of rural communities to manage their water supply.
- To enhance research and support capacity of partner organizations.

The project was funded by the Netherlands Directorate General for International Co-operation – DGIS – and was carried out by IRC and six partner organizations in Africa, Asia, and Latin America.

The project grew out of the need to get to grips with the problem of how to implement community management – then a relatively new concept – and to allow it to become a more mainstream approach to water supply. The PAR methodology was selected because it not only provides information through questioning and observation, but also assists people in a community to go through the various processes of change. Participatory action research shares the same roots as other 'putting the last first' approaches developed during the 1980s and early 1990s. It seeks to put communities in the driving seat of the development process, and to give them the skills to work together with external support agencies (NGOs, donor projects, etc.) to identify the key priorities and constraints in their own development needs, and to address these efficiently (Lammerink et al., 1998).

The PAR project was carried out within existing rural water supply programmes, implemented or supported by government agencies or NGOs in the respective countries. It was not, therefore, a classic 'water supply project'. While, in some communities, work did take place on upgrading or developing new infrastructure, the primary objective was to test and develop methods of strengthening the capacities of communities to manage their water supplies after they had been implemented.

The PAR project operated as a facilitator of the communities' own efforts rather than as a provider of resources. This gave it a unique opportunity to carry out a form of research where communities identified the key issues and reported on them in their own voices. The project went through a number of stages.

1994 – project inception

The main work of the project started in 1994 as partner organizations formed research teams, gathered information on existing community-managed rural water supply systems in their countries, and visited selected communities to learn about key issues. Based on this scoping process, four communities per country were selected in Nepal, Pakistan, Kenya and Cameroon, and three communities per country were selected in Colombia and Guatemala. These 22 communities represented a broad range of environmental, socio-economic and cultural conditions, and showed a range of managerial capacity.

Various groups were formed at different levels. At community level, Community Research Teams (CRTs) made up of local people became the intermediaries between the community and the research teams. They were trained in participatory methods to identify problems and search for solutions, and to strengthen management capacities in the communities. These CRTs played a crucial role in subsequent stages and were frequently the driving force behind the participatory process. National Reference Groups (NRGs) were formed in each of the six countries to create a platform at national level for recognition and discussion, and to ensure that the problems of national organizations in the water and sanitation sector were also addressed within the framework of the research project. An International Advisory Group (IAG) was put in place to provide expert support at the international level to the project teams of partner organizations and to IRC.

In accepting the PAR process, research teams in partner organizations were embracing a shift in professional attitudes towards mutual learning and towards sharing experiences in a structured but flexible way.

1995–96 – participatory field investigations

During this stage of the project, the research teams and the CRTs carried out an in-depth examination of local conditions and used participatory research to assess the demand for managerial improvement. As part of this community diagnosis, they assessed water-related environmental conditions in the communities and general sanitary conditions, and they included a study of the gender aspects of the establishment and management of water services, together with appraisals of possible solutions. A range of participatory methods was used to identify problems and search for solutions.

1996–97 – development and field testing of problem-solving strategies, methods and tools

Armed with the outcomes of this process of community diagnosis, the PAR research teams, in close collaboration with CRTs, developed strategies, methods and tools to address managerial problems and to monitor their effects on service performance. Each community drew up an agenda for experimentation, implemented the agenda and chose monitoring indicators to assess progress. Many of these experiments have led to improvements in the performance of the water supply systems. The PAR research teams in partner organizations documented these experiences in the communities, in reports and case studies which provide a wealth of information on the efforts of rural communities to get to grips with the management of their water supply systems.

1998–2001 – disseminating the results of the research – the MANAGE dissemination project

Following the official end of research activities in 1998, the IRC and its partners then entered a second phase; a three-year period with the emphasis on disseminating lessons and experiences – which ended in July 2002. The project produced a number of outputs including training courses, national workshops, international conferences, videos, training materials, a website and this book. Taken together, these represent a significant addition to the body of knowledge on the theory and practice of undertaking community management.

Partners in six countries

The PAR project was carried out by local NGOs in the six countries, supported by IRC. These partners ranged from long-established resource centres with close links to universities to small, new NGOs with practically no previous research experience. In the course of the project, two of the original NGOs were replaced by other NGOs in the same countries. In 2000, the South African NGO Mvula Trust joined the project. A brief description of the partner organizations will illustrate their diversity.

Guatemala	The initial partner in Guatemala was an NGO called *Agua del Pueblo* (ADP). During the first phase of the project, following an internal split in the organization, *Servicios para el Desarrollo* (SER) was formed and continued the PAR project. SER is a small NGO in the north of Guatemala providing technical and advisory services to facilitate construction, operation and maintenance and management of improved water and sanitation systems.
Colombia	CINARA, *Instituto de Investigación y Desarrollo en Agua Potable Saneamiento Básico y Conservación del Recurso Hídrico*, is based in Cali, Colombia. CINARA is a non-profit foundation with close links with the University of Valle in Cali. The centre is involved in research, development and technology transfer in support of improving the water supply and environmental conditions in rural and peri-urban communities.
Kenya	NETWAS (Network for Water and Sanitation), based in Nairobi, Kenya, promotes training in community-based water supply and

sanitation in collaboration with government and other organizations working in the sector. Programme activities are focused in four main areas: training; technical information dissemination; project development for community-based water supply and sanitation; and applied research.

Cameroon   At the start of the PAR research project the project partner was PAID-WA (Pan African Institute for Development – West Africa). PAID-WA is an international African NGO, with regional offices in Burkina Faso, Zambia and Cameroon. PAID-WA promotes integrated and participatory development activities and does so by designing and undertaking regular and tailor-made training events and action-oriented field studies. In 2000 PAID-WA was replaced by Water and Sanitation Management Consultants (WSMC) in Yaoundé, Cameroon. WSMC carries out short-term advisory missions but is mainly involved in training NGO and government staff in improved, participatory, project implementation.

Nepal   Nepal Water for Health (NEWAH), Kathmandu, Nepal, is an independent NGO set up to provide water and sanitation services to community-based organizations. Services include advice on project formulation and proposal writing; technical work on system design, budgeting and planning; supervision of construction; advice on health education and hygiene promotion; training for community management; and project operation and maintenance. NEWAH serves as a resource centre for the water and sanitation sector in Nepal.

Pakistan   In Pakistan the project started with the Water, Sanitation, Hygiene and Health Studies Project (WSHHSP). WSHHSP was a project under the Aga Khan Health Service. When the WSHHSP project came to an end, activities transferred to the newly established Water and Sanitation Extension Programme (WASEP) under the Aga Khan Housing Board for Pakistan. WASEP implements water supply and sanitation projects on a demand-responsive basis in northern Pakistan.

South Africa   In 2000 the Mvula Trust joined the project. The Mvula Trust implements water and sanitation projects in South Africa at the request of the South African Government and international donors. The Mvula Trust is also involved in policy advice, advocacy and information dissemination.

CHAPTER 3

Countries and communities

THIS CHAPTER GIVES a brief overview of the countries and communities involved in the research phase of the PAR project, with a focus on indicators describing water resources, water supply and sanitation coverage and policies for the water sector in the six countries. Short profiles of each of the 22 communities are presented as well as the state of their water supply systems and management at the start of the PAR project (see Appendix 1).

This is drawn from the rich material in the original project documentation (IRC 2001). General indicators on economic and social development of the six countries are presented in Appendix 2.

Kenya: water from God, donors and self-help groups

Table 3.1 Water supply and sanitation coverage in Kenya 1990 and 2000[1]

	Population ('000)			Water supply coverage			Sanitation coverage		
	Total	Urban	Rural	Urban (%)	Rural (%)	Total (%)	Urban (%)	Rural (%)	Total (%)
1990	23 552	5 671	17 881	89	25	40	94	81	84
2000	30 080	9 927	20 123	87	31	49	96	81	86

(WHO, UNICEF, WSSCC 2001)

Kenyan public policy immediately following independence in 1963 was to provide basic services for all its citizens. However, the provision of services increasingly became a function shared between the government and the voluntary sector such as local groups (self-help groups, women's groups and church organizations), NGOs and ESAs. Local NGOs and ESAs support a variety of water and sanitation programmes in all parts of the country. Local groups have become the backbone of much of Kenya's services provision.

---

1 Water and sanitation coverage figures are often presented to show the state of water supply and sanitation in a country or a region. The figures should be interpreted with much caution. Because of lack of information they often do not say anything about the safety of the water – quality – or the reliability of the water supply – quantity. The figures presented here are taken from the Global Water Supply and Sanitation Assessment Report 2000. The definition of coverage used in this report is based on technology type. It assumes that some technologies are safer than others. The population with access to 'improved' water supply and sanitation is considered to be covered. (WHO, UNICEF and WSSCC 2001).

In the early 1980s the philosophy of the NGOs and ESAs changed, shifting from simple charity and relief activities to community development programmes. Those programmes embraced institution building and popular participatory approaches. Local communities were encouraged to take responsibility for the operation and maintenance of water supply systems. The new approach met two obstacles. First, a lack of a sense of ownership on the part of communities, which hindered their meaningful involvement. Second, a lack of legal status of management committees, which hampered their involvement in decision making. Problems with management often started after 'handing over' the water project (Oenga and Ikumi 1997).

The Kenyan government aims to provide its population with improved water services by the year 2010. Institutional changes in the water sector will be needed to make this possible (Hukka 1998). Parliament enacted the National Policy on Water Resources Management and Development in 1999, stipulating a change of government role from provider to facilitator, and drafting guidelines to transfer responsibility for water supply management to rural communities where the need arises. However, decentralization of responsibilities and power is still far from obvious in the Kenyan political arena, and legislation to implement the 1999 policy is still being debated (Njuguna et al. 2000).

Most rural water supply systems are constructed with donor funding and that is how the four communities in the PAR research project got theirs: two through the Catholic Diocese of Machakos, in the eastern province, one through Finnish Aid and one through the Rural Domestic Water Supply Program (RDWSP) funded by the Netherlands government. Water management committees in Kenya are mostly self-help groups and do not have any legal status. Although most committees and caretakers are trained during project implementation, many of them face technical and managerial problems. Management often breaks down due to inadequate communication between committees and community members, poor leadership, fraud or general lack of management capacities. Often a committed individual or a small group of members dominates the water committee and the success of the system depends largely on their perseverance. Politicians and tribal leaders often use water supply systems as trade-off for support and votes. Cost recovery programmes are undermined by politicians saying that water is free and a gift from God.

Many of the water supply systems constructed in the 1980s and 1990s have broken down. Donors and government have recently started a rehabilitation programme (Oenga and Ikumi 1997; Njuguna et al. 2000).

Sigomere: many systems, little responsibility

Sigomere is located in a semi-arid region in the western part of Kenya, near Kisumu town. It is a village of some 5000 inhabitants who live mainly from subsistence agriculture. Many elderly people who have retired from active public service form the richer part of the community. There is a health centre in the

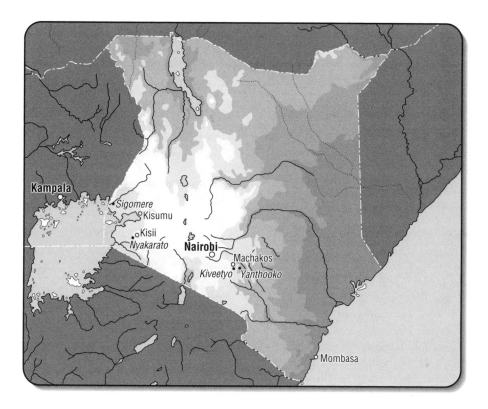

Map 3.1 Kenya with the location of the four communities

area and a number of primary schools. An electricity grid serves the area and drives the water pump.

The initial water supply was a piped scheme constructed with the support of UNICEF in the 1960s. The scheme broke down and was abandoned. Community leaders approached the Kenya Finland Western Water Supply Programme (KFWWSP) which provided shallow wells equipped with hand-pumps. A third gradation was initiated by the richer community members who had lived in towns and wanted household connections. They obtained a bore-hole equipped with an electric, submersible pump and piped distribution to their houses. Poorer households had to get their water from traditional water sources and the shallow wells. Later, communal water points (kiosks) were constructed to serve the poorer households. The 369 members of the water system pay a monthly tariff and participate in the decision-making process. Non-members have to pay at the kiosk for water. At the start of the PAR research project the different water systems were managed by different committees. The biggest management problem in Sigomere was therefore the fact that consumers had access to different water sources and nobody took responsibility for any of them.

There was also a problem with a treasurer who defrauded one of the committees of large sums of money.

Kiveetyo: water committee not responsible to the community

Kiveetyo is located in Mbiuni, in the Mwala division, about 50 km from Machakos town. The area is semi-arid. Kiveetyo has a population of about 2500 people who live mainly from small-scale agriculture. There are several primary and secondary schools in the area. There is also a health centre. Electricity is provided to only a limited number of houses.

The traditional water supply is by scooping the dry river beds. Water scarcity is a predominant problem, threatened further by the harvesting of river sand which is ferried to Nairobi as construction material. In the 1970s the government of Kenya constructed the Athi Water Project which served part of Kiveetyo. The water source is the Athi River which is heavily contaminated and carries high sediment load. Due to the high cost of pumping and water treatment the supply became unreliable.

In 1988 the Roman Catholic Diocese of Machakos implemented the gravity-fed Kiveetyo/Kathyioli Water Supply system, which gets its water from a protected source. It serves the communities of Kiveetyo, Kathyioli and Mutitu. Even though the system has very low water yields, it gives a steady flow of water that is distributed to each of the three areas in a rotating fashion during the day, while at night water is allowed to flow into the storage tanks of the schools. Water is provided through public stand posts and kiosks. Consumers get water for free, except at the Mbiuni market communal kiosk where KSh2 is paid per 20-litre container. The Athi Water Project and the Kiveetyo/Kathyioli Water Supply system are both functioning but are not connected to each other. At the start of the PAR research project the community faced a range of problems. The biggest problem was that large parts of the community did not pay the operational and maintenance costs. Another problem was that the water committee held itself responsible to the implementing agency and did not communicate with the community. There was also a dispute with the owner of the land around the water intake.

Nyakerato: rivalry between clans

Nyakerato is located in the hills of the Ibencho range, the source of the Nyakerato and Getacho rivers, in the Kisii district of the Nyanza province. The steep hill of Ibencho houses the clans of the Abatabori and of the Abakione. The majority of inhabitants, some 1000, are peasant farmers. There are several primary schools in the area and a few secondary schools. There is no electricity serving the area. The area receives plenty of rainfall.

The Nyakerato river is the boundary between the two clans of the Abatabori and the Abakione. The Abatabori live west of this river, the Abakione live on the eastern slopes of the Ibencho range. In the 1980s a small group of families from the Abatabori clan requested and received a spring protection which was converted to a small gravity scheme, implemented by the RDWSP. With time, other families of the Abatabori further away demanded a water service and, with donor support from the RDWSP, the gravity lines were extended. As time passed those living up on the hill, where a gravity system was not feasible, were given a shallow well, also by RDWSP. During this period, the Abakione realized that they could benefit from the developments as well. They asked RDWSP for a gravity scheme to serve the eastern slopes. Because of problems during construction the gravity line in this area is much shorter and has fewer distribution lines than the scheme serving the western slopes.

The biggest problem at the start of the PAR research project was competition, conflict and rivalry between the different clans. In addition, one person was claiming that the well was located on his land and wanted financial compensation. Illegal connections further undermined the system.

Yanthooko: women take the lead

Like Kiveetyo, Yanthooko is situated in Mwala division, Mwala location, Kibau sub-location, about 40 km from Machakos town. Yanthooko has a population of about 33 000 people who live from small-scale agriculture. The area is semi-arid. There are several primary schools.

Traditionally, water was harvested by scooping the sandy river beds of the river Mikwani. High population growth exerted pressure on the limited water resources. The self-help Yanthooko women's group decided to solve the problem of persistent water shortages, especially during the dry periods. After recurring cases of water-related diseases the community was also alerted to the need to use clean water by the Ministry of Health.

After consultations with different agencies, the Yanthooko women's group opted for a shallow well. They identified a location, purchased the plot, and requested the Roman Catholic Diocese of Machakos to supply technical and financial assistance. The communal shallow well is operated by a handpump. Water supply is augmented with household rainwater harvesting systems using roof catchment, water jars and ferrocement tanks. The shallow well also has facilities for washing clothes (washing slab/basins) and bathrooms. The Yanthooko women's group runs the shallow well as a small enterprise. There are 34 members who pay a very small monthly fee. Non-members pay cash on the spot as they collect water.

In the past the main problems were poor record keeping and lack of communication between the committee members and the project members. There was no constitution and, as a result, no clearly defined rules. Another problem was that the group is a closed society that does not allow new members.

Colombia: decentralization without capacity

Table 3.2 Water supply and sanitation coverage in Colombia 1990 and 2000

	Population ('000)			Water supply coverage			Sanitation coverage		
	Total	Urban	Rural	Urban (%)	Rural (%)	Total (%)	Urban (%)	Rural (%)	Total (%)
1990	34 970	24 291	10 679	95	68	87	95	53	82
2000	42 322	31 274	11 048	98	73	91	97	51	85

(WHO, UNICEF, WSSCC 2001)

In Colombia the distribution of wealth is very unequal, and this is one reason for the violence for which the country is known. Drug trafficking and a history of wars and guerrilla fighting contribute to continuing conflict between left-wing guerrilla groups, paramilitary groups and the national army. The violence particularly affects rural areas and the peri-urban zones of the big cities. Guerrilla and paramilitary groups all try to exert power on community-based organizations (Gomez and Rojas 1997).

In terms of water coverage, there are large differences between rural and urban areas. The percentage of the population with access to safe water is lower than the figures in Table 3.2 suggest, due to poor service and low water quality. The Ministry of Health estimates that in towns with fewer than 2500 inhabitants, safe water coverage is only 10 per cent. Official policies aim to close the gap between urban and rural (including peri-urban) settlements. A decentralization process has been introduced, and in 1994 Law 142 transferred responsibility for providing public services to municipalities. The *Junta de Acción Comunal* (JACs)[2] were allowed to administer public services, water supply being one of them. Responsibility for regulation and control continues to be with central government entities. There is clear and transparent legislation accompanying this process, and municipalities have also obtained the necessary financial resources to take over their responsibilities from central government. In practice, however, the municipalities lack both the capacity to manage their public services and the economic instruments to regulate water supply services. For day-to-day management, Law 142/1994 allows users to set up, or take part in, four general types of organization: public, private, mixed, or community-based. In small rural settlements, the community-based organization is predominant (Smits 2001).

---

2 JACs were created by the government of Colombia in 1957 to allow the involvement of communities in their development. They consist of seven elected community members who work on a voluntary basis. They work in different areas of community interest: health, education, water and sanitation, culture, recreation, etc. Since 1970 they have been officially allowed to administer water and sanitation services. However, other organizational forms are allowed as well, such as user associations and co-operatives. In 1998 a survey of the Ministry of Development showed that of the registered community organizations responsible for water and sanitation, only 33 per cent were JACs.

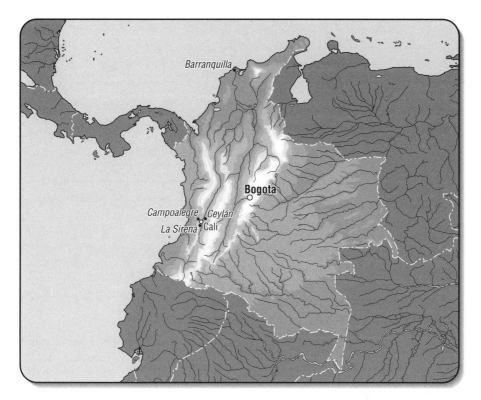

Map 3.2 Colombia with the location of the three communities

La Sirena: groups wrestle for control

La Sirena, a community of 4000 people, is located southwest of the city of Cali in the western mountain chain of Colombia at an altitude of 1100 m. It is densely populated, with a migratory flow from the nearby town of Cali and from the south-western part of the country. Some sectors of the community live in high-risk areas, where inhabitants have no legal holding of their plots. Many settlers survive through informal economic activities in nearby Cali.

The first group of settlers in La Sirena built the first water intakes in the 1970s and installed the first hoses to bring water to the community. In 1987 the water supply system was upgraded with a water treatment plant. The current gravity-piped system was constructed in 1983, using a number of intakes from different rivers. The water supply system is managed by a legally recognized community-based organization. Apart from technical problems with the water supply system, the biggest problem in La Sirena at the start of the PAR project was rivalry in the community. Many groups tried to exert control on the community. Another problem was that the users of the water supply system wanted their own community organization to manage it instead of the JAC that was created

31

as part of the decentralization to administer public services, including the supply of drinking water.

Ceylán: the civil war intrudes

Ceylán has 3000 inhabitants. It is located in the north of the department Valle del Cauca at an altitude of 1350 m and falls under the jurisdiction of the Bugalagrande municipality. The community has three primary schools and one secondary school, a telecommunication centre, a health post and a library. Ceylán is well known for its economic activities. Coffee, its most important crop, and plantain are sold in the region through co-operatives set up by community leaders. In 1973 after a struggle over land rights, local leaders and peasants started the Association of Peasants, which acquired land and redistributed it among peasant families most in need.

The first water system was established by Father Hector Salazar around 1946, with a water tank on the banks of the Elvira stream and a gravity system made of bamboo pipes. Thanks to strong community leadership the water supply system was modernized, a drinking water treatment plant constructed and an organization created to administer and operate the system.

As in La Sirena, the people of Ceylán refused to dismantle their community-based organization which had been in existence since 1989. The civil war had repercussions in the community and at the start of the PAR research project, guerrilla and paramilitary groups tried to gain control over the community-based organizations.

Campoalegre: illegal connections

Campoalegre is in the vicinity of the city of Cali, and was founded in the 1950s when many people migrated to the area to work in the stone crushing company El Chocho. Due to lack of state support, many of these migrants illegally occupied abandoned areas of land and started spontaneous, clandestine settlements. Natural disasters and the crises in agriculture have caused more migration to Campoalegre and contributed to its rapid growth. It now has some 1700 inhabitants. Most work at the stone crushing company or on poultry farms.

The gravity-fed water supply system was built in 1988 with 120 registered users. By 1996 the number of users had grown to 336.

The biggest problem at the start of the project was the continuous development of new settlements near Campoalegre, which resulted in great pressure on the water system. Only Campoalegre and nearby Montebello had their own water supply systems. New settlements forced unauthorized connections to these two systems, causing a decrease in water volume carried to the storage tank. At the start of the project there were some 150 illegal connections to the Campoalegre water supply system. These problems caused conflicts in the community and the users could not agree on solutions.

Guatemala: public confidence in municipalities eroded

Table 3.3 Water supply and sanitation coverage in Guatemala 1990 and 2000

	Population ('000)			Water supply coverage			Sanitation coverage		
	Total	Urban	Rural	Urban (%)	Rural (%)	Total (%)	Urban (%)	Rural (%)	Total (%)
1990	8 749	3 333	5 416	88	72	78	94	66	77
2000	11 385	4 515	6 870	97	88	92	98	76	85

(WHO, UNICEF, WSSCC 2001)

The legal framework of the water and sanitation sector in Guatemala consists of the Constitution, the Health Code, the Municipality Code and Government Decree 367–97. The last of these assigns responsibility for sector policies, strategies and co-ordination to the Institute of Municipal Public Works (INFOM). A General Water Bill, which will regulate the exploitation, use and conservation of water resources, has been in Congress since 1996.

The Health Code lays overall responsibility for universal access to water services on the Ministry of Health in co-ordination with INFOM. It explicitly mentions community management as a means to guarantee the sustainable use of water resources. However, the formal responsibility for the delivery of potable water lies with the municipalities. They receive 10 per cent of the state income for investments in infrastructure, including water systems. Municipalities also carry the final responsibilities for operation and maintenance of water supply systems. They are entitled to collect contributions for this service. Unfortunately, the municipal management of the systems suffers from lack of capacity, from political interference, and from changes in the political identity of municipalities and national government. As a result, the confidence of the population in municipalities has been eroded.

Investment in rural water and sanitation was part of the 1996 Peace Agreement between the Guatemala Government and the URNG (*Unidad Revolucionaria Nacional Guatemalteca*). Since then, government social funds have been invested in the construction of rural water supply systems. The sustainability of these systems has not received enough attention. Some of the social funds have been used to strengthen collaboration between municipalities, beneficiaries and NGOs. These experiences contributed to new decentralization policies under the aegis of INFOM.

Government Decree 441–2000 created the Commission for the Reform and Modernisation of the Water Supply and Sanitation Sector. This inter-institutional commission will work towards the creation of three separate entities in the sector: a legislative body, a regulative body and an operative body. The 331 municipalities will constitute the operative body.

Of the many NGOs that construct water systems, only a few are specialized and cover all the organizational and educational aspects that are necessary to ensure sustainable community management in rural areas. Most NGOs consider community management to be an easy way of securing a local supply of labour, materials and financial support. A variety of international NGOs and donor organizations provide financial support to the sector, usually under a mandate of supporting the development efforts of indigenous groups in rural areas (SER 2001).

Aguacatán: seven communities, one water system

Aguacatán is located in the department of Huehuetenango in Guatemala and comprises 49 rural communities. Seven of these, Chex, Chichoche, Tucuná, Aguacatán Canton, Patzalam, Agua Blanca and Río Blanco, are home to 550 families (3600 inhabitants) which have organized themselves to establish a water project. The communities are of indigenous ethnicity. The men are rarely, and the women very rarely, literate. Most of them speak only their own indigenous language.

In general, the men work the land, in 10- to 12-hour shifts, while the women do the domestic work and take care of the domestic animals. Every year in April,

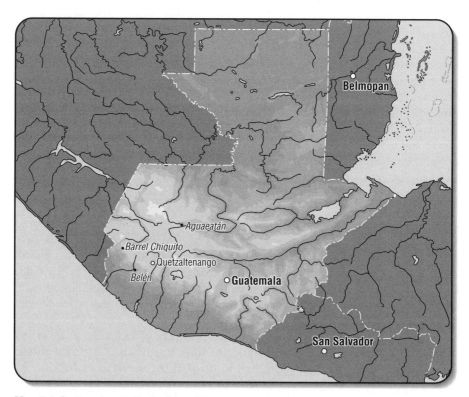

Map 3.3 Guatemala with the location of the three communities

July and August, men, women and children go to work on the coffee plantations in miserable conditions and often for less than a dollar a day.

Until 1986 the seven communities in Aguacatán did not have a clean drinking water system. Women and children would get water from rivers, streams and home-made wells in the area. They spent on average three hours a day bringing water back to their homes. The water was of poor quality. Without health services at their disposal or the economic means to pay for a doctor, many children died of diarrhoea, dehydration or water-borne diseases. In one of the seven communities, Patzalam, three leaders persuaded the community to create a fund and to look for support for a water system. After five years of fruitless searching, they came to *Agua del Pueblo*[3] (ADP). The community realized that it would be cheaper to involve other communities as well and to build one big system. In the end, ADP constructed a gravity water system with one source serving seven of the communities.

After a few years there were serious technical and administrative problems with the water supply. By the start of the PAR project the community was struggling not only with the technical features of its system, but also with its management. The water committee lacked motivation and there were often severe conflicts between the seven communities using the system.

Barrel Chiquito: fee too low to cover costs

Barrel Chiquito is a small town with a population of 1875 inhabitants, part of the municipality of Flores Costa Cuca in the department of Quetzaltenango. It is a green area with fertile soils at an altitude of 600 m. Most of the families have small plots near their houses where they grow coffee, papaya, tomato, avocado and lime, which they sell in small quantities. The town is surrounded by big private landholdings. Some families rent land in faraway places to grow corn, the principal component of tortillas. They cannot cultivate enough land to satisfy their food needs. That is why the men have to work in the coffee plantations, leaving the women to take responsibility for managing and doing the work in the village. From November to January the children do not go to school and the whole family works in the plantations.

Before the construction of the water supply system, women and children were responsible for hauling water from waterfalls or from small springs. A trip would take them one and a half hours; the average family water needs took four trips a day. The water was used for all sorts of domestic chores, as well as for watering the family gardens and for the domestic animals. During the rainy season people harvested rainwater and stored the water in barrels, buckets or jugs.

In 1988 the neighbouring community of Belén approached Barrel Chiquito to propose purchasing a spring. After purchasing the spring, the community

---

3   *Agua del Pueblo*: a Guatemala-based NGO supporting the implementation of water and sanitation projects.

went to the municipality to ask for support to construct a water system, but the municipality refused. In 1989, a committee was formed to look for a sponsor. The agency ADP agreed to support the construction of the water system. In May 1991, construction started. In November 1991, the water and latrine project was inaugurated.

At the start of the PAR project in 1994, Barrel Chiquito had major problems with its water supply. Waste water ran out of the houses, there was a lack of maintenance, partly due to a lack of tools, and the fee was too low to cover administration, operational and maintenance costs. Another problem was that in order to acquire legal status the committee had become a Pro-Improvement Committee, which is committed to a variety of community development projects. After a while, other activities such as the establishment of a school, the hiring of teachers, and the purchase of electricity and stoves, started to interfere with the water project.

Belén: too many connections

The village of Belén is part of the Palmar municipality in the department of Quetzaltenango. It consists of 290 houses, inhabited by 2038 people, most of whom have migrated to the village from surrounding towns or plantations. The people are generally very poor, and have to work long days at the plantations cultivating coffee and macadamia nuts. Most of them have coffee bushes and fruit trees around their houses, and rent land to plant corn and beans for family consumption.

Until 1975, Belén did not have a water supply system. The women used to go to the river to haul water in addition to a full day's work in the plantations and their other domestic work. In 1975, 18 people from Belén went to the mayor of Palmar to discuss community needs, such as improved roads, a school, electricity and water. They were advised to organize themselves into a Pro-Improvement Committee. In 1982 the committee signed an agreement with UNEPAR[4] to build a water supply system. This gravity-piped system with house connections was inaugurated in 1983, supplying at that time 86 families and a population of 516 inhabitants.

After three years the system started to develop many problems. Not all the sectors received water, there were problems among committee members, and the treasurer and secretary took decisions without consulting the community. One cause was the fact that the population was growing due to the violence in the country. The secretary and treasurer kept on selling new connections without considering the capacity of the source. A few years later a new source was bought and 100 additional connections made, but again the secretary and treasurer sold too many taps for the source to bear. Many members stopped paying their fees.

---

4 UNEPAR: *Unidad Ejecutora del Programa de Agua Rural* – a government agency in Guatemala responsible for the provision of water supply and sanitation services in rural areas.

Cameroon: ministry does not trust communities

Table 3.4 Water supply and sanitation coverage in Cameroon 1990 and 2000

	Population ('000)			Water supply coverage			Sanitation coverage		
	Total	Urban	Rural	Urban (%)	Rural (%)	Total (%)	Urban (%)	Rural (%)	Total (%)
1990	11 472	4 622	6 850	76	36	52	99	79	87
2000	15 085	7 379	7 706	82	42	62	99	85	92

(WHO, UNICEF, WSSCC 2001)

Because of its varied topography and climate, each zone in Cameroon is best suited to a different type of water supply technology. In the Sahel zone, 95 per cent of drinking water for communities is provided from large groundwater reservoirs, using mainly manual pumps and wells. In the Savannah zone, gravity networks have a wide coverage. Some systems have more than 70 public stand-pipes managed by a single community (Tayong 2001).

In the 1980s the government of Cameroon implemented a programme to supply drinking water to rural and urban areas. Two government departments were assigned to undertake this task: the Ministry of Mines, Water and Energy (MINMEE) and the department of Community Development (CD) of the Ministry of Agriculture. CD took a participatory approach to implementing systems managed by rural communities. Some of the funds for the programme came from the government itself, but most of the investment was provided by foreign donors and agencies such as CARE, Helvetas from Switzerland, DED from Germany, various embassies and a wide variety of charitable organizations. Foreign contractors were involved in the construction work, the best known of which was Scanwater, a Danish company that constructed some 350 water supply systems in villages and small towns.

The results of the investments were disappointing. Many systems broke down not long after construction, partly due to poor management and planning, and partly due to lack of community participation in the implementation of the projects. This was most notable in projects in which Scanwater and MINMEE were involved. Today, the implementation of most water supply projects, including construction and training, is contracted out by the ESAs to local NGOs and private firms (Tayong 2001; Nchari, Nformi and Amouye 1994).

Until 1988, the government managed water supply systems free for consumers, and trained and paid community caretakers. During the economic crisis of the late 1980s the government had to stop this programme and it transferred maintenance responsibility for rural water supply systems to communities. The government authorized communities to form Village Development Associations (VDAs) to lead them towards self-help initiatives. In some parts of the country the VDAs have developed well. They carry out development projects including the management of water supplies.

In 1998 the National Assembly adopted a law that emphasizes the protection of water resources and expresses the value of water for human life and the environment. A section of the law allows any conflicts that result during the process of construction, operation and maintenance of community water supplies to be settled at community level and gives legal protection to such locally based rulings (Tayong 2001).

Although the daily practice is that most water supply systems in Cameroon are in one way or another managed by communities themselves, the most important and powerful ministry, MINMEE, still considers water supply to be its own responsibility and questions the capacities of communities to manage their systems. Decentralization and the transfer of management responsibility to lower, more local, levels was accepted in policy texts and in the 1998 law, mostly through pressure from donors, but willingness to implement these principles has drained away. Corruption is another barrier to the effective implementation of water supply policies and projects (Tayong 2001; Nchari, Nformi and Amouye 1994).

Bokito Rural: poor system construction

Bokito Rural is located 200 km north-west of Yaounde in the Centre province of Cameroon. Although located in the highland savannah grassland zone, it is generally flat. The total population of 1500 is quite widely distributed. The community is relatively accessible by tarmac roads, but has no electricity.

People in Bokito Rural grow a variety of both cash and food crops. Many are involved in cocoa farming, where women and children provide labour but men 'own' the crop. Coffee and raffia palm wine are also produced. The coffee producers have formed a co-operative. The village is headed by a chief, who leads the VDA consisting of all quarter heads of the community.

Water is scarce. Traditional sources of water for drinking in the village are unprotected and often dry up in dry seasons. The most reliable water source is called Nobela. It has a spiritual importance and people say that no matter how dry the season, Nobela will always supply water. However, the water is of poor quality.

The first attempt to improve the water supply dates from 1984, when the community dug a well 10 km outside the village. In 1985 the community profited from a project which dug a borehole equipped with a manual pump. But this system was also far from where people lived. In 1990, government ministries constructed a water storage tank to provide water through an engine-driven pump to 10 tap stands in the village. But the quality of construction was poor, pipes were exposed to the surface and the tap at the chief's quarter did not function. The system was hardly used and fell into disarray soon after construction. At the start of the PAR project the people of Bokito Rural were using traditional water sources, the well and the borehole. They were thinking of looking for funds to rehabilitate the system constructed in 1990, but their hopes were not high.

38

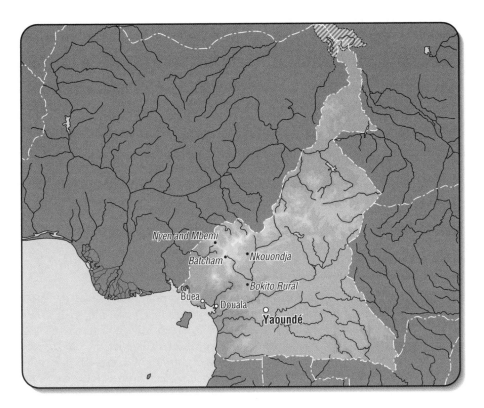

Map 3.4 Cameroon with the location of the four communities

Nkouondja: trust and water in short supply

Nkouondja village is about 2 km from Foumbot town in the Noun Division of the Western province in Cameroon. It has some 2500 inhabitants divided between six quarters. The village is located between the highland savannah zone of the Western province and the drier mountain savannah zone of the Adamawa province. The soil is very rich volcanic ash and the climate is very suitable for agriculture. The main activity of the community is farming. Agriculture in this area is highly commercialized, and produce from the area is exported to other parts of Cameroon and even to neighbouring countries.

Nkouondja village is well organized and has farming groups, youth groups and marketing associations. Whenever there is a development project, all villagers are levied an amount to contribute.

The community is predominantly Moslem. The village is headed by a chief who rules with the help of village elders, who are all men.

Traditionally, the women of Nkouondja got up at 4 a.m. to fetch water from traditional sources, before going to their farms. Sources were dirty and often dried up in the dry season. The women complained to the chief, threatening to divorce their husbands if nothing was done. The chief contacted SATA, Swiss Association for Technical Assistance the predecessor of Helvetas. Together with CD, SATA constructed a gravity system covering the entire village and part of the nearby village of Fosset, where one of the two sources is located. The system has 21 standpipes. A water management committee was set up comprising influential men close to the chief.

At the start of the PAR project the committee had many problems. The president of the committee took all decisions by himself. Books and financial accounts were not transparent and the president was accused of fraud. Users had become unwilling to pay their fees. The caretaker could not be paid regularly and he in turn started to cut off quarters of the community from the system as a kind of punishment. In dry seasons the water supply became unreliable and, faced with an acute water shortage, many women returned to their traditional water sources.

Batcham: nobody knew how to repair the pumps

Batcham is in the western highlands in the Western province, one of the most densely populated areas of Cameroon. The vegetation is grassland with a few trees in the valleys. The total population of Batcham village is about 57 182 divided over 60 quarters. Each quarter is administered by a quarter head, and these are centrally co-ordinated by the chief and a group of seven advisers.

The community is generally poor and the main occupation is farming. Food crops are produced mostly by the women, while the men take care of the cash crops, raffia palm tapping and small livestock production. Due to the increase in population, land has become a scarce commodity. For this reason many families migrate out of the village during the farming season to acquire farming land.

The village does not have surface water and depends on groundwater. In 1988 the government funded an engine pumping system with a borehole drilled to extract groundwater, constructed by the Danish company Scanwater. The technology was so complicated that the system soon fell apart. When water distribution was limited to half the village, people started to return to their traditional, scarce sources and unprotected wells. Sister Lola at the maternity clinic in the village decided to help by providing seven manual pumps distributed across the village at wells dug by community people. The handpumps soon revealed technical problems, nobody knew how to repair them and spare parts were not available. People again returned to traditional sources.

Nyen and Mbemi: a dedicated caretaker

Nyen and Mbemi are two villages sharing the same water supply system 8 km from Mbengwi in the North West province of Cameroon. Nyen has 3000 inhabitants and Mbemi has 2000. People live from farming; men in charge of cash crop production, mainly palm oil, and women taking care of the food crops.

People traditionally collected water from a range of sources in the villages. These provided enough water, but of poor quality. In 1974 a community leader in Nyen formed a committee of five men to develop an improved water supply system. They approached SATA for technical assistance and the community raised money to contribute to the construction of the system. In 1981 the system was inaugurated and in 1982 it was extended to Mbemi village. The system extracts water from five catchment areas, and the water flows under gravity into a 1000 m³ storage tank. There are several standpipes in the two villages and four taps are located at the market place. The Nyen water supply system is well designed and constructed. The system is not only large, it has an office and a store, equipped by SATA with spare parts and tools.

The management committee was created in 1988, six years after the system was constructed, as a result of the prompting of a Divisional Officer. Until then the system had been managed single-handed by the caretaker. The committee consists of 28 members representing the various quarters, with an executive board of eight members who handle urgent issues.

At the start of the PAR project the caretaker was still active, but the government had stopped paying his salary two years earlier, and he was working on a voluntary basis. However, since he had to take time away to earn an income in other ways, the maintenance of the system declined. Leakages and broken stand pipes were the first signs of neglected maintenance. The chairman of the committee was a retired civil servant with a lot of power in Nyen. He ran the committee on his own behalf and charged water fees at his own liking. Because of his position and status, the community of Nyen could not replace him. Their only way to express discontent was by not paying the fees for operation and maintenance. The people of the other community, Mbemi, are in a minority so they could not remove the chairman at elections. This caused tension between the villages of Nyen and Mbemi.

Pakistan: no standards, no responsible ministry

Table 3.5 Water supply and sanitation coverage in Pakistan 1990 and 2000

	Population ('000)			Water supply coverage			Sanitation coverage		
	Total	Urban	Rural	Urban (%)	Rural (%)	Total (%)	Urban (%)	Rural (%)	Total (%)
1990	119 155	37 987	81 168	96	79	84	78	13	34
2000	156 483	57 968	98 515	96	84	88	94	42	61

(WHO, UNICEF, WSSCC 2001)

In Pakistan there is no legislation for the national drinking water sector, there is no national standard for drinking water quality, and there is no ministry responsible for water and sanitation services. Co-ordination between the government departments working in the water and sanitation sector such as the departments of health, community development and municipal administration is lacking. NGOs play a pivotal role in the water and sanitation sector, but there is lack of recognition of NGOs by government institutions (UNICEF Pakistan 2001).

Especially in dry and semi-arid areas, handpumps are privately owned. Cost recovery for water services is well accepted, with some 80 per cent of water users paying a water fee. More than 90 per cent of the piped water supply systems have been constructed by the local government, often with the support of international donors such as the World Bank, UNICEF, DFID, the government of Japan and KfW. However, total investment in rural water and sanitation service is low compared to other public sectors; US$ 12 million in the period 1996–2000, compared to US$ 91 million for education and US$ 48 million for health. Girls and women suffer most from lack of access to water and sanitation services. Socio-cultural taboos make it difficult for them to benefit from these services, even when they are close at hand (UNICEF Pakistan 2001).

The four communities involved in the PAR research project are all located in Northern Pakistan where the partner in the project, WASEP, has its working terrain in the Northern Areas and Chitral. Half of the Northern Areas is above 4500 m. The summers are hot and the winters cold, with temperatures ranging from +40°C in summer to −20°C in winter. In this area 97 per cent of the population is Moslem belonging to the Shia, Suni, Ismali and Norbakhshi sects. The major source of income is agriculture, in particular apples, apricots and mulberries, and livestock. Rural communities are isolated and far from government services (WASEP 2000).

A number of agencies are active in the delivery of water and sanitation services in Northern Pakistan. The Local Bodies and Rural Development Department (LBRDD) initiated a community-based approach in the 1980s with the assistance of UNICEF. The Social Action Programme (SAP) was initiated in 1993 in partnership with AKRSP (Aga Khan Rural Support Programme), aiming to increase community participation. This was achieved through the use of village organisations (VOs) and women's organizations (WOs) in the communities. In 1997 the Aga Khan Planning and Building Service (AKPBS) initiated the Water and Sanitation Extension Programme (WASEP) with the objective of reducing the risk of water and food-borne diseases in Northern Pakistan (WASEP 2000).

In Northern Pakistan only 16 per cent of the population has access to clean drinking water. The main traditional water source is glacial water, which reaches the scattered communities through streams and man-made channels and is stored in underground water pits. Harsh winters create major problems for the water supply as traditional irrigation channels used for domestic water freeze, and even the PVC pipes in improved systems fall victim to the cold temperatures. Drinking water resources have high levels of human and animal faecal contamination (WASEP 2000).

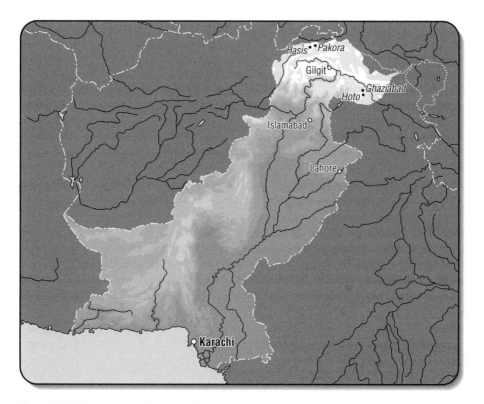

Map 3.5 Pakistan with the location of the four communities

The four communities have strong traditional patterns of governance, mostly based on the Moslem religion and tribal hierarchies. Village organizations, initiated by AKRSP, have a legal responsibility for development in the villages. VOs are mostly dominated by traditional leaders. Women have their own women's organizations but do not integrate in the affairs of the men. Gender divisions supported by religious practices have been an obstacle to involving women in the management of water supplies (WASEP 2000 and UNICEF 2001).

Ghaziabad: Lieutenant sets an example

Ghaziabad is located in the Bultistan district, 25 km from the district capital Skardu. The village has 38 households divided into three *muhallahs* (clusters of households) with a total of 280 inhabitants. The community has a village organization (VO), which organizes weekly meetings.

The first settlers in the village constructed an irrigation channel and built their houses along the channel which gave them easy access to water for domestic use. Another channel was built when the population increased and more irrigated land was needed. With an increase in both human and livestock population, the channels became contaminated. The community appointed *chowkidars* (caretakers) and banned activities along the channels that would contaminate them. Retired honorary Lt. Mirza Muhammad, aware of the contamination problems, constructed a very small water tank 300 ft above his house to get water into his compound, kitchen and bathrooms. He also used the tank to store water in winter. This system acted as a demonstration model for other community members. In 1991 the village organization (VO) requested LBRDD to fund an improved water supply system. A gravity-fed system with yard taps was inaugurated in 1993. A caretaker was appointed to repair major breakdowns and to inform the community members when they had to clean the water tank. The caretaker is accountable to the VO.

At the start of the PAR research project there were several technical problems. Community members at the upper end of the village did not get enough water because of low pressure in the system. They accused people at the lower end of leaving their taps open. The water quality was bad because storage tanks were not covered, and the caretaker was not trained to repair broken taps. Poorer families were not able to pay the fees. Women were not involved, nor did the women discuss the water supply in their own WO as they regarded it as the men's responsibility.

Hoto: hard work led to disappointment

Hoto is situated in the Bultistan district. It comprises of six *muhallahs* with 174 households, and 1200 inhabitants. Some inhabitants claim that Hoto consists of only four *muhallahs*, and that the other two are independent. However, all *muhallahs* have equal rights to use the water sources, pastures and forests.

The village has two water sources, a *nallah* (stream) which is fed by the snow-melt water in the summer and a spring. Nallah water is used for irrigation and drinking in summer, while spring water is used for drinking in winter. In 1983, Aga Ahmad, a community leader, proposed contacting the AKRSP to form a VO in Hoto and to ask them to support the construction of a water supply system.

In 1985, staff from AKRSP, accompanied by the Deputy Commissioner and a district council member, came to the community and explained the terms and conditions for support. AKRSP consulted only the male members of the Hoto community. The VO started constructing a gravity-fed system with yard taps in 1985. All 83 VO members worked on the system for 60 days and the VO took up the task of managing the system. Aga Ahmad became the first president of the VO.

The system operated for one-and-a-half years. Then problems started. The water tanks had been poorly built because the community could not afford enough cement, and water in the tanks became contaminated by insects. There was no caretaker and the president of the VO tried to maintain the system as well as he could. Although an initial fee for operation and maintenance had been agreed, only a few people paid it. As the PAR research project started the system was no longer operational. The community was disappointed and did not know what to do.

Pakora: caretaker lost community salary and the will to work

Pakora is located in the Ghizer district. It is divided into two sections: Pakora Bala, the upper part, and Pakora Paeen, the lower part. In total there are 1700 inhabitants in 180 households.

In summer people used to fetch drinking water from irrigation channels. In winter, when the channels froze, the women had to walk to a nearby spring for drinking water. In 1992, LBRDD constructed a gravity-fed system with yard taps to supply water to both Pakora Bala and Pakora Paeen. The community appointed a paid caretaker. Members of the VO social committee were responsible for collecting fees that community members promised to pay. Neither LBRDD nor AKRSP trained anyone in Pakora, not even the caretaker or the social committee members responsible for fee collection and book-keeping.

At the beginning of the PAR research project the water tank was poorly covered and broken at different places. The water was contaminated by frogs and insects living in the tank. The water in the pipes froze and burst in winter because they were not well protected. The system did not function any more.

Social committee members said that some members would not pay fees for the caretaker's salary on time, and that this was why the caretaker did not care for the system properly. The caretaker had donated land for the construction of the water tank, hoping that one day he would be appointed by the government to become a paid caretaker. However, the government does not pay caretakers and so he later asked the community to compensate him for the land. There were no regular meetings to discuss these problems.

Hasis: water system divided the community

The village of Hasis is located in the remote valley of Punyal in the Ghizer district and is divided into four sections: Hasis Bala, Hasis Paeen, Hasis Khari I and Hasis Khari II with a total number of 115 households and some 1000 inhabitants. Each section has its own VO and WO. The four VOs hold joint meetings every month.

Traditionally, in summer, irrigation channels and streams were used as the major sources for drinking water. In winter, springs and open rivers are used. Collecting water is hard work, especially in winter. Some families dug *ghulks* (water pits) in their houses for storing water in winter. A *ghulk* held enough water for four days and these *ghulks* later became the major systems for providing cool water in summer.

In 1980, the VOs of Hasis Bala and Hasis Paeen approached LBRDD for an improved water supply system. LBRDD constructed a gravity-fed system in Hasis Bala. Hasis Paeen did not support this system because they were afraid that every year the river that runs through Hasis would wash away the pipe linking them to the tank, which the engineers of LBRDD said must be located in Hasis Bala. Of the 65 households in Hasis Bala, only 55 households got tap connections because they were able to pay. The other 10 households collected water from nearby tap stands and the traditional water sources.

At the start of the PAR project there were disputes between the different sections of the community caused by the fact that only one section was provided with a water supply system. There were also constant quarrels between the care-taker and users about fees and about people who were not willing to help to clean the tank. There was no separate water committee and the VO was not able to solve the problems. Nobody had been trained by the implementing agency.

Nepal: efficiency damaged by lack of co-ordination

Table 3.6 Water supply and sanitation coverage in Nepal 1990 and 2000

| | Population ('000) | | | Water supply coverage | | | Sanitation coverage | | |
	Total	Urban	Rural	Urban (%)	Rural (%)	Total (%)	Urban (%)	Rural (%)	Total (%)
1990	18 772	1 680	17 092	96	63	66	68	16	21
2000	23 931	2 844	21 087	85	80	81	75	20	27

(WHO, UNICEF, WSSCC 2001)

Several stakeholders are involved in the water and sanitation sector in Nepal: the government, ESAs, international and national NGOs, community-based organizations and private companies.

The leading ministry for water supply and sanitation, the Ministry of Housing and Physical Planning (MHPP), was created in 1988 and has responsibility for formulating sector policies, co-ordinating budgets and strategies and for planning. It has a Department of Water Supply and Sewerage (DWSS) with responsibility for sector planning, co-ordination, setting technical standards, managing design and construction of large water and sanitation schemes, incorporating health and hygiene education into projects and constructing sanitation facilities. Although DWSS is mandated to operate as a facilitator, its main focus is on implementing water supply systems through its network of District Water Supply Offices (DWSO) in the 75 districts in Nepal. DWSS allocates over 80 per cent of its total expenditure to direct project work. Support services make up only 4 per cent of its budget, while expenditure on monitoring and evaluation, sector co-ordination and NGO/private sector support is non-existent.

At local level, the government is represented by district development committees (DDC) and village development committees (VDC), which are usually responsible for several rural communities. The DDC is responsible for co-ordinating planning and implementation. DDCs and VDCs play an increasing role in evolving and implementing water and sanitation strategies. Community-based organizations such as water user committees (WUC) are responsible for maintaining rural water services.

ESAs have a great influence on sector priorities and developments. They include multilateral agencies, such as the Asian Development Bank (ADB), UNICEF, UNCHS-Habitat, UNDP, WHO and bilateral institutions such as the governments of Austria, Finland, Germany, Japan, the Netherlands, Switzerland and the UK. Each agency has its own programme and approach, and invests in different parts of the country. Donor contributions in the sector went up from 40 per cent in the 1980s to 60 per cent in 1999, and are concentrated in rural areas.

There are at least 19 international NGOs active in the water and sanitation sector, primarily supporting smaller projects in both rural and urban areas. They generally implement their projects in collaboration with local NGOs. Lack of co-ordination and a high degree of pluralism in the NGO sector has resulted in poor overall efficiency and in the marginalization of the government as the key agency responsible for guiding the sector as a whole.

The Water Resources Act and regulation 2049 of 1992 provide umbrella legislation for hydropower, irrigation, drinking water and other water uses. There are problems in enforcing legal regulations and in assigning specific duties and responsibilities to the public stakeholders in the sector. (WECS 2001; Whiteside and Shrestha 2000; Rai and Subba 1997; Otte and Budhathoki 2002)

Yampaphant: system exhausts water source

Yampaphant is located in ward 8 of Bandipur Village Development Committee (VDC) of the Tanahu district of Gandaki zone in the western development region about 130 km west of Kathmandu, the capital city. Around 90 households and 544 people live in Yampaphant, representing a rich variety of ethnic groups, with Brahmins and Chhetris as the dominant ones. People in Yampaphant can be characterized as middle class and well-off. The caste system is still deeply rooted in this community. Besides the caste division there is also a strict gender division. However, both boys and girls go to school and the literacy rate of the younger generations below 40 years of age is nearly 100 per cent. Agriculture is the predominant occupation and main source of income for the village. Hard-working farmers have established a dairy which produces milk products.

Community people used streams, springs and irrigation water for domestic purposes until 1992, when a gravity-fed water system with 14 tap stands was implemented by the Nepal Red Cross Society (NRCS). During construction, a

47

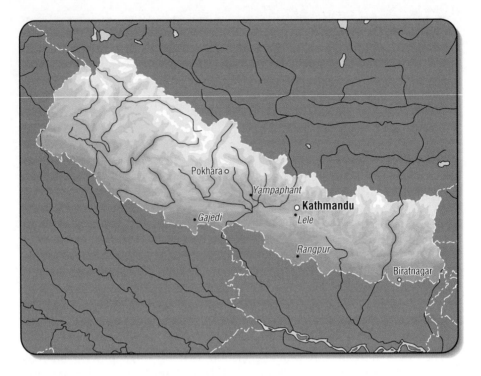

Map 3.6 Nepal with the location of the four communities

WUC with 13 members was formed and 21 people were trained as technicians. The community collected NRs 2000 as an initial donation to the operation and maintenance fund, while NRCS put in NRs 500. The project included a sanitation component and with NRCS encouragement, more than 60 per cent of the households constructed pit latrines during that period. It soon turned out that the water source was insufficient for the system that had been installed, and the water supply was open for only two hours in the morning and two hours in the evening.

During construction, WUC members were very active. When the problems started with the supply some people refused to pay money for the watchman, while others returned to their traditional sources. WUC members became worried because nobody took any notice of their decisions. The WUC became inactive. One of the trained village maintenance workers left the village to find a better job elsewhere.

Lele: activity drained from the pipes

Lele Mahadevkhola is in ward 4 of Lele Village Development Committee of Lalitpur district in Bagmati zone in the central development region of Nepal.

Lele is famous in Nepal for Saraswati Kunda, the pond of the goddess of learning. Lele consists of 79 households with 354 inhabitants. Ward 4 has a diverse ethnic composition, with Tamang as the biggest ethnic group. The caste system is still deeply rooted in the village, as are gender differences. Ninety-nine per cent of the women over 40 years old and 75 per cent of the young women are illiterate, although all young children are now supposed to go to school. The existence of a health post in the village means that minimum health services are more accessible than in many other rural villages.

The main sources of income are agriculture and stone quarrying. Land holdings are too small for subsistence farming, which is why almost everyone works in stone quarries close to the village. Women crush the stones for aggregates and men excavate stones from the cliff. There is a considerable migration of young people to Kathmandu in search of better job opportunities.

Traditionally the people used unprotected springs for water. In the early 1990s a group of social workers in Lele requested a water supply system from the DWSO of Lalitpur district, which in turn asked community leaders to form a water user committee. This WUC then assisted in the design and construction of an open flow gravity-fed system with tap stands, which was inaugurated in May 1993. Two men and two women were trained as village maintenance workers. Only 68 households use the system; the remaining 11 were too far from the system or were above the level of the source.

At the start of the PAR research project the WUC was inactive. Members said they were too busy and frustrated because nobody listened to them. The four trained village maintenance workers were also inactive. There were technical problems. The system was an open-flow gravity system without a reservoir tank, so when taps in the lower parts of the village were open, there was no water coming out of the taps in the upper parts. One tap was built too high above the source and did not provide water at all. Pipes were not buried well and people in the upper parts of the village had started to cut into the pipes to get water. This caused conflict in the community.

Rangpur: disputed leadership, inadequate funds

Rangpur Uttarbadi consists of wards 1, 7 and 8 and is a part of Rangpur VDC of Rautahat district of Narayani zone in Central Development region. It is situated in the Terai region, about 300 km south of Kathmandu, and contains 300 households and 1934 people.

Rangpur is an old settlement and people live close by one another along the village road and keep their cattle by the roadside. The community has a wide variety of ethnic groups, with Tharus as the main group.

Poor landless people of the Musahar caste, who are considered to be 'untouchable', earn money through daily labour work whereas middle-class people have their own land and produce enough food for their families throughout the year. A small group of rich people produces surplus grain for sale at the

49

local market. The literacy rate of men is higher than that of women. Most children now go to school, but Musahar children work at home and help their mothers.

The most common water sources are traditional wells and rivers, which people have been using for centuries. These water sources are still used for watering cattle and washing clothes. The development of Rangpur's water system started in 1992 at the request of the community and was completed in 1994. NEWAH provided technical and financial assistance to implement a water, health education and sanitation programme, installing 72 boreholes fitted with handpumps throughout all wards in the VDC. Before the system was built, a project management and maintenance committee (PMC), was formed, representing members from all wards, along with sub-water committees for each handpump. The responsibility of the PMC was to implement the programme and take responsibility for the operation and maintenance of the system. The responsibility of the handpump sub-water committees was to maintain individual handpumps, educate water users in matters of hygiene, keep the handpumps and surroundings clean, and raise maintenance funds. Members of the PMC, the water committee, health volunteers and caretakers received basic training in management, hygiene education and minor repairs.

Despite successful community participation during the implementation of the project, the PMC and the water committees were inactive by the time the PAR research project became involved. Not enough money was collected to keep maintenance funds up to date, because people were suspicious and did not know who was keeping the funds. Major repairs on the handpumps could not be carried out by the village maintenance worker. Political groups were also fighting about the leadership of the PMC and the water committees. These were some of the problems at the start of the project.

Gajedi: sand discharge and insufficient water yields

Gajedi Belbhariya is located in ward 2 of Gajedi Village Development Committee of Rupandehi district of Lumbini zone in the western development region. Ward 2 consists of 251 households and 1633 inhabitants.

Gajedi has two categories of inhabitants. The indigenous settlement of the Tharu has registered land while other caste and ethnic groups, newcomers to the village, live on unregistered land. All children go to school without social or cultural discrimination and the young generation, below 40 years of age, is literate. An adult literacy programme was implemented by the World Education Program through the District Education Office, and the community built its own school for adult education.

The main source of income is agriculture. People also earn a living from livestock, vegetables and daily labour. Production of crops depends on rainwater, which is why the people of Gajedi repeatedly asked for an irrigation water system.

For centuries, traditional wells provided water to the Tharu settlement. Around 1990, when landless people settled in the village, the Gajedi VDC provided one handpump for the new settlement. The Red Cross provided another tubewell, which helped to serve more people. Some people in the village found out about the Lumbani Rural Water Supply and Sanitation Project[5] (LRWSSP). They wrote an application for a water supply project and submitted it to the DWSO in Rupandehi. At the same time, there was an outbreak of cholera in Gajedi ward 1. As a result LRWSSP immediately implemented a water supply project in all nine wards of Gajedi VDC. A WUC was formed before the project was implemented.

At the start of the PAR research project Gajedi VDC faced several problems with its water supply system. Some of the wells were not deep enough, causing sand discharge and insufficient water yields from the handpumps. There were irregular committee meetings, the committee did not inform the community about its decisions, the village maintenance worker performed badly, the committee was not registered, and accounting and bookkeeping was poor.

---

5 LRWSSP is a Finnida-supported project particularly in the Lumbani zone. Finnida supports the DWSO in implementing water and sanitation projects.

PART 2
THE STORIES

Community management in practice

IN THIS PART we look at community management from three perspectives: that of the community itself, the management of water supply systems, and the enabling environment – drawing in each case on the experiences of communities, and how issues impacted on their ability or inability to sustain their water supply systems. Our red thread runs throughout this part, and we continuously draw attention to the gap where institutional support to communities is missing.

Each chapter describes key factors affecting community management, using the stories from the 22 communities. These are the factors that need to be addressed if sustainable management is to be accomplished. There is no attempt to rank these factors hierarchically, since the reality of community management is complex and it is largely meaningless to talk about one factor being more important than others. Part 2 ends with a discussion of the lessons learned from the experiences in the communities. These experiences were recorded in numerous documents written by the research teams in the six countries and by IRC staff members, including progress reports, reports of meetings and workshops, reports with the results of the different phases in the project, etc. It would be tedious when quoting from community experiences to keep reminding readers of this fact. Where such a passage is quoted without attribution, we have taken it from the reports of the relevant PAR partner. References to the main documents used to write this part have been included as Appendix 4.

CHAPTER 4

Living communities –
complex and dynamic

Community dynamics

We start our story with 'community dynamics' a phrase that suggests that communities are active, not passive, that they change all the time and that they are full of energy, and perhaps also of tensions. What is a community? How do its form and internal dynamics affect implementation and management of water supply projects? This would seem to be a logical place to start with an investigation into the concept of community management, but surprisingly, the community is seldom at the centre of research into how to do better. The focus is almost always on technologies and institutions – designed for some sort of homogeneous 'rural community' that can be found anywhere in the world.

Do communities exist?

Many on the 'new-right' deny the existence of community at all, seeing it as an artificial left/liberal construct with no basis in reality. To them, 'community' is nothing more than groups of individuals, mainly competing, but sometimes coming together in interest groups for a common purpose. The true unit for looking at humans and their interactions is the individual or household. Applying this approach to water supply, it is possible to see the 'user community' as nothing more than all the individuals who use the water supply system. By taking such an approach, questions of social inclusion, equity, etc. simply cease to matter. Anyone who pays the requisite fee joins the 'community' of those served by the water supply system; anyone who does not has nothing to do with the water supply. Water supply becomes like a private club where success or failure is measured simply by how well the 'members' (those who pay) are served. What happens to non-members is irrelevant, except that they may at some future date be persuaded to join. This approach is attractive because it makes building and managing 'effective' and 'efficient' water supply systems easier.

We are not going to use this definition of community. Neither would most people working in the development world. We bring it in here simply to show the extent to which we all take certain key assumptions for granted. In this case the assumption is that, however hard it may be to pin down, a community must have something more to it than a shared interest in a resource or service. Ties of mutual obligation, kinship, etc. are crucial on some level.

Communities are fluid, and difficult to define, but they do exist. If sliced finely with an analytical razor, a community may look like the sum of the

individuals who make it up – yet to suggest that 'community' does not exist is completely counter-intuitive to anyone who has experienced a rural community. Communities do contain interest groups and they are made up of individuals, but they are more than interest groups and more than the sum of the individuals who make them up. The individual men, women and children, some rich, some poor, do not just co-exist in a shared space. They interact in many different ways, some visible, some invisible. The existence of 'community' is not something that can be demonstrated – it is a philosophical point of departure that is shared, albeit implicitly, by most of the key players in our story.

Taking into account the many different ways of looking at a community, it is probably simplest to say that a community exists if the people who make it up think that it does. This is an unsatisfactory definition for the engineer, to be sure, but one to which he or she would do well to pay attention. History is littered with examples where water engineers brought technical solutions to communities, which failed spectacularly because where they saw a single community, the people who lived there saw several diverse communities.

If we accept that communities exist then it becomes meaningful to talk of them owning and sharing things, and then to speak of the equity with which these are owned or shared. Equity includes both a sense of equality and a sense of being entitled to a share in ownership. Equity is crucial to community management. It implies that, although communities are diverse, everyone in the community should profit in the same manner from a water supply system. It accepts that communities must mean more than the rich getting together to buy themselves an expensive water supply system. To deal with this view of community means to acknowledge diversity.

As Visscher and Lammerink state: 'Men, women and children have different needs, different access to resources and different areas in which they can take decisions. Yet all have the right to equally contribute to and benefit from development activities, thus making it necessary to strike a gender balance in programme activities, problem identification, conflict resolution and joint management of common interests.' (Visscher and Lammerink 1998:4). Making this come true – equity in using a water supply system and in making decisions on its management – is one of the most difficult tasks in rural water supply, as the implementing agency NEWAH honestly confesses (see box).

Communities are not homogeneous . . .

So, communities exist. But this does not mean that they are homogeneous or static entities. Rather, they are melting pots of continuous negotiations, discussions and conflicts. They are dynamic and change constantly in their power balances, wealth, size, water availability and so on. Within one community there are rich and poor people, people with high and low status, women and men, old and young people, people from low and high castes, ethnic minorities and majorities, highly and poorly educated, powerful and powerless, farmers and

---

Those who have most to gain, are least involved

'... all the people covered by a project, irrespective of gender, caste or class have access to clean water. However, they may not all have equal access to all the benefits which are part of the work. Many important decisions made during project implementation are made by well-off and influential men in the village. Women and poor men are not equally involved and both are poorly represented in project management committees. NEWAH recognises that its current project approach has maintained existing gender, caste or class disparities, which hampered community management and hence the long-term sustainability of the water supply and sanitation systems. Those who probably have the most to gain from these water supply and sanitation systems, mainly poor women and men are the least involved in management of these systems.'

---

cattle raisers, land owners and the landless. Diversity and unclear boundaries are characteristics of communities and they are arguably the characteristics that have the most important impact on community management. In the past, project staff, engineers and social workers have often ignored them.

Galvis et al. describe the community as a 'group of people with some common but also some conflicting interests and ideas and different socio-economic and cultural backgrounds. The water supply system may be one such common interest, but at the same time can be a major source of conflict. The identity of the people in the communities is shaped by their history and their socio-economic and environmental conditions. Some of them, often the economically better off, may be better informed, may know more of the world, but may on the other hand, have certain interests in keeping the status quo and therefore may not be willing to solve certain problems. Women may have interests different from those of men and may not have been heard in the past, or their position may make it difficult to achieve changes on their own.' (Galvis et al. in Visscher et al. 1997:33).

Guijt and Shah state: 'Despite the stated intentions of social inclusion, it has become clear that many participatory development initiatives do not deal well with the complexity of community differences, including age, economic, religious, caste, ethnic and, in particular, gender. Looking back, it is apparent that 'community' has often been viewed naively, or in practice dealt with, as an harmonious and internally equitable collective. Too often there has been an inadequate understanding of the internal dynamics and differences, that are so crucial to positive outcomes. This mythical notion of community cohesion continues to permeate much participatory work, hiding a bias that favours the opinions and priorities of those with more power and the ability to voice themselves publicly. In particular, there is a minimal consideration of gender issues and inadequate involvement of women' (Guijt and Shah 1998:1).

... nor are they islands

Communities are not islands. They are linked to, and have shared boundaries with, other communities, and they interact continuously with the outside world. Surprisingly, this reality is often overlooked because many of those who plan projects see communities as self-contained clusters of humanity littering the rural landscape. Communities are strongly affected by developments in both neighbouring communities and also in the larger groupings within which they fall – the district, the country or even the 'global village'.

The outside world constantly intrudes on the community. Opinions of religious leaders or national party politics change the opinions and objectives of groups in the community. There are numerous cases where local politicians, part of a network of patronage, give away water projects to win votes. Numerous also are the cases where politicians use the slogan 'water for free' as a way to gain sympathy and votes among rural dwellers. Having spent years implementing a programme of rural cost recovery, the government of South Africa, when faced by its first election as incumbent, decided to give a first 6000 litres of water per household away for free.

National and international economic development will change community composition and projects. Growth of wealth will create better opportunities for water projects. On the other hand, reduced state budgets will have the opposite effect, as in Cameroon where the government had to stop paying local caretakers in times of economic crisis. A small downturn in the global economy can result in untold damage at community level as national governments find their room for manoeuvre reduced. The damage is literally untold, because these small catastrophes are all too rarely reported. And when international donors and development paradigms and projects come into the community they often have unforeseen impact on social divisions and the balance of power.

CHAPTER 5

Factors that affect community cohesion

W E HAVE ESTABLISHED that communities not only exist, but are in fact often highly diverse. However, diversity alone is not a guide to how united or divided communities feel, how they pull together, or suffer from conflict. The ability of a community to unite around a water project will depend to a great extent on the degree of social cohesion.

Project donors often suppose that everyone in the community celebrates equally the arrival of a water system, everyone agrees on how to manage it, no one is excluded from decision making and all share in the costs and benefits. This degree of social cohesion is indeed a myth. Reality in communities is dominated by heterogeneity, division of interests, and differences in power. These divisions are based on deeply rooted cultural patterns and beliefs, or on economic or political differences.

A water supply system does not differ fundamentally from other communal resources such as schools, health posts or electricity, or indeed forestry or range land. Communities have managed some of these for a long time, especially productive resources such as land, labour, forests and agricultural produce. Despite the diversity, there is some kind of acceptance and stability in who manages these resources, and how. That does not mean that everybody profits in the same manner; simply that there is an historic but temporary acceptance. Such arrangements may favour some members of the community because of class, gender, clan or caste, or exclude others because of civil conflict. It would be a naïve perception of community reality to expect a new benefit, such as a water supply system, no matter how well implemented, to do away with these differences. In the first instance this new 'alien body' (Minnigh and Moeliono 2001) may in fact highlight existing disparities and inequalities. To overlook this reality is a guarantee of an unsustainable project. Many things affect social cohesion in a community. We shall look at some of them, in particular leadership and gender issues because these factors came out strongly from the research.

Caste, tribe, elites and politics

Caste troubles in Nepal

In Lele village one can observe the caste differences and the consequences for water supply. The Nepal research team reports: 'White and red coloured tiled roofs look very attractive for anyone who passes through the village of Lele. Houses peeping through Lapsi and Kaphal trees are of Tamang and Chhetri. A separate drinking water tap for Sarki families indicates that there is still the caste system deeply rooted in the village.' Mr Bishnu Ghimire is the former chairman of the water user committee (WUC) in the community of Yampaphant. He says: 'People of this village are not united, they do not know cohesion on the level of the community, only on the level of the tribe or caste.'

In Nepalese communities, social arrangements based on the caste system are well accepted. Over the centuries caste differences were incorporated into, or were the basis of, communal arrangements for joint farming, irrigation, Parma (exchange of labour), Pooja (an act of worship) and forest management. Other communal activities are managed at a community level. For example, once a year each household pays Katuwal the village messenger; Kami, the blacksmith; and Damai, the tailor. Such social arrangements are rooted in the (caste) history of the community society. However, arrangements for the management of a water supply system have much lower acceptance. The system is a newly imported technology and decisions about its management offer new opportunities for old grievances to be aired. The PAR research team of Nepal reports: 'In meetings on the water supply lower caste people stay at a distance. The higher castes present themselves as being the community representative.' The higher castes determine the water fees. If people from lower castes complain that paying the fee for water involves selling the rice from their second daily meal, the answer is: 'old woman you have to pay, no matter what'.

Politics and civil conflict in Latin America

Party politics also cause inequity and conflicts over the management of water supply systems. Political rivalry has long caused problems in communities in Colombia, and political groups often struggle for power over public services in communities. Armed groups also have a great influence on community institutions. Since the civil war in Colombia (1948–1952) conflicts between guerrilla groups have had repercussions on social organization in the community of Ceylán. Intimidation is used. So-called urban militias often control the management of community organizations. Doña Fabiola, chairwoman of the JAC in La Sirena and elected by the community assembly, was under pressure from a militia to resign. In the year 2000 paramilitary groups killed her predecessor, because they regarded him as liberal and left wing. Conflicts between political clans disrupt the management of public services when water committees or JACs are being elected. Even between elections, some groups express discontent with elected members of committees and JACs and refuse to accept their decisions. Under such circumstances the 'sustainability' of a committee can become fragile.

Clan conflict in Kenya – the role of the honest broker

Conflicts between clans or tribes in a community can also disrupt the management of the water supply, particularly where they are accentuated by faults in the design of the water supply system. In Nyakerato, in Kenya, rivalry between two clans, the Abakione and the Abatabori, has been causing problems in the management of the water supply for many years. Unfortunately, a donor agency constructed a piped gravity-fed system, which accentuated these divisions. One of the clans was served by the gravity-fed system. The other clan lived on higher ground which gravity pipelines could not reach. They insisted on contributing money to the gravity system in the false hope that one day they too would be considered for such a system. Constant fights between the clans paralysed the management of the water supply system. The local district administration had to intervene to put the record straight. In a general meeting it was decided that Nyakerato had to be divided into different sections, each with its own water committee, bank account and constituency. The committees would then constitute a central management committee to co-ordinate issues of common interest. Our red thread becomes visible in a positive way, because here, for once, the community was not left on its own. The intervention of the district administration is a good example of the need for an external 'honest broker' to come in and solve problems which, if left to the community, may become entirely intractable.

Gender issues

The relations between women and men are a pertinent aspect of social cohesion. This is true of all aspects of development, but doubly true for water issues because in most communities men and women use water in different ways and for different things. Of course, both sexes need to drink, but domestic water is almost invariably seen as a woman's affair, while water for irrigation is often largely the responsibility of men. As the examples below illustrate, decision making about almost anything is mostly seen as 'men's work'. In relation to water supply this often means that the 'participatory involvement of the community' is, in reality, a group of men making decisions about a system that will be used exclusively by women.

Women suffer most from poor water supply

In Hoto, Pakistan, women collect water for drinking, washing and bathing from communally-managed irrigation channels. But in winter the channels freeze. The women then have to fetch water from a far-away river. This is a precarious job because in the winter the paths become covered with ice and snow. One of the women from Hoto says: 'Water collection is our biggest problem. We have to carry jerry cans on our shoulders to fetch water from a distant river, which takes more than two hours for one trip, and sometimes we are injured while walking over dangerous tracks packed with ice.'

The women from Yampaphant, Nepal, expressed their problems with domestic water supply in a meeting: 'We used to spend two hours to get one container of water. You need to stay more then ten days to listen to the previous problems that we had to face to get water.' Similar stories were heard in almost all of the communities, and are well known to anyone remotely familiar with the water and sanitation sector. In fact, together with improved health, saving women's time and energy is frequently one of the main economic justifications given for investment in rural water supply. It is women who suffer most from a bad water supply, and new systems will reduce a lot of physical suffering. Nevertheless, when a system is being introduced, it is the men who take decisions.

Patriarchal societies

In many communities, women take no part in implementing water projects. While women may be discriminated against in all kinds of societies, in patriarchal societies the subservient position of women is formalized and they are often prevented from taking any effective decisions. Many religions have historically stressed the role of men as decision takers and women as domestic care-takers. Today this may be the case in traditional Islamic communities. There are many Islamic societies where women play an active role, but there are others where their role is almost totally domestic, and these do tend to be rural and poorer communities. Mr. Issiaka, president of the VDC in Nkouondja in the West Province of Cameroon explained that Muslim culture would bar women from becoming involved in project implementation because it separated men from women in public. Men in that community never allowed 'their' women to go to public places such as meetings, and women were not informed about or educated to recognize their role in the management of such an important resource that plays a key role in their domestic activities. In Pakora, Pakistan, the role of the women during project construction was limited to their traditional roles, cooking and taking food to the sites where the men were working on the construction of the water system. In Hoto, also in Pakistan, where women follow the strict rules of purdah, men in the community did not allow the research team to meet with the women. The men distrusted these 'outsiders' and feared that they would prove to be 'agents of negative change'. The women in Hoto are responsible for domestic water and for some of the irrigation works, but the men have traditionally been the ones who take decisions that affect the management of resources. How far this is a result of religious belief and how far religion is used to underpin existing practice is open to debate. However, in some Islamic societies it is often not possible to have meetings in which both men and women are present, or if both groups are present, women are not allowed to speak out loud.

The same phenomenon can be seen in some Hindu communities. In Lele, Nepal, the women were not allowed to take part in the exchange visits with other communities. When asked for the reason the men said that the women 'do not like to go out of their homes and travel far from home'. And in Yampaphant, also in Nepal, the first WUC consisted of 13 men, although women had participated in the physical construction of the system. Gender division is not only restricted to Muslim or Hindu communities. In Belén, in Catholic Guatemala, the participation of women during construction was limited to making food for those working. The implementing agency involved the women only by giving them a few talks on the use of water, the latrine and hygiene in the home. The Guatemala team writes: 'An important constraint for the women was the fact that they were married. The decision to participate did not depend on the women, but rather on their husbands.'

In some communities women were not even allowed to take part in communal construction of the system, although change could be implemented once trust was gained. In Hoto the households were organized in labour teams, and all men and women were required to work together to move rocks, sand and other materials to the construction site. Women had never participated in this type of communal labour so this was a very new experience for the entire community. In Nkouondja it was only after the intervention of the chief that women were involved in the construction work, and it was a surprise to many people in Nkouondja to see women moving around with men during community labour days, which were formerly organized on separate days for each sex.

When unequal gender roles are deeply ingrained in a society they can be upheld by both sexes. It is a mistake to think that the only problem is to convince some recalcitrant men to drop their opposition to women's involvement. In Hoto the men did not allow the research team to meet with the women for a year. Later, after confidence and trust between the team and the community started to grow, the female research team member was allowed to meet with the women about their role in improving the water supply. The women did not perceive their role as important and were not offended by the decision of the men to exclude them. 'The men didn't tell us about the meeting, otherwise we were free to come. Anyway, what are we supposed to do in the meeting? What concern is it of ours? This is the men's duty and not ours.' However, after a few meetings, the women of Hoto began to realize that decision making on the water supply was not just a duty for men.

Women motivated for change – the external catalyst

However excluded women are from decision making, because of their role in water supply provision they are often very motivated to improve the water supply in their communities. If they get a chance, they take it and come up with all kinds of creative solutions. Importantly, with reference to our red thread, such chances often have to be generated by outsiders, such as research teams, who by operating with respect and patience can act as catalysts of social change.

Don Felipe from Belén in Guatemala says: 'In 1975, UNEPAR started the construction of our water system. Steps were only taken because of pressure from the women. They protested about the lack of water.' Women in Belén started to participate in the water committee. They were the driving forces behind the committee. Don Juan, also from the community of Belén, says:

'These women are really determined, these women "pusieron pilas", are the batteries that power the water committee. Although it is difficult for us to accept, thanks to them we have water.' And another resident from Belén says: 'The women are more intelligent in obtaining and spending resources. They know when to say yes and when to say no.' Not everybody in Belén had the same opinion. The former secretary of the water committee said: 'Those women now in the committee are very nosy, they want to know everything.' Other residents who were invited to come to the meetings commented: 'Maybe these women don't have anything to occupy their time.' The participation of the women in Belén is appreciated, but it also remains new and strange. One of the men on the committee said: 'It was me who had to go to the houses to collect the contributions to pay for the debt on the repair that was done. It seemed that the men were embarrassed that a woman was collecting from them, so I had to go to collect the money.'

In much of central America it is common to assure resource sustainability by purchasing the water source and surrounding area, which may then be subject to some form of management intervention to preserve it – for example by fencing it off and banning tree cutting. In Aguacatán in Guatemala, it was women who pressed the community to buy the spring as a resource.

The women also worked on the construction of the new water system. Doña Calixta from Aguacatán says: 'Our husbands are working on the plantations in the southern lowlands. That is why we have to do this work.' The women carried the rocks, gravel and plastic pipes. Doña Jacinta says: 'The truth is that the local materials that we needed to construct our water supply system were not there. The men were not in the community. They had gone off to the plantations. So the women took advantage of the fact that a road construction company was filling the potholes on the highway with big rocks. We would hide, and when the trucks had left we'd bring the rocks to the community. We women could do that work because the men were not around. They sent money only to pay the "hired hands". These hired hands were doing only the heaviest work, such as the digging of the ditches and the hauling of cement, iron, pipes and blocks. We women also got training for the handling of the water cocks.'

Once women are convinced that a water system will reduce their burden and improve family health, they are always ready to pay. The people from Pakora in Pakistan are very poor and have very little money to contribute to the operation and maintenance fund. Women members of the community research team started to collect five rupees per month and deposited this in a separate bank account. Bibi Nargis, a young and enthusiastic member of the team says: 'We get the money for the O&M fund from the women because the men are never ready to give money. The women manage to get the money by selling eggs. Women are always ready to pay because they think that five rupees for the maintenance of the system is nothing, compared to their suffering in the past'.

Women's participation may be an obvious necessity from the perspective of those implementing a water project and pursuing universal inclusion. It may not be obvious for communities and it often touches on deeply rooted traditions and beliefs. It takes time and patience, and almost invariably the external catalyst of a 'project team', to involve women in decision making on the water supply and to help them take up a manager's role. However, with time, patience and confidence building it is possible, and normally leads to greatly improved project success.

In La Sirena, Colombia, the women play an active role in the leadership of all community activities. Doña Fabiola says: 'Truly speaking, at the beginning it was tough since all organizations were mastered by the men, and when women wanted to participate they had to impose themselves with force. It was a hard task, but we showed them that we were capable enough, and we did better than them and were never discouraged.' Women now play an important role in the management of the water supply system, and also in other communal organizations. This can be a mixed blessing. Doña Mercedes Astudillo, chairwoman of an enterprise that makes brooms and mops and cleans the schools, says: 'Some women are supported by their families in their household tasks; others have seen their work doubled.'

Sometimes indirect methods have to be sought to enable women's participation. In Pakistan, women selected female members for water committees giving representation to every ethnic group and *muhallah* (separate cluster of houses in a village) and running their committees in parallel with the water committees of the men. The two committees of men and women are considered to be an integral part of a single body, called the Community Research Team (CRT). In Cameroon the PAR research team organized a workshop in Nkouondja for water committee members from all communities, including women members. 'In Nkouondja they are now experimenting with the two committees system. It functions as follows. During male meetings, the president of the women's committee attends as an observer and if necessary presents ideas or issues from women. During women's meetings, the male president attends as an observer. This system permits women to discuss freely without the fear of disrespecting the men, which is very strong in their culture.'

Women as part of the project team

Women in research and project teams are of crucial importance, especially in communities where the division between women and men is great. The research team in Kenya writes: 'The gender balance in our own team made it easier to participate in activities of the women groups such as singing, serving meals and occasionally helping on the women's plots.' The Colombia team found: 'Recognizing the inequity in men's and women's participation in water supply programmes is a starting point to work with a gender perspective, which in the end can result in democratization of utilities. It involves rethinking of the traditional power divisions and facilitating that interests are negotiated.'

What goes for women goes for other marginal groups. Involving low-caste people in water projects in Nepal is very difficult. Involving poor people, land-less people or ethnic minorities in water management is difficult as well. The divisions of power are there. Beliefs and attitudes are deeply rooted.

With intensive and wise facilitation during project implementation, power issues may be dealt with to increase equity in the use of a water supply system and in decision making. A project team may succeed in overcoming the divisions and including marginal groups. But such new balances of power may be very fragile, and after the project team has left old grievances may come back and old patterns of power be restored. Community groups should have the opportunity to call on outsiders for support if they are excluded from the use of a system or from decision making, or if they face any other intractable problem such as conflict between clans or castes. Although in many countries laws and policies prescribe inclusion of all, in rural communities traditions are stubborn and social patterns based on social division are deeply ingrained. Mediation at times of disagreement or conflict between different community groups is a crucial part of the support that communities need to be given. This is our red thread – one of the missing links in community support.

A long and winding road

Feeling satisfied with the job and the result, the chief of Nkouondja in Cameroon said: 'Since you have been coming here, you talked to us about the importance of involving women but we never could imagine the difference we now see. We wish that you would continue to train them as much as possible. I would like to see them drive a car like the woman I saw in Foumbot town. You are now our light and we are ready to follow. It will be our pleasure to provide you with land and a wife from Nkouondja so that you become one of us.'

Dynamics of leadership

'Government agencies and NGOs are expected to provide the energy for improved water supply, but they need to know the limitations or frameworks set by the community leaders. They need to know how to work with these leader-ship structures,' writes the Cameroon team.

Leaders in rural communities derive their position from various sources: from tradition, from tribal arrangements or from administrative structures. Their styles of leadership differ. They can be the driving force or the constraint in improv-ing the water supplies of communities. They can act as advocates of improved water supply and they often play a crucial role in the settlement of local disputes.

Styles of leadership are often deeply rooted in social economic and cultural patterns of the community society. Leaders can change, but styles of leadership are more stubborn. In La Sirena, Colombia, three groups had been fighting over the management of the JAC for 15 years, using an autocratic style of leadership. After the PAR project had pleaded for a more democratic style, Doña Fabiola was elected as the new chairman of the JAC. Initially things changed, but after a while she started to make the same mistakes as her predecessors, using a top-down management style that resulted in low participation. The problem had not been the individual leaders who hindered a more democratic approach, but rather the style of leadership, itself deeply anchored in society.

The 'big man' – meritocratic leadership

In many rural communities an individualistic style of leadership is used, referred to in West Africa as the 'big man'. Big men are frequently leaders who have the best intentions and who want to guide the community, but often act in isolation. They speak for the whole community, saying what they know to be best. They turn water supply management into a one-man show.

In Campoalegre in Colombia this style of leadership hinders collective action and people do not identify with community projects and public services. 'There will always be someone who will do it for us', is a phrase often heard. In Campoalegre this someone is Edgar Guevarra. He has been working in all kinds of community projects such as electricity and telephone lines. He also is dedicated to improving the water supply. Edgar Guevarra is a former national boxing champion and, thanks to that and his good connections in the political party system, he has been able to source help from as high a person as the President of Colombia.

Management of the water supply system of Nyen and Mbeni in Cameroon suffered from the dictatorial behaviour of a chairman who did not share tasks and did not want to work with the elected Water Management Committee. He imposed rules and regulations which people rejected by not respecting them. A meeting of the committee was organized to discuss the problems but nobody was ready to speak out because of fear of the chairman's presence. It should be noted that this chairman was a senior civil servant now on retirement in the village with a lot of power over the people.

Big men may inherit their position, or like Edgar Guevarra earn it through becoming famous or rich. Another, more meritocratic type of leadership is that of the 'educated' person. Mr Rajendra in Lele in Nepal holds positions in many community projects. He is the secretary of the electricity management committee, secretary of the school construction committee, secretary of the village development committee and secretary of the BOVO (Build Our Village Ourselves). Why is so much power concentrated in the hands of Mr Rajendra? 'Because we don't have an experienced and literate person as Rajendra,' says Mr Nani Babu. Both Campoalegre and Lele profit from the specific skills of their leaders. However, concentrating so much power in the hands of one leader is hazardous, not least because of the vacuum left when they leave the community or die. In Lele rumours were going around that the secretary of the WUC was using the money in the account for his own personal projects.

Reading and writing make not a leader

It was taken for granted that someone who cannot read or write could not aspire to leadership. However, Tresia Mutisia saw in herself the wisdom that age brings with life experiences and maturity. She had the leadership that time brings. She saw the lack of clean and acceptable water and the high prevalence of diseases as a real life problem, and not an essay writing competition. She saw the problem as women becoming beasts of burden, travelling long distances in search of water, not as an exercise in grammar. She saw the problem as the wasting away of their soils and an ever-reducing yield over the years, not as 'environmental science' or 'agro-forestry'. She saw communication as passing a message, not as speaking fluent Kiswahili. Her local Kamba language would do. Tresia is now the chairperson of Yanthooko women's group. In her own quiet way she has kept the project going. The problems are many but so are her life experiences. Her illiteracy has not stood in the way of composing many a welcoming song for the visitors who come from far and wide, and how she can sing and dance! She is proof that illiteracy is not a handicap to leadership. Her members see her for what she is. A hardworking, fair and honest leader.

Traditional chiefs

Traditional chiefs play an important role in community projects such as water supply. They have the power, and all decisions in the community have to pass through them. The chief of Nkouondja in Cameroon is the symbol of respect and order. Meetings always take place at his palace, gathering notables and quarter heads of the whole community. In that way a broad support for change is created. Every community project needs the approval and participation of the chief. On the other hand a saying in Cameroon is: 'money that comes into the palace, will never come out'. Funds for improving the water supply are collected in the palace, but you never know if they will be used for the water supply or for other things. That is up to the chief.

Traditional leadership does not necessarily mean conservative leadership. In Hoto, in Pakistan, the traditional leaders felt that people with an education would be better prepared to take on the responsibilities of implementing the water supply system. They stepped aside. However traditional leaders may also be ill equipped to deal with the management of new technologies and institutional structures required for the management of improved water supply. In Campoalegre, leaders with modern management perceptions wanted to open a shop that would sell spare parts as well as plumbing materials for the whole of the community. They came into conflict with leaders with more traditional ideas.

In many rural communities the traditional leaders take decisions regarding communal resources, land, agricultural produce and water. In Hoto, Pakistan, the village elders and the Numberdar (village notable) have been responsible for the management of water in the community and for ensuring that all members of the community receive an equal allotment of water for their fields. These systems of leadership and resource sharing must be known and respected.

Working with leaders

Leadership is part of the social and institutional structure of a community. It is part of the balance of power and it is reinforced by the community itself. Styles of leadership are not dependent only on individuals but are part of social history. The style is often individualistic because democratic representation is not traditional in all communities or countries. Leaders are part of systems of patronage and their decisions are often arbitrary. Outside projects become subject to that style of leadership. That can be positive or negative, depending on individual leaders and the room they get from their community to manoeuvre.

What leadership will do to projects is not always predictable. Strong leaders are often seen as a blessing by project staff – they make things so much easier. Yet the strong leader may be too strong and, as the story of Mrs Mutisia demonstrates, leadership is not always related to high educational standards. Projects must obviously try to adapt to the leadership norms of the country or culture in which they operate. At the same time, they must make every effort not to become dependent on strong leaders to 'push things through'. Leaders should not be excluded, but they should not be given a stranglehold. This is easy to say, but difficult to implement.

Again coming back to our red thread, an enabling institutional environment may counterbalance some of the negative impacts of bad leadership. Policies, clear rules and regulations can bind leaders to standard agreements and control their behaviour. On the other hand, we know how difficult it is to enforce such rules and regulations in rural areas and how powerful traditional leaders are. They are often part of a system of patronage that extends from the community and links them to national politicians and decision makers. These complex systems of patronage and dependency often hinder the rational management of water supply services.

CHAPTER 6

Water flows through the lives of communities

Community perceptions and uses of water

It is not only community social dynamics that interact positively or negatively with the management of a water supply system. The way that people perceive water, its importance and use also affect how an improved water supply system is viewed and managed. What are people's perceptions of water? What role does water play in their lives? Does a water supply system harmonize with these views or not?

Water has always been an integral part of rural lives, productive lives, healthy lives and sometimes ceremonial lives. It plays, and always has played, a much bigger role in people's lives than just something clean to drink, which is sometimes the only role that the water supply and sanitation sector recognizes. In the perception of rural people, water is not always divided into potable and non-potable water. It is needed for crops, for cattle, for drinking, cooking and cleaning, sometimes for transport and sometimes for rituals.

In one way or another, people have always managed their water sources. If water was neither too plentiful nor too scarce, management was simple. If water was scarce, technologies and management were set up to deal with the scarcity, and there are many ancient, highly sophisticated technologies and management systems, especially for irrigation purposes. Who collected water, who decided about its allocation and distribution, which technologies were used, these were all aspects arranged within the community – be it a small rural collective in present-day Zimbabwe or in ancient Egypt. Some kind of balance existed. Sometimes the balance was questioned and disputed until new arrangements were made, and of course, as societies changed so the arrangements changed. Water as an ephemeral resource that is always in motion provides the perfect metaphor for society itself. Take a snapshot and you create a false image. Water and societies and their relations are always in motion – always coming from somewhere and going somewhere.

What has changed in the modern era is the pace of change. Now, rather than having generations to adapt to new ideas, people are supposed to make major adjustments every few years. In South Africa, rural water supply has gone from being ignored (but free) under the Apartheid government, to being focused on (but paid for) under the first post-independence government, to being still focused on (and partially free) all in less than ten years.

Another major change in people's perception of water is the introduction of water supply technologies for safe and clean drinking water. The technology

70

itself and the major assumptions that are built into the technol
people. To many rural communities improved water supply sys
bodies', prone to rejection or partial assimilation unless carefully
sustained by an outside agent.

Rural people don't separate out drinking water

Communities do not look on water as only for drinking – or only for irrigation, or only for washing or only for livestock. Water plays all these and many other roles in their whole livelihood. The tap is not opened only for domestic water supply – a fact that has traditionally been ignored in the water and sanitation sector, which has focused exclusively on the way that improved water supplies improve health and reduce women's drudgery.

Of course, the role of water for drinking is crucial: 'With the construction of the treatment plant many things have changed in the community. For instance, diarrhoea and other children's skin diseases have been reduced, as well as cholera outbreaks. When there were outbreaks of cholera in the nearby city of Cali, here in La Sirena, due to the good quality of the water there were no cases,' says Doña Fabiola Gomez. But better health may not be the only reason for communities to invest in water supply. Other reasons include the productive uses of water. People in Barrel Chiquito, Guatemala, recall how women's hard work in collecting water for a wide range of household chores was improved by the new project. 'Before the construction of the water project, the women hauled water to the houses from waterfalls or from small springs. It was used for food preparation, drinking and bathing the young children, as well as for the family gardens close to the house and for the domestic animals: horses, cows, chickens and pigs. To wash the clothes, the women had to go to the river. The older children, adolescents and adults would go to the river to bath, or else use the waterfalls. After the construction of the system, the water from the system was used for drinking but also for washing and bathing, for the family gardens, domestic animals and sometimes for coffee processing.' In Gajedi, in Nepal, people started to use the water from the newly installed hand-pumps not only for drinking, cooking and bathing, but also to water their animals.

A more traditional view of domestic water supply is taken in Belén and Aguacatán, Guatemala, where the management committees regard water for production purposes as inappropriate due to the low overall capacity of the system. Whether the system could have been designed to give more water is unknown. The point is that few water supply systems are ever designed with more than the domestic water supply in mind.

A particularly striking example of using the productive value of water to raise income for the community as a whole comes from Lele in Nepal, which sells water from its source to a nearby mineral water factory. However, it is seldom so easy, as demonstrated by the story in the box, where, despite water having a clear role in the local economy, it has been impossible to capitalize on this for the well-being of the community. Because the system was never designed with

71

iroductive uses in mind, the community was not helped to put institutional structures into place to deal with the matter more effectively.

Tad market day in Nyen, Cameroon

Preparations for Tad market start a day early. Women prepare for market. They clean the bars, cook food to sell, wash their clothes to look neat, wash the bottles for the sale of palm wine, and prepare corn beer. For all this they require water. Water shortage would be a disaster because this is one of the few chances the women have to make an income. On market day it is not only the people who are buying and selling who need water, so do the pigs, goats, sheep and chickens. There are also children who come to market – some primary schools even close on market day.

Market day is an opportunity for men to meet with the women of their choice. Everybody tries to attend the market because it is the only place where they can meet loved ones, friends and family members who live far away. All these people will need to drink water at some point during the day.

But Mr Tassi, chairman of the maintenance committee in Nyen, explains that the storage tank often dries up on market day, causing serious problems. 'It is difficult to control because everybody is busy and no one likes to come and sit here to control the use of water.' Why not build a fence around the tap stand in the market place? Mr Tassi suspects that people will push the fence down. What about employing someone to sit here and charge a small fee? The money could be used to maintain the system and even to expand it. Mr Tassi starts to laugh: 'You ask people to pay for water? Those are things you people do in towns. Water is a free gift from God and cannot be sold. That is not possible.' Don't you think that water use on market day is a burden on the community? Mr Tassi replies: 'The council in Mbengwi is responsible for this. We have asked them to compensate us for maintenance. No answer has been given, but every market day they come and collect market fees without giving us anything.'

Mr Tassi has to admit that the problem is serious, because he receives a lot of complaints from women who go back to their homes after the market and find their taps dried up. They insult Mr Tassi, asking if he has any problem with the women since he has decided to stop water flowing to their quarters. They will not accept any explanation.

There's more to life than water

Not only is drinking far from being the only use to which water is put in communities, water itself is only one of a range of factors – albeit a critical one – that affect communities' livelihoods. It is often not the only public service that communities have to manage. Besides their productive work, communities are involved in all kinds of development activities.

Don Carlos says: 'The mayor of Palmar, Don José López Rodríguez, came to Belén canton to offer us the water supply system, but we asked first for a school and electric power. My worry was the school because I already had one nine-year-old child and there was no school in the district.'

People are not always able to make water a priority. They have to make choices on how to spend their limited resources – cash, labour and time. Paying the fee for water may not always be at the top of their list. Like Don Carlos, they would rather invest in a school, or new equipment for agriculture, or a new roof, or just having a second meal each day. Such choices will hamper the management of the water supply system, even more so if alternative water sources are close by.

Rural livelihoods reflected in system planning and design

Let us pick up our red thread and consider it from the perspective of multiple uses of water. Would a more holistic approach to planning and designing water systems contribute to their sustainability? Should the perspective of water in rural livelihoods be incorporated in system design? The answer to both questions is yes. For too long the water supply sector has been dominated by health and hygiene considerations alone. For too long sector boundaries have imposed a narrow perspective of water supply on rural people. The opportunities are there and should be considered in planning and managing water systems. Institutional support could strengthen these opportunities.

It will not be easy to build on the opportunities to increase the sustainability of water supply by catering to the livelihoods of rural people, especially since there is so much institutional segregation in government institutions and ESAs between those responsible for water supply, those responsible for irrigation, those responsible for water resources management, those responsible for rural credit, and so on. Institutional support to community-managed water supply systems should include a more holistic perspective to water planning and management and increased co-operation between ministries and departments, in particular at district and community levels.

Pressure on the water supply system

Communities often struggle with the capacity of their systems. There are constant changes, in particular as populations expand rapidly. Water supply systems are usually not built for the future. Their design is static, taking into account only existing water sources, quantities and service levels at the time of construction. They take no account of the essentially dynamic nature of communities, and seldom allow for population growth or demands for higher service levels. As soon as pressure on the system increases due to population growth or illegal connections, the management committee gets into trouble. They have problems in enforcing rules on illegal users, problems with legal users who complain about lack of pressure, problems identifying new sources of water, and problems in extending the system with new pipes and taps.

The water committee in Belén, Guatemala, faces multiple simultaneous problems linked to rapidly changing community dynamics. The population grows as people migrate into the area due to the violence in the country. New taps are connected without taking into account the capacity of the source. In addition, more and more water from the system is being used for productive purposes such as watering cattle and coffee production.

In Campoalegre, the committee struggles with illegal connections as new settlements are built. Campoalegre and nearby Montebello are the only communities with their own water supply systems. New settlers have forced some 150 illegal connections through to these systems, causing loss of pressure and water shortages. The committee proposed a number of solutions. One was to use galvanized pipes, through which connections could not be forced, depriving illegally connected families of water. Another was to enforce the law better to make people respect the rights of the inhabitants of Campoalegre. Another was to negotiate with the families to legalize the situation, and to ask them to pay the monthly fee. The inhabitants of Campoalegre did not accept this idea as it meant that they would not be able to improve their service and extend it to those in their own community who were waiting for a connection. Lack of water in Campoalegre caused such a crisis that the president and the other board members were forced to resign.

In Yampaphant, in Nepal, the demand for water is also increasing, not because of population growth or increased productive demand, but because people in the community want a better level of service; namely household connections instead of standpipes. However, the water source is inadequate for such a service.

This highlights two issues. First, it is important to take future growth into account while designing systems, for example by over-designing the main network to allow for later connections. Second, support to help communities to extend systems to deal with increasing demand is one area in which continuing interaction with external support agents is critical. The red thread warns us that it is unrealistic to expect a community which benefited from external funding for a water system to be able to find the money and expertise itself to double the size of the system a few years later.

Conflicts over the use of a water source

Some communities face resource conflicts, typically where different villages use the same source or where ownership of a source is disputed. Often there are no agreed ways to settle disputes over resource use. Especially when water is scarce, conflicts can be harsh and communities are left on their own.

Settling the dispute

The water supply systems of Nyen and Mbemi are connected to the same water source. This has been a cause of many disputes, and has paralysed the functioning of the water committee. A meeting is organized to discuss the problems. Tension is high as members from Nyen and Mbemi enter the hall. Nobody speaks. The inability of the management committee to function is soon identified as the cause of many problems. Solutions are brought forward, including dissolving the management committee and electing a new one. The chairman stands up to put forward his opinion, but heavy protests prevent him from speaking. It turns out that the leaders of the Mbemi community have mobilized their entire population to outnumber the members of Nyen at the meeting. An old man from Nyen argues that an election for a new management committee would not be honest because of unequal representation. The people from Mbemi respond that everyone knew about the meeting. The old man explains that during the night somebody died and many people had gone to pay their respects. The groups discuss whether the election should proceed. An old woman, highly respected by both communities, says: 'When a child is at fault but accepts its faults, do you send the child away or do you tell it never to do it again?' The people from Mbemi cool down and decide to give the management committee another chance.

For a long time the Andhimul source provided people from Rangpur in Nepal with plenty of water. A 300 m pipeline ran from the source to the community. Then a neighbouring village, Sarasaya Phant, claimed water from the same source. The two communities quarrelled, but a solution could not be found, not even after mediation by the district administrative office. When the Red Cross came to Rangpur to support the community with its water supply, they identified an alternative source. However, the capacity of this source is insufficient. The water supply is open for two hours in the morning and two hours in the evening. People from Rangpur are not satisfied. They blame the Red Cross, saying that it came to Rangpur only to train people, and that it was incapable of resolving the more acute problem of the source.

The community of Pakora in Pakistan also has a dispute over resource use with a neighbouring community. This community says that it has the right to use the source for irrigation for a defined period of time during summer. But the source is being used to feed the gravity-fed system of Pakora, and the people of Pakora are afraid that the source will dry up in summer if it is used for irrigation by their neighbours.

Ownership is often a delicate issue. In many countries, ownership is unclear and often it is not well protected by law. In water supply management, ownership plays a role on different levels. Who owns the water supply system? Is it the community or is it the committee? What is the legal status of the committee vis-à-vis the community and the government? Who owns the source? Is it the owner of the land where the source originates? Who owns a country's water resources in the first place? Where ownership is not clear, water management suffers. Legislation to clarify and protect ownership is a classic red-thread factor in the success or failure of community-managed systems. Communities can do a lot themselves, but they can do a lot better when supported by an enabling web of legislation and law enforcement. Often matters of resource conflict have to be negotiated without much legal or policy support.

The Kenya research team describes how confusion can complicate water resource management, but also how the presence of external facilitation and knowledge of the appropriate legal mechanisms can help. 'There are a number of problems in the community of Kiveetyo. These include the destruction of the water intake, and the problem of the ownership and use of the land around the water intake. This was resolved with the help of the sub-chief. It involved sensitizing the owner of the land to the importance of the water supply system, by telling him how immense his contribution to the water system would be if he surrendered his land to the committee. It also involved holding a meeting between the land owner, the local administration and the water committee emphasizing the need to respect each other's rights, to ensure that the land around the intake and particularly the crops are not trampled, and that the committee reserves the right to inspect the intake. To date the problem has not recurred. However, we advised the project on the need to formally acquire the land through the relevant government agency, or to seek the consent of the land owner that it is surveyed and registered as public land entrusted to the project.'

Friction can be creative

Although community dynamics often create friction between water supply systems and their management, they can also have positive impacts on water supply management, especially in cases where there is strong and respected leadership. In Yanthooko, Kenya, for example, the women's group took the initiative to demand a water system and took responsibility for managing it on behalf of the whole community. Because they had the respect of the whole community, their management was quite successful.

Ceylán, in Colombia, is well known for its economic activity, coffee being the most important crop, followed by plantain. These products are sold in the region through co-operatives, which have been created by community leaders and have a long history. The organizational dynamics of the region, and the skills already developed through the co-operatives, help to explain the early creation of an organization called 'Public Services', which manages the local water system at an administrative and technical level and which is regarded as a successful model.

Development is a cyclical process; success brings skills which breed more success. However, early failure breeds disenchantment and cynicism.

To make the most of the positive energy in a community, solutions must, as far as possible, be tailored to fit in with community dynamics. Hoto is a village in Pakistan of some 180 households divided into four *muhallahs* based on family or clan membership. Each clan has its own identity and ways of looking at its position in the community. The traditional leaders decided that it was better to organize *muhallah*-based water committees. These committees would then be responsible for communicating with the households in their *muhallahs* and for organizing their *muhallahs* in by means of community-wide meetings. Division was not the breaking point, but became the starting point of the management system.

More often than not, conflicts in communities are counterproductive and communities struggle with the management of their systems. Our red thread is needed to repair the damage. Outside mediation and facilitation will be needed to overcome disputes. Clarity of ownership, clear rules and regulations, backed by national policies, can function as a safety net for community management and can guide communities.

CHAPTER 7

Instruments and techniques of management

How management fits in with community dynamics

THE PREVIOUS CHAPTER looked at how the dynamics of the community itself affect how people use and regard water. This chapter looks at the way management issues are critical to successful community management of water systems. We look specifically at the instruments the community uses to manage its systems – committees, technicians, rules and regulations. We see that management and community dynamics are inextricably linked.

Management problems in Belén, Guatemala: a cycle of despair

The committee in charge of the water system in Belén dedicated itself to collecting the fees, presenting accounts to the revenue administration, and selling new connections. At first, since the system was new, there were no problems. Maintenance consisted of cleaning the distribution tank and, occasionally, the collection tank.

Committee member Don Herminio Pérez recalls that they met only a few times. Three years after it had been constructed, the system developed many problems. People protested because the water was not reaching every part of the community.

There were also problems because the treasurer and secretary, backed by the water engineer, were taking decisions without consultation. The president and two members of the committee resigned because they did not like this way of working, and because of the problems that were arising. The treasurer and secretary remained on the committee for 12 years.

Over this period, the water spring that had been bought was no longer sufficient to provide water for everyone, yet new taps were sold without taking capacity into account. Water was used for productive purposes, especially for cattle and coffee, and demand increased as people moved in to escape violence in other places.

Eventually, the committee asked people to chip in money and bought the spring in the Morelia plantation. In 1992, UNEPAR started work and in 1993 the new system was up and running. One hundred more users were installed, and now the community had a total of 190 water connections, septic tanks for waste water and 190 improved latrines.

The treasurer and secretary continued taking the decisions without

---

consulting the community, and directing everything related to the water system. They collected the fees, they cleaned the collection and distribution tanks, they repaired taps in houses and presented accounts to the government three times a year.

And they continued to sell services without considering the capacity of the new spring. By 1994 the number of connections had reached 315. Problems began anew. Doña Dora said: 'We don't have water all the time. There's a shortage because the committee sells new taps; there are water leaks, and the community of Belén is growing.' The committee did not seem concerned. Don Santiago said: 'Essential repairs aren't done, nor do they review all aspects of the system. The committee does not hold itself accountable to the community.'

When the water system became unreliable, people despaired. Only 75 members continued to pay their water fee in full, and this was only enough to pay the water engineer to clean the tanks and for constant repairs because of water leaks.

The committee decided to ration the water supply, dividing the community into five sectors, and refilling the tank at night. This increased costs since they now had to have a full-time water engineer to open and close valves in the sectors on a daily basis. The fee increased from Q17 to Q27 per beneficiary per month, without giving families the minimum water they needed. People continued to protest. Doña Hermelinda said: 'In the high lands of the community the water no longer arrives, and in the sectors where it does arrive they have water for only three hours, and not every day. Still, the committee does not do anything.'

Doña Eugenia said: 'We don't know what was done with all the money from the sale of the new taps. The committee doesn't give information about how much was brought in from the sale of new connections, nor about the investment of this money. Neither do they inform us about the total number of beneficiaries.'

Doña Cheli commented: 'We're fed up because our project doesn't function well and we do not agree with the way that these three people are working.'

UNEPAR did not want to have anything more to do with this community and its complex problems. At the same time, the community was angry with the institution. According to one user: 'The only thing UNEPAR has given us is a promoter who reviews the books with the treasurer every four months.'

Management of a modern water supply system can often cause problems. It can be misunderstood, clash with existing authorities and management structures, make unrealistic assumptions about the available capacity and time, place too much reliance on the skills of a handful of individuals, and so on. Sustainability in management is therefore about matching requirements to capacity, systems to physical reality and technical ability, costs to ability and willingness to pay, system delivery to requirements, and so on. Get these right and the system will be sustainable. Get any one of them wrong and failure will inevitably follow, as was the case in Belén. Past struggles for water – walking for hours, contaminated water, diseases, water shortages – have been replaced by new struggles – managing a system, managing technology and managing community dynamics.

We start this section by looking at issues intrinsic to 'management' itself, examining how management is affected by community dynamics, and the dynamics of ESAs. Next we look at the components of the management system and what is needed to make them work: committees, chairmen, treasurers, training, financial skills, etc. In subsequent chapters we look at how management interacts with three crucial elements for sustainability: cost recovery and financing, system design, and resource management.

Institutional dynamics (ESA-community-committee)

At its worst, community management is nothing more than the dumping of what used to be government's responsibility on to the community. At its best it is a system in which government and communities work together, each doing what it does best, and with mutual support. The director of water in Cameroon does not believe that water committees are capable of managing the system alone. He argues that committees have a life span and will eventually die. He asks what will happen if trained community members leave the village, and he doubts the ability of the committee to handle major repairs. He believes that community management does not imply that agencies relinquish all responsibility. 'It is more a question of sharing, where the agency and the community know where each other's responsibilities and tasks start and end.'

This admirable vision can fail on two counts. First, when community-managed schemes are implemented as 'projects' with an implementation phase followed by 'handing over', the time and work to develop the skills and capacities of water committee may not be sufficient. Second, even when it is done, if there are no permanent support structures in place, the communities will be left facing insurmountable problems once the implementing agencies move on.

In Pakistan, committees were often formed on an ad hoc basis with varied interests. They were responsible for the systems, but not enough time and attention was given to making clear the role of post-implementation management. As a result, the management systems rarely lasted long enough to take over the operation and management of the systems. A study conducted in 1996 in 502 communities in the Northern Areas in Pakistan revealed that in only 5 per cent of the communities were the originally created water committees still functional (Ahmed and Lagendijk 1996).

Developing links between an ESA and a community can be a slow process, as can creating trust between a committee and community. It is therefore particularly wasteful to do all this, only to break the links with the community and move on after four or five years. Developing trust is a process. No single action or set of actions can give a committee legitimacy, or convince a committee of an ESA's ability to provide support and help. Success slowly breeds success, while failure can quickly lead to disillusionment. People's time is precious and they need to see that it will not be wasted if they become involved in ESA- or committee-led activities.

In Ceylán, Colombia, the process started with a handful of interested community leaders. Along the way, other community leaders became involved; still later, the community members themselves became protagonists. This passage from spectator to actor occurred only once they saw that the meetings, assemblies and discussions, which initially seemed like a waste of time, could come to life and show results.

By contrast, in Bokito Rural, Cameroon, repeated failure led to complete disillusionment. In the words of a rural councillor: 'You may have some good intentions, but we're tired of hearing about the issue of water all the time. The population you have here could have been doubled if we had been talking about something else. People are totally discouraged when it comes to water, because many of your friends have been here, said the same things year in year out, yet we still do not have water. So I am afraid that you might have wasted your time.'

In Aguacatán, Guatemala, not only was there incredulity and no small amount of cynicism when yet another group of outsiders from yet another institution came offering 'stuff', but the community was also suspicious, because paramilitary groups in the region used any pretext to obtain information about the community.

Problems with external support agencies are not confined to local government or NGOs. They also arise when donors decide to implement a system which reflects their own values and beliefs, but omits to negotiate these with the community. A Kenyan case study reported: 'It was noted from the discussions that in many cases donors come up with guidelines that are rigid for communities. This is quite a concern as, although it is important to have these guidelines, they should be flexible, be in line with what exists, and also allow the communities to sort their problems.' It is particularly unhelpful for a donor or other ESA to impose a set of guidelines when the organization has not the slightest intention of remaining in the area to provide the community with long-term support.

Building a relationship between an ESA and a community takes time. This, more than anything else, will overcome the initial hurdles. However, ESAs often do not have time. They have a planning routine to follow, and a budget that decides how they operate. But cutting corners will simply lead to failure, which is, of course, the greatest waste of people's time and money. The process must be allowed to develop at the right pace. Rural people are often not used to the 'professionalism' of cities, where people who have never met each other sit down and do business after a brief introduction. Personal relationships and long-term interaction are crucial.

All the more reason, then, returning to our red thread, that once the hard work of building these relationships has been done during an initial three-year project, it is not thrown away when the ESA moves on to the next project. Indeed, given the realities of operating as an ESA, rather than building a short-term relationship, it is surely better to facilitate those who have a long-term presence and mandate for community support, such as local government and local NGOs, to build relationships with communities.

Institutional turmoil in South Africa

We conclude this section with an example of a mismatch between community and institutional dynamics in South Africa. South Africa is a special case because since the introduction of the Water Services Act (RSA 1997) so many new actors have entered the water scene. In this case, lack of communication and transparency, political games, problems with cost recovery, and in the end vandalism and distrust, have brought the water supply system to its knees. Community dynamics and the dynamics of the external support agencies are out of sync.

The case of the community of Maboloka is described by a project officer of the Mvula Trust.

Competing institutional interests in Maboloka

Maboloka is located on the eastern side of Brits, falling under the Eastern District Council in the North West Province of South Africa. Work on the Maboloka water project started in 1996 and was completed by 1998. Responsibility was transferred to the Brits Transitional Local Council (TLC) as the water services provider and to the Eastern District Council (EDC) as the water services authority.

In 2000, The Project Steering Committee (PSC) established a development fund to allow the community to upgrade the scheme from communal standposts to individual household yard connections. Each household was asked to pay SAR 17.00 in addition to the set tariff of SAR 3.00 per kilolitre of water. The PSC presented a range of explanations and procedures at a meeting at the EDC's zonal office in October 2000. However, while people generally felt that the idea of a development fund was good, this well-intentioned development went tragically wrong. Why?

Lack of proper communication
When households were asked to pay for the development fund to allow the installation of household connections, the broader community was not adequately brought on board. Some households paid the initial fees, but the majority refused because they did know what the money was for. PSC representatives were supposed to promote the idea within their areas, but to a large extent this did not happen. Confusion was the order of the day.

Lack of co-operation between role players

There was a battle for legitimacy over who should champion local development. The EDC did not fully agree with the development fund and turned it into a political football game. Some claim that councillors of the EDC influenced people not to pay, saying that the community was being robbed, and that local government would provide people with household connections.

The Tribal Authorities were not supportive, because they felt undermined by the new democratic local government structures which reduced the role of traditional leaders in providing basic services.

Lack of clarity on legal issues

There are three categories of land in this community: state land (Lethabong Community Authority), communal land (Bafokeng Community Authority) and private land (Bataung Tribal Authority). There was confusion because the PSC did not give feedback to the community about how the different categories would be affected by the installation of the household connections.

Vandalism

The Bambamanzi pre-paid system, as it is commonly known in the village, was vandalized. It seems that the scheme stopped functioning due to lack of cost recovery, and vandalism was triggered because people were not getting household connections as promised by politicians. Criminal elements added to the vandalism and people stole batteries from meters. Some accused owners of private boreholes of vandalizing the scheme so they could sell their own water. The system has since been totally vandalized. A new system will not come cheap, a double tragedy since the cost of the existing system was SAR 30 million.

Reaping bitter fruit

The community of around 7000 households has lost all the intended benefits of a clean water supply and is now in misery. Women and children again have to walk long distances to collect water from the old handpump system. Others pay between SAR 6.00 and SAR 10.00 for 50 litres from private handpumps or vendors, which lasts a family of two about a week.

It may be that someone looking at this disaster would say that it was a community failure. However, it should also be clear that the initiative to upgrade the system of Maboloka, however well-intended, triggered a range of institutional conflicts over competencies, historical rights, political aspirations and interpretation of policies and laws. The case shows that the support institutions surrounding the community are not able to support the upgrading of the system to household connections. The policy is in place, but the institutional dynamics prevent it from being implemented.

The project officer of the Mvula Trust who described this case states that on other issues the community of Maboloka was perfectly capable of organizing itself. The project officer concludes: 'I think that if this community was given a fair opportunity the upgrade would have been successful. It is very important for us as development institutions to understand that the communities know best what they want. We have to identify community dynamics and make sure that communities are part of a project's decisions and have all relevant information. Our role is to give guidance, turn weaknesses into strengths, raise awareness about policy issues and identify existing strengths.'

The case shows that institutional dynamics have as great an impact on the outcomes of water supply projects as community dynamics. Having the support institutions in place, as is the case in South Africa, is not itself a guarantee for success.

Reinventing the wheel or working with existing structures?

We have seen how communities already have mechanisms for managing issues of common interest and for resolving disputes. Wherever possible, outside agencies should recognize the local institutions and structures that exist, pay respect to their strengths and legitimacy, and work with them.

A common error made by project staff when they are trying to work quickly is to parachute in fully formed management structures as a 'blueprint' for the 'social' part of the project. There is no quicker way to earn the hostility of a community than to ignore existing structures and norms, and to alienate local elites. However, existing committees and management structures can become overburdened. A sympathetic approach is needed to explore with communities the most suitable structures.

The choice of a management system, and who is to fill the various functions in that system, is key. In communities that already have a management structure before intervention, it is not always useful or necessary to establish a new water committee: instead this could be an added task for the existing (local) management structure.

In Uganda, when a new water committee was formed, care was taken to ensure that clear agreements were made between the new and existing structure, for instance local government, on the roles and functions of the different councils and committees (Arebahona 2000:4).

Applying a blueprint for a committee needs to be done carefully and with respect for existing ways of doing things. In Aguacatán there was already a well-entrenched tradition of communal decision making, backed up by traditional norms and regulations. Assemblies, led by formally recognized traditional community leaders, were part of community tradition, and although their form of functioning is not written down, what is discussed and agreed upon is respected and carried out. 'The assembly helps the beneficiaries of the water system to understand and realize what the central water committee and local water committees are doing,' writes the Guatemala research team.

Ignoring traditional ways of working created problems in Belén, Guatemala. It was established during participatory assessment that the water regulations were not up to date. However, in drafting new regulations the implementing agency, UNEPAR, did not take into account the established community practices. Regulations were made from behind a desk and addressed only the interests of the agency. They did not refer to the rights and obligations of beneficiaries, but to the functioning of the committee and its commitment to the agency. UNEPAR, basing itself on government resolution 293-82, defined how water fees would be charged and also nominated members of the water committee. They chose members of an existing pro-improvement committee in Belén, failing to realize that this committee did not have the full support of the community. Many community people were not satisfied with their work. After two years the pro-improvement committee was discharged, and the water committee went as well. For those two years it had hindered the management of the water system.

More often, experience from other management structures provides valuable skills for incorporation into a new one. In Nepal, Lele already had a forest users committee, a school construction committee and a committee aiming to bring electrification to the village. These all fed into the larger village development committee. The skills developed in all these committees provided a strong base for managing water in a similar manner.

Similarly, in Ceylán, Colombia, it was discovered that the business tradition that the community had established had an impact on the level of management and administration of the public services. Some small coffee producers had organized themselves into an association to commercialize and distribute their product, overcoming problems with transporting products to storage centres. This organization was extended to other products, such as honey and clothes made by women who had joined together to create a small business. Organization of the public services, which includes the water system, sewage, rubbish collection and, at one time, the post, was not difficult for the community because it had experience of working together. It has been easy in Ceylán to create a legal organization, to negotiate legal status, to draw up rules and regulations, to allocate functions, to elect the managing board and to keep accounts. Easy, both because of the skills of the community, and because of the existence of legislation that was tailored to the sort of co-operative structures that people were accustomed to working with.

Clarifying roles and responsibilities

The single most important issue related to institutional dynamics is clarity of roles and responsibilities within water management institutions. This is closely related to the transparency with which the committee operates. Clarity is crucial at all levels, both within the community and between the community and external agencies. How is the committee linked to the community, and how does it interact with the ESA? Who does what? Who needs to be seen when something breaks down? What is expected of people? Who reports to whom? Who collects fees? Who audits?

The research teams did much to clarify roles and responsibilities in the communities. 'Before the PAR interventions in Ghaziabad, Pakistan, planning in the village was very difficult and complex, but as a result of the community research team's involvement, management has become easier and more systematic. All activities in the community are now documented, including meetings of the village organisation and the women's organisation, a record of visitors, the duties of each CRT member, the funds collected for the maintenance and operation of the water supply system and the fines for households who left the standpost taps running.'

In Belén, Guatemala: 'The contents of the new regulations served to clarify the users of the water supply system on the rights, obligations and sanctions as well as the principal norms for water use. The objective of the regulations is to guarantee that the users, the committee and the water engineer are responsible for fulfilling their functions. It also helps the users to take ownership of the water system and to be able to have strict control, applying sanctions that the committee itself, together with the users, have made.'

In Nyakerato, Kenya, lack of clearly defined roles and responsibilities between the District Programme Office, the District Water Office and the community meant that they all had different views and concepts about the water supply. 'Due to lack of clarity in the division of roles between the water management committee and the local administration, animosity was high. The local administration stayed aloof, to the detriment of the proper running and management of the water system.'

It is also crucial that people know whom to talk to about problems, that responsible people are reasonably accessible, and that issues raised will be acted upon, both within the community and, with regard to our red thread, outside it as well.

The CRT in Hasis, Pakistan, made adjustments to ensure that water users could report faults more easily. 'Whenever the Zatoon goes to collect the fees, he has to hear complaints from the people. So it was decided that the households could go to the president and the secretary of the CRT to express their complaints. However, sometimes it was difficult to contact the president and the secretary, and people started complaining to the other CRT members. It was then decided that all CRT members had to receive complaints. Several interest groups, men and women, now complain if there is anything wrong with the tap water. The most vocal group are the women. When a woman is not getting enough water and hears the sound of air in the tap, she goes to the house of the nearest CRT member and informs him about the problem. Community members also check the distribution line to see if there is any abnormality in the water supply. All such problems are brought to the attention of CRT members. CRT members make a routine visit once a week to check for leakages and to listen to complaints from the users. This makes the community conscious about the condition of the water supply system and maintenance has become the priority of the community members.'

It is thus not only essential that the roles and responsibilities of all actors are clearly defined; they must also be acted upon. Knowing that your complaints are going to be heard and acted on proves a powerful incentive to co-operate with a management structure, as was also the case in Lele, Nepal, where a functioning system, an active committee and trained caretakers with appropriate tools has been linked to improved record keeping and transparency of actions. Now, if there is a problem in the taps or in the pipeline, the villagers don't touch the pipeline or taps without informing the WUC. In the past villagers tried to solve the problems themselves, sometimes even to the extent that they broke the pipes near to their houses to get water. Mr Rajendra, chairman of the WUC, says: 'Villagers have set a good habit. Even when there is no water in the taps for three days, the villagers don't touch the taps or the pipeline, without informing the caretaker and the WUC member.'

When people see that breakdowns are fixed efficiently, their support for the water committee is strengthened. In the words of Doña Teodora from Barrel Chiquito in Guatemala: 'After the work was done to fix the project, and when everyone had water again, the people loved us because they saw our work and because we talked with them in the assembly. They knew what we had been doing. It's better for us if people know about our work; that way, they help more.'

The work of Miguel

Workshops can play a useful role in allowing people to clarify their own duties and those of other people, as shown by a workshop in Ceylán, Colombia. Miguel, the water engineer, reports to workshop participants: 'I am happy that the administrators and everyone else recognizes that my work is difficult and involves great responsibility on my part. I see that I have made serious mistakes which have affected the management of the treatment plant and I think that I was one of those who has most benefited from this workshop. Not so much for myself, because I already knew all this, but for the Water Administrative Board and the people in charge because they didn't know the system. They didn't know about all the work on the plant and when they found out, they could judge better. This has meant better relationships and everything has returned to normal.'

Mrs Gloria Lida Soto, financial controller of the Water Administrative Board, concluded: 'Really we weren't aware of the importance of the work carried out by the operator and the degree of responsibility in the management of this plant. There is a need for the collaboration of the administrator in order to distribute the workload better... Sometimes, when we criticize or judge a person without really knowing his work, I think we are not acting correctly.'

Representation to resolve conflict

Water committees are the backbone in sustaining a water supply system. They decide who has to fulfil which tasks, who bears which responsibility and the level of the water tariffs. They also keep the accounts and enforce the regulations. Control and decision making are in their hands. However, they can function only if their decisions are shared and supported by the whole of the community. That is why representation of the community in its committee is crucial for sustainable and equitable water services.

In particular in communities with deep divisions based on class, gender, ethnicity, or religion, getting good representation in one way or another is essential. The question of who is and is not on the committee can lead to confusion and conflict. Women are often left off committees despite taking part in work and being largely responsible for fetching water. Different groups and power structures in the community must be included if they are to feel ownership. As we saw in the previous chapter – particularly in the section on gender – helping to ensure proper representation of marginalized groups is a critical role for outside facilitators and honest brokers, and should be underpinned by appropriate policies and legislation.

Democratic elections to posts such as treasurer are one way to strive for ensuring a representative mix, but they are not the only way, and not always the best. The combination of people represented in some of the committees in Cameroon reflects a mix of elected and unelected positions. Traditional hierarchies, important stakeholders (the cotton industry), and paid positions are mixed with an elected committee in which gender representation is enforced by assigning gender roles to certain positions.

However, it is not always possible to enforce gender representation on the central water committee. Sometimes parallel committees of women and men need to be created separately. As already seen in some communities in Pakistan, two committees of men and women are considered to be an integral part of a single CRT.

In Hasis, the water committee consisting of 15 members – nine men and six women – was formed with the help of the whole community. The Pakistan research team explains: 'Priority was given to notables, influential and educated people. The membership was based on clan membership. The role of the committee was clarified as: to take care of the water supply system, to bring water-related issues to be discussed at the community level and to gain experience in action research to help the community in development in the future. The committee is powerful because the traditional organization is supporting the committee. The significant factor is that the committee selection was based on clan, so now the whole community is bound to support the committee.' Ensuring a representative committee may lead to extensive institutional set-ups, but it is often the only way to avoid conflict.

While having an entirely elected committee may cause problems, so can having one composed entirely of elites. The committee in Sigomere in Kenya was handpicked by a group of retired public servants who had a patronizing approach to the management of the water system, giving little room for input from the general community. The role of the committee was divisive.

A sense of ownership

Developing a sense of ownership is typically seen as a crucial part of the implementation of water supply projects, principally with the aim of making communities accept responsibility for maintaining their water system. Often a community contribution to the construction of the system is regarded as an expression of a sense of ownership. However, we think it is more complex than that. What is ownership, and how can the dynamics of community management help to engender it?

Ownership issues lie at the heart of the seeming paradox that communities with long histories of water resource and supply management are often no more successful in managing modern water supply systems than those with none. In Northern Pakistan, the concept of community management is as old as the settlements that started there about 1000 years ago, and ownership and management of irrigation channels independently by communities is common. Despite this, the management of water supply systems failed because communities never 'owned' the systems and saw maintenance as the responsibility of the outside agencies who did, in their opinion, own them.

Spirit of togetherness, respect for traditional authority and a sense of responsibility

Dudu Mnisi, an engineer in one of the regional offices of Mvula Trust in South Africa questioned Mr J Makgoka, chairperson of the Village Water Committee of Mohlajeng.

DM: What is it about your community that allows you to manage your scheme in a sustainable manner?

JM: We work in a collective manner in this community. There is a spirit of togetherness and Mvula Trust told us at the official opening that the scheme belongs to us. It is our responsibility to take care of it. For instance, there is a need for yard connections in the village, but Mvula has explained to us that if people want a higher level of service, a thorough investigation should be done on the availability of enough water and on the cost and management implications of yard connections. So those issues have been discussed with the community and we now wait for a reply from Mvula.

DM: How do you collect and spend your tariffs?

JM: The Tribal Authority plays an important role in the community. People pay the Moshate (Tribal Authority) . We have agreed as a community to pay SAR 20 per annum per household.

DM: Do you think SAR 20 per annum is enough to carry out all the necessary operation and maintenance works?

JM: Yes and no. 'Yes' because we are able to buy diesel in bulk once per year. We have negotiated with Northern Oils whereby they have given us a big tank which carries 2210 litres of diesel. 'No' because there are some who don't pay for their service and this affects our saving account. We are unable to save for major breakdowns.

DM: But how do you maintain that spirit of togetherness while others seem not to contribute to the sustainability of your scheme?

JM: We are not a big community and we respect our Tribal Authority. Once someone is called by the Tribal Authority to account for non-payment of the service, they respond positively.

DM: What would you say to other communities that are fractured by politics or personal ambition?

JM: My advice is let us do things for our own communities. No one can bring development to you unless you make development happen in your area. Second, be prepared to volunteer your services. There are many challenges in community-based management, such as no wages for the Village Water Committee (VWC). It will take time for communities to understand that they need to thank the VWC for the service rendered.

DM: How long will you be able to volunteer your services to this project?

JM: I was born in this village, so I feel responsible to assist the people for as long as I am able. Second, I cannot imagine our community without water because water is life.

In Kiveetyo, Kenya, it was also apparent that the community perceived the project to be owned by the agency that assisted in financing the construction. The community contributed no resources to operation and maintenance. Records were poorly kept and information was not shared with the community as the committee considered itself to be accountable only to the funding agency. General meetings were rarely convened, and when they were, no systematic approach was used to inform the community about them. Leadership apathy and wrangles split the committee members and the local administration was viewed with suspicion.

A community member in Bokito Rural, Cameroon comments: 'When they came to build the water project we said "this is Father Christmas coming with his gifts", but when we encountered the first problems with the pipes, we found out that Father Christmas had left to go back to the Pole.'

Creating ownership

How can you create ownership? The PAR principle is to involve the whole community in research into problems and solutions. A community research team may do the actual work, but they must report back to the community.
In Belén, Guatemala, the community research team made a careful participatory assessment of the community's water and sanitation situation.

First: The community research team was trained in the investigative work that they had to do. A list was made of what needed to be investigated and ways to obtain information.

Second: The community research team did the fieldwork. It began with a walk through the whole community, where everything being observed was sketched out according to the list of topics that had been selected – water uses, current condition of the project's structures and latrines, garbage, black water (sewage), etc. Meetings were held with the committee and with groups of women to become familiar with the water situation. Other techniques were applied, including structured interviews, ranking different options, and drawing up a historical timeline of events.

Third: The community research team prepared a report and presented it to the whole community in a communal assembly. Specific water problems were discussed in work groups.

Fourth: Ideas and alternative solutions were established. In the assembly, Don Rubén said: 'The first thing that we have to do is to get the water to all the houses and for a longer time.' Others expressed a view that 'if it is necessary to give an economic contribution, we are willing to give it.'

A key question in the water sector is whether ownership is possible in the absence of payment. One of the most commonly voiced complaints from those implementing cost recovery within community management programmes is that 'nefarious politicians' mess everything up with promises of free water they can never keep. Certainly, in their view, payment is crucial to developing a sense of empowerment and ownership. This viewpoint is supported by the experience of Aguacatán, where a combination of work and economic contribution strengthened the identity that the community had with their water system. This translated into the feeling of ownership, as expressed by Don Reginaldo: 'We all feel like owners of the water project because we always have to watch what we're doing so that everything works out well and that we have water in our houses; also because we pay our fee.'

Repeated failure of the old 'owners' to take their responsibilities seriously can be a powerful incentive for ownership to be taken up by new owners – the community. In Belén, the new committee at first insisted that UNEPAR would come to solve their water problems for them again. Several applications were made for UNEPAR to improve the system or authorize another institution do it, but there was no response. Faced with this, members of the community research team declared: 'The best thing is for us to solve the problem ourselves and not wait for UNEPAR to come. We, the residents of Belén, must solve the problem in Belén instead of looking for outside resources.'

In Aguacatán, Guatemala, inhabitants decided that, in the regulations, they were not to be called 'beneficiaries' because that implied that they received only the benefits of the project. Nor should they be called 'users'. Instead, the community members agreed to call themselves 'associates' because this meant that they were owners of the water system and that they had responsibilities as well as benefits. This feeling of ownership made them assume more responsibilities regarding the management of the water.

Of course, one of the best ways to engender a sense of ownership is through actual (legal) ownership. Communities are more likely to protect assets that they themselves own. In Pakistan, the ownership of pipes and construction materials was clarified. In a meeting between the PAR team and CRT members a place was identified to store the pipes. However, WASEP engineers dropped them at the house of the village notable, where they were usually delivered. The CRT president, and later the whole CRT, refused to accept responsibility for the pipes because they were stored in the wrong place where they could be lost or stolen. The CRT urged the engineers never to do this again. Shukrat Wali, president of the CRT, said: 'The engineers have done a wrong thing. The pipes mean a lot to the community and if someone had stolen them who would have been responsible?'

Ownership creates a sense of maturity and responsibility. In Aguacatán, when there was no water supply system the leaders always thought about looking for an institution to 'make them a project', 'hand out financing', 'train them to handle it', 'bring them regulations' and even 'put in technicians'. With that attitude, the leaders imposed solutions and made decisions about community matters. Now the community takes advantage of the new water system and manages it, but also continues using its different water sources – wells, rivers, streams – to wash clothes, irrigate crops and water their animals. Assuming ownership means that they have also assumed responsibility and have internalized management of the water supply system within their existing community practices and regulations.

Ultimately, ownership comes to mean not just ownership of pipes and projects, but ownership of the whole problem and the means of finding the solution. In Belén, Guatemala, after finishing the evaluation of the project, Doña Dora handed over diplomas at a community assembly to community members who had directed the research process. She said: 'I am happy because we now have water. Those of us on the committee worked in spite of having several problems to resolve. The people pay their fees and love those of us on the committee. Now, it certainly is a pleasure to be on the committee. [...] They did not bring us pipes or money or material things. Together with them we learned to solve our water problems. The rain ruined our project again and we are sad, but at the same time we are happy, because we already know how to solve this problem. Now we know that it is not enough to have money; one must sit down, talk and sometimes fight among ourselves to find a solution.'

A sense of ownership, brought about by paying for the system and its operation and maintenance, or by other processes or incentives, is crucial to the success of community management. Our red thread asks a crucial question – can it be done without legal ownership? A sense of ownership becomes a farce if a district official can just take away the pump because he needs it to buy political support in another part of his district. Shouldn't a sense of ownership, be supported and embedded in a form of legal ownership and shouldn't it be protected by policies and rules and regulations for institutions above the level of the community? Is ownership, actual, legal ownership – along with process control – not in fact a cornerstone of community management? We elaborate on this in Part 3, 'The Way Forward'.

Rules, regulations and enforcement

This final section of this chapter deals with the issue of the rules and regulations necessary for effective system management, and with their enforcement. How are rules made, how do they gain legitimacy, and how can they be enforced? How are these aspects related to the dynamics between the various community management actors? As with everything else to do with community management, there are no simple answers and no blueprints. The reasons why some regulations will or won't work are deeply embedded in community dynamics. At its simplest, where there is little conflict in a community, and existing power structures are working well, there is a good chance that new rules created to manage the water supply system will work well and be easily enforced. Where this is not the case, because there is conflict, existing power structures are under challenge, or rights are not clearly defined, rules for system management are difficult to implement.

Rules and regulations need to regulate the behaviour of water users and also the behaviour of its management committee. The rules for the committee are essential to ensure transparency of action and communication. They must set out the proper relations between the various actors, and their respective roles.

Where a community is relatively conflict free and secure in its internal management, a strong system of management can be maintained with relatively little external support. However, where this is not the case, the presence of an external legal framework that allows enforcement and intervention by outsiders is essential. Our red thread applies to legal structures, rules and regulations as much as to maintenance and support for water systems and community-based management institutions. Sensitively developed and enforced, such networks can underpin and support communities' efforts; poorly or inappropriately designed, they make management almost impossible.

In Aguacatán, Guatemala, various efforts were made to develop rules and regulations, none of which gained the support of the community. Here, the agency that had supported the system construction in 1986 also brought a set of written regulations. These regulations did not help the community much, principally because their content was highly technical and because they espoused a different vision from that of the community. Later, a member of the WUC made other regulations, but these contained only his ideas. Once again, they did not work out. Don Aurelio Gómez commented on the problems: 'We are not familiar with the regulations that we have. They are only known to committee members. It seems like the committee members who made them thought more about their own interests than those of everyone else.'

In Belén, Guatemala, the experience was more positive, because rather than an imposed set of external regulations, they were devised in consultation with the community. Because of this, the committee managed to legitimize itself.

In Barrel Chiquito, also in Guatemala, committee members, the water engineer and three water users met, with the support of the community research team. First, a questionnaire was put together with three themes:

- rights and obligations of water users
- functions of the committee
- functions of the water engineer.

Everyone could give his or her ideas. They were discussed and a first draft of the regulations was made. Other aspects that had not been addressed in the questionnaire were also incorporated. After modifying the document, the committee organized a meeting for the community to present the regulations.

The enforcement of regulations is normally done through some sort of social sanction or fine. It is critical that where sanctions are imposed they are respected. In Lele, Nepal, consistent problems with illegal connections were solved by a system of fines. Anyone who cut the water pipeline was fined NRs 50 for a first offence, NRs 500 the second time, and NRs 1000, with a recommendation to the local authorities for further punishment, after the third time. The threat of punishment by the local authorities was critical to the efficacy of the whole system. The chairman of the water committee in Lele says: 'In the beginning the people just cut the pipes if there had been no water for three-to-four days. Now they warn the caretaker and do not touch the pipes. That is what happens if you impose sanctions of NRs 50 to NRs 1000 for cutting the pipes.'

In Nkouondja, Cameroon, public ridicule was used as a means of censure for the obstinate behaviour of the caretaker. The caretaker was told in public: 'Mama, you have abused our confidence. Be informed today that we are going to train another caretaker so that never again will you block water from us.' In Aguacatán, Don Chico illustrated how the assembly continued to be a control mechanism to apply pressure and to enforce the regulations: 'I know the case of a person who has a tap connected on his land but hasn't told the committee about it. If I go to tell him not to do it, he'd tell me to go to hell. It's better if I say it in the assembly. That way, he feels ashamed and doesn't do it again.'

In Hasis, Pakistan, the person who collects fees within the community is traditionally known as the Zatoon. He is responsible for informing people when there is need for communal work by visiting each house in the community. For doing this job he gets a fixed amount of grain or cash from the households. If someone from the community does not participate in communal work (e.g. repairing irrigation channels or repairing paths) the Numberdar, the village notable, sends the Zatoon to collect a fine. The CRT responsible for the water supply continued this traditional way of collecting fines from those who violated management rules. If any household refuses to pay the fines, the CRT has the authority to seize axes, a plough or a cooking container. If this is not possible, the CRT can disconnect the water supply, which is thought to be a shameful thing to happen to someone. To date, there has not been any such case.

A democratically elected committee on its own may not have the necessary 'respect' in the community to ensure payment of fees and fines. The involvement of widely accepted authorities, traditional or otherwise, gives essential support to community management.

To return to our red thread, it is clear that for a committee to enforce any type of control other than social it is essential that it derives some legitimacy from a wider framework of laws and statutes. The legislative status of the committee is essential – from where does it draw its legitimacy? In Guatemala, water committees are legalized by registration with local government, and this is seen as a key step in acquiring legitimacy. They gain additional legitimacy from being embedded in customary norms. In all four Nepalese communities, registration of the constitution was essential (and considered so by the communities), before the committee was able to function.

This Cameroon story from Nyen and Mbemi illustrates the importance of acquiring legal status. 'We did not have a legal water users' committee, so we discussed it with a lawyer and he advised us to prepare a constitution. We prepared the constitution of the WUC and started a lengthy process to register it with the District Administrative Office. After four months on 16 June 1998 we were able to register the constitution of the WUC. From that date we have never had to apply the constitutions' laws, because its legitimacy is respected.'

Let us give the final word to the secretary of the WUC of Nyen and Mbemi, who recognizes that legitimacy comes from a mix of legal and community acceptance. 'We registered the WUC, we are in a strong position and we are satisfied with it. But on the other hand it may not be useful or effective if we use only the laws. Public awareness is the most important aspect.'

CHAPTER 8

Management capacities

T HIS CHAPTER LOOKS at the question of management capacity. What is the ability in the community to undertake management of a water supply system? What are the skills needed to become a committee member? How do these relate to the type of system used? What are the possible roles of training in strengthening the capacities? What are the training needs, and what are the experiences of implementing training? Our red thread prompts us to ask what is needed to maintain those capacities once they have been put in place.

Once again, the differences between the systems in the different countries are instructive. The complex systems of Latin America require more management than the relatively simple ones of Kenya. Each level of system complexity brings a new level of management complexity. The more that is expected of the community in terms of operation and maintenance, the more that is needed in terms of management. The more money that needs to be recovered, the more complex the financial systems will be.

A report from the Cameroon research team raises the importance of this issue: 'Capacity-building for both community members and agency staff is fundamental for efficient community management. Advocacy has created awareness of community management, but how to make it operational is still a major obstacle in many organizations. Staff with limited skills, using inappropriate training methods and strategies, mostly end up frustrating the villagers because they [the villagers] are given responsibilities that are outside their capacity. Imagine blaming a treasurer for not keeping documented records when he or she does not even know what that means.'

Management skills and operational skills

Management capacity is essential for two largely different groups of people in the community: first for the technical people such as pump minders, caretakers, operators, network managers, engineers, etc.; and second for the managers themselves, the 'committee', who are responsible for overseeing the former while also taking more strategic decisions such as what tariffs to set, or what service level to adopt.

In Cameroon, this separation of management roles was not well recognized, and, as a result, training and capacity-building of communities concentrated on training in operation and maintenance rather than in management. The agencies themselves hardly distinguished between O&M training and community management training.

Typical roles of a committee include:

- representing the community in contacts with government officials, support agencies and the private sector
- co-ordinating roles with other community institutions and decision-making bodies
- ensuring efficient and effective overall management
- ensuring equity of water use and distribution
- ensuring equity in decision making
- financial planning, calculating and organizing contributions
- organising and supervising effective O&M
- enforcing rules and regulations
- maintaining accurate records, including financial records, minutes of meetings and important data such as member lists
- promoting hygienic and effective use of facilities
- holding and leading regular meetings.

Operation and maintenance skills needed include:

- upkeep and repair of systems
- monitoring system performance
- problem analysis, with the ability to decide when a problem can be fixed locally and when outside help is necessary
- collecting user fees
- enforcing regulations and bylaws.

An important difference between these two groups of people is that of voluntarism and professionalism. While management committees are almost invariably voluntary, only in the most simple systems should operation and maintenance be an unpaid task. In more complex schemes it represents a full-time job for one or more people. As this role is increasingly played by community members, finding money for these people represents an important part of cost recovery.

Dealing with the private sector

Being able to deal effectively with private sector operators is a skill that will become increasingly essential. This involves learning how to negotiate contracts, and how to ensure fulfilment of contractual obligations with local contractors working on part of the system, and with agencies that implement a complete system. It means knowing how to avoid being ripped off, and how to avoid signing contracts that cannot realistically be fulfilled. Communities seldom have expertise in contract administration. It is clear that while the private sector has many potential roles within community management, there is need for a framework to oversee these relationships, and to help communities (and contractors) to ensure that obligations are fulfilled and that communities are not exploited by unscrupulous contractors. Again, the red thread warns of danger and connects the need for outside support. Water committees also need legal status to be able to sue defaulting contractors.

Conflict in Nkouondja, Cameroon

The village chief
We dug the earth to build a new tank, which has still not been constructed. We bought the materials needed and transported them to the site where they now lie to rot.

The caretaker
This contractor deceived us. He has embezzled our money. I want an explanation from him before I go mad. I am stopping here for now. We signed an agreement authorizing us to manage the money together. But he never respected this. Once he got the money, he disappeared. He has even abandoned his office. Our project is now blocked.

The treasurer
He is the boss. He spent money without consulting me.
He took advantage of my illiteracy and made me sign the receipts.
This man is dangerous.

The contractor
I can't stand your accusations any longer.

Another committee member
Why did you disappear with our money?
All the technicians are now gone because you refused to pay them.
How do you expect our project to proceed?

Professionals and volunteers – getting the mix right

'Voluntarism' is used to describe the assumption of willingness to give of time and effort for the long-term management of community-managed systems – for example, by serving on a committee or undertaking repairs and maintenance. In the sense used here, it is the opposite of professionalism which means people who are paid to do a job. This is not to say that volunteers do not know what they are doing. Volunteers can act in a thoroughly professional manner, while some professionals would be put to shame by volunteers. The story of John Muno, who went from being a paid government employee to an unpaid volunteer, illustrates that it is possible to retain professional standards in either role.

John Muno's story – from employee to volunteer

Nyen and Mbemi are two communities sharing the same gravity water supply system that was started in 1974 and completed in 1980. It comprises the following components and facilities:

- 5 spring catchments
- 1 storage tank with a capacity of 9000m³
- 1 interruption chamber
- 3 public fountains
- 1 flushing fountain at the Fon's palace
- 1 shower house with an attached office
- 8 washing places
- 28 stand pipes.

John Muno was the first caretaker of the system. As one of the villagers working with the team that constructed the system, he was elected as caretaker and sent to Kumba town for training at SATA, now known as Helvetas). After training, he returned to the village and was given a monthly salary on the state payroll. This kept him satisfied and motivated him to work well. He did the job well with support from village institutions such as the traditional council and the village development association. After 16 ½ years he retired from the caretaker's job.

Before retiring he put in four years of voluntary work, after the government stopped paying caretakers. The four years were also used to train a young caretaker who was elected by the villagers and is now doing the job. Muno now regrets the situation because he says that the caretaker is not motivated enough. The young man cannot concentrate on the job or react promptly to complaints because he has to do other paying jobs to survive. John Muno recommends proper training of management committees to take caretaker support more seriously and to request state support through municipal councils.

The communities of Njen and Mbemi did not take over the payment of their caretaker. They hoped that the government would soon restart paying the caretaker and they decided to wait for that.

Not only does this case study illustrate the sort of 'caretaking' that is undertaken by the community on an ad hoc basis, it also illustrates one of the problems of having such a crucial position on a voluntary basis. Volunteerism requires enthusiasm and this can wax and wane. As more interesting, profitable opportunities arise people move on and training and skills are lost.

In Kenya, we see the lightest form of management, useful for the O&M of very simple systems. 'Most of the water points operate on an ad hoc basis, and the communities meet to address the problem if the water point breaks down.

The majority of trained caretakers are young women, which causes a problem because after they marry they often leave the area.'

As soon as systems become more complex it becomes necessary to formalize the position of the caretaker, normally through payment of a fee. However, paying the caretaker brings with it its own risks, with failure to pay resulting in system failure as surely as the marriage of a volunteer. In Pakora, Abdul Manaf, the provider of land for the tank construction, was appointed caretaker of the tank and the pipelines. The committee decided that he would receive PRs 800 per month. It was the committee's responsibility to collect PRs 5 from each household and pay him. However, he was not paid regularly so he did not perform his duty. Cost recovery is a topic in its own right, addressed in Chapter 9.

As the above examples show, there are limits to voluntarism, and once the limit is reached it is necessary to put operational issues on a professional footing. In general, the approach seems to be that in simple 'point' sources, such as the boreholes with handpumps in Kenya, maintenance relies on voluntarism by the whole community, by a dedicated individual or by a large group. More complex distribution systems with networks of water pipes and multiple taps tend to have a more formal system with paid caretakers, who have more status because the complexity of their job is visible. In developed countries, such as in the USA and Switzerland, caretakers of community-managed water supplies have a high reputation. In Switzerland they are called 'Brunnenmeister', the master of the source, and are professionals who undertake regular retraining. Caretakers in developing countries often lack that reputation and the respect that goes with it (Saladin, 2002).

While caretakers quickly become professionals, committee members are almost always voluntary. They often make great personal sacrifices to give time to their work, as did the villagers in Batcham in Cameroon. 'One interesting moment was when they had to participate in a workshop in another village. Information sent to them never arrived and when we got there to collect them, they were already at the market. When we explained what happened they immediately abandoned the market and hurried home to pick a few things so that we could move immediately. This was when we saw how committed these people were to the project. Generally, villagers would hardly sacrifice market days just like that.'

While voluntarism in committees seems the norm, it is not without a number of problems. The first danger is that the important offices will be taken by the well-off who are in a position to dedicate time to the committee. These may be educated people, retired civil servants, high-caste people, or people 'who have seen the world'. The second danger is that one day the volunteer sets his or her priorities differently and does not show up any more. The third is that the volunteer cannot resist the temptation to 'play around' with the money in the maintenance funds. Without both external and internal auditing this is easily done and was reported in a number of the communities.

It is difficult to overcome these problems. What is clear – and here we return to our red thread – is that it helps a great deal if committees are not left isolated, but are rather part of a larger support structure, with a clear legal status acknowledged in state policies and institutional set-ups. Training and capacity-building needs to be a regular activity instead of a one-off effort. The functions, rights and obligations of a committee should be clearly spelled out and backed by wider frameworks. External audits should be carried out. If committees and their office bearers are part of a broader structure, rather than operating in isolation at the community level, the voluntary job becomes more stable and even attractive.

Training – a vital task

Training follows two main paths – 'management' skills for committees and 'technical' skills for caretakers. There are several examples where lack of capacity leads to poor work, which in turn leads to rejection by the community. Training in aspects such as book-keeping and record keeping is essential if transparency is to be achieved. In Kenya, this led to improved relations between the community and the committee.

In Yanthooko, trainees are selected by the members of the water supply system. Thus accountability and transparency are enhanced. Trainees provide feedback after they have attended a training course. Records of training events are available to the members on request and regular sharing of information has become common. Training thus becomes less an investment in individuals and more an investment in the community.

'In the past, records were poorly kept and shared. The accounts were not audited. In Yanthooko only one person kept both financial and secretary's records, as the women shied away from this responsibility, mainly because they felt insecure towards the superiors from the ESA. Having completed the training, they now know that their primary accountability is to the community. The secretary and the treasurer have accepted the challenge. Membership records have been updated, management of financial resources enhanced, and time spent in meetings has been greatly reduced. The agenda for meetings has been streamlined, while transparency and accountability has been improved. Records are made available to any member on request, especially those that pertain to that member. This has increased confidence and trust among the members.'

Training can expand roles and skills that have a broader application in building community capacity. As capacity improves, management institutions can take on more activities. In Ceylán, Colombia, the committee has expanded its role to manage a small shop where spare parts are sold. The reputation of the committee is so good that it is now a community model. They also have an opportunity to sell their skills to other communities.

In Aguacatán, Guatemala, the association of water systems APAGUA (*Asociación de Proyectos de Agua para Aguacatán*) improved its management capability to the point where it moved beyond supplying water and began to promote integrated community development, benefiting the seven communities in all kinds of other ways. Neighbouring communities have sought APAGUA's support to train their committees and the Public Health Ministry invited APAGUA to present its experience to the directors of national sector institutions.

However, a word of warning comes from Barrel Chiquito, Guatemala, where the water committee turned into a general pro-improvement committee and bit off more than it could chew. It took on so many community duties involving the school, electricity and stoves that it ended up neglecting the administration of the water system.

Some carefully targeted training can greatly increase levels of confidence and ownership. In Belén, Guatemala, one of the training sessions on the elements of a water system – such as tank volume and capacity for supplying water – was extended to both the water engineers and the committee members. Committee members felt more confident as a result: 'Now we know when it is possible to hand out a new tap and when it is not', said one. The committee took steps to budget for the new tank and planned its construction.

It is tempting to avoid the need for training by using the abilities of an 'elite' within a village, and indeed there are ways that a management body can be structured to play to the strengths of different members. For example, the involvement of experienced retired public servants who are resident in Sigomere, Kenya, the inclusion of chiefs and sub-chiefs and the involvement of other government departments (water, health, social services) results in a capacity to absorb and assimilate concepts such as participatory action research with relative ease.

However, as discussed in the section 'Dynamics of leadership' in Chapter 5, over-reliance on a handful of gifted individuals is a two-edged sword. Better to take the time and effort to train people rather than rely on a single retired civil servant. The presence of a relatively well-educated person – often a semi-outsider – can undoubtedly make the community work more effectively. Equally, they can act as powerful agents for generating conflict and must not be taken for granted to the extent that a whole programme is built around them.

People must have the capacity to undertake the work required of them. In Nyakerato, Kenya, it took a whole training session before an illiterate book-keeper realized that he was not the man for the job. As well as the ability, people must have time and motivation to carry out the work. In Pakora, Pakistan, the first secretary was the most educated man in the village – however, he was also a businessman who was often away. He was not able to carry out his work properly.

In summary, it is clear that training is crucial to the development of capacity. However, great care has to be taken in ensuring that the training given is suitable, sustainable, and fits with community realities. Training, judiciously applied, can help a community to manage more complex systems and other development projects, but it cannot work miracles. Even with training, you cannot implement a complex system of community cost recovery in a village where no one is literate or numerate. You cannot expect a community where people have primary school education to monitor, unaided, contracts with the private sector. Both training and other forms of external support are needed, and our red thread demands that we define the right mix.

Training for the long term

Capacity-building needs to be designed for the long term and this is typically a task for support institutions. In the past, training has usually been connected with projects. But projects come and go, and when agencies conclude their training in the community capacities are both unprotected and endangered. Capacity-building for the management of water supplies should therefore be part of a support structure that looks beyond the project towards sustainable management. Training should not only focus on operation and maintenance, but also on management institutions, which must have a capacity for self-renewal as trained people die, leave the area or just get tired of volunteering. They must be able to train a replacement themselves, or send them on a training course or, preferably, both. Such training strategies are not typically considered by projects, so must become part of the framework for institutional support.

In Lele, Nepal, the community learned about the need for institutional sustainability the hard way. Mr Jit Bahadur Moktan and Mr Jhalak Bahadur Silwal were selected by the water committee to participate in the first volunteer training in Birendra Nagar, in the central region. They became the key volunteers during the diagnosis phase. A few months later Mr Jhalak left the village for a better job somewhere else. The committee realized that training one or two volunteers would not be sufficient to mobilize the community. When the second training course was organized, the committee sent six people from Lele, including two women.

In Sigomere and Kiveetyo, in Kenya, they ensured that the founding office bearers stayed involved as resource persons even after they left their posts. The founding chairman and other previous committee members still work closely with the current committee. In Barrel Chiquito, in Guatemala, the committee observed: 'Now that we know how to make the extensions, we are going to tell the people that there is enough water, and that more taps can be sold so that they won't oppose us. Also, we have to see to it that another water engineer gets trained, and if he resigns, have him teach someone who is going to stay on.'

Monitoring

Monitoring is a particularly crucial aspect of management, and one where perhaps least stress is currently placed. Much training teaches people to react to problems as they occur, while effective monitoring can head off problems before they become serious. The institutionalization of a monitoring framework will lead to better and more efficient systems and community management, whether through monitoring leaks or user satisfaction. It is important to consider what resources are available for monitoring, and whether they match the capacity and the requirements of committee members.

Monitoring in Belén, Guatemala

The new committee divided the community into two sectors in order to rationalize and improve the water supply system. First, one sector got water for 24 hours and the other did not. This was then reversed for the next 24 hours. This was done to check if the flow and pressure was enough to supply water to the houses in the different sectors and also to check for leaks in the system. It revealed that one sector consumed more water than the other, mainly because there were more connections but also because water was being used for productive purposes. This was discussed in a meeting with the community.

Monitoring can be as simple or difficult as required. In Barrel Chiquito, Guatemala, the committee visits homes every six months to monitor the water and latrine use. Doña Teodora recounts: 'When people found out that the committee was going to visit their homes, they'd get worried and clean all around their cisterns, not to leave signs of water being spilled. But we knew, of course, from what the neighbours told us that the water was spilled. They also swept the latrine so that it was clean when we made the visit.'

In La Sirena, Colombia, where monitoring water use was a problem, investment in technology and training led to a considerable improvement. 'The water supply system has 510 members but no water meters. Right now the meters are Oscar and Luis (the operator and the plumber) who are constantly knocking on doors so that people close their water faucets and pick up the hose. It was decided that water meters had to be installed in households with high consumption. Residents were prepared in a meeting. Two months after 20 meters were installed there was another community meeting. Oscar, the plumber, says: "People did not like it at the beginning, but they allowed it to be installed, and after the second month consumption was reduced almost by half. Now the neighbours also want meters. One can say this: there was more control of the use of water."' The committee decided to gradually increase the installation of water meters, although not everybody accepted them. The community research team members held meetings with people in the seven sectors to help them understand the value of water and the benefits for their health.

There is a range of aspects that should be monitored in the community itself. Users should be able to monitor their own household water use, especially if the fee is linked to consumption. Users should also be able to monitor the water committee through regular meetings, and by having access to financial accounts and minutes of meetings. System performance monitoring is a task for the caretaker, engineer or operator, and they often use innovative ways to do this

105

without much technical equipment. Committees have to keep payment records and monitor the proper use of taps and wells.

However, monitoring should also be part of the institutional support to community-managed water systems. To date this is seldom the case, largely because without a proper support framework in place, there is not much to monitor. Depending on the type of support framework, tasks for institutional monitoring of community-managed systems could include: auditing the financial records, monitoring source capacity and quality, monitoring equal participation of all sections of the community in decision making, monitoring equal access to facilities, monitoring the capacities of operators and caretakers, etc. Support institutions should also train communities in monitoring and provide them with the necessary monitoring tools and procedures.

A crucial aspect of monitoring is that it should always lead to action – or at least the knowledge that action will result if the monitoring identifies a problem. Knowing to whom to report the results of monitoring is as important as carrying out the monitoring in the first place (Shordt 2000). As with all the other tasks and responsibilities in managing water supply systems, communities can do a great deal, but they should not be left to carry the entire responsibility.

CHAPTER 9

Cost recovery and managing finances

OUR STARTING POSITION is that cost recovery is essential and must not be over-looked. How much it will be, and what the share between community and ESA should be, is discussed in Part 3, but we take it as given that some cost recovery is essential for community management.

Financial management of a water service is a complicated matter. You need capacities to set budgets, manage and administer finances, monitor payments, keep records and report to the users. Above all, the users of the service need to trust the system and those who manage it. They must feel that the financial system is fair and that the managers are honest. On top of that, users must be willing to pay for water from the system both in times of limited cash income, and in times of high water availability from alternative sources. What is more, all of these core factors – capacity, trust and willingness to pay – must be present to make cost recovery work. They are not always evident in rural communities.

All kinds of community dynamics threaten these pillars of sound cost recovery: different interests, poverty, gender inequity, fraud, different views about paying for water and simple lack of capacities. Communities mostly have to deal with these threats by themselves. The implementing agency may assist in the initial phases of a project but, after handing over, the community is on its own. One of the biggest hurdles to cost recovery is persuading people that they should pay in the first place. As we have seen, the issue of free water remains very much alive and politicians frequently promise it, whether it is in their power to give it or not.

Many different factors influence cost recovery, and they are all interrelated. The experiences in this chapter show how much time it takes to settle a sustainable and trusted system of financial management. Things can go wrong every step of the way.

Willingness and ability to pay

'They thought the water supply system was provided by the government free of cost.' Such a perception is expressed not only in Lele. In many communities people perceive the water supply system as something that comes from the outside, either from the government or from a foreign agency. If the system breaks down, they turn to the closest government official or agency to get help. Politicians and government officials themselves often propagate the perception that a water supply is a gift. But it is not only politicians who think that water should be provided for free. The local administration and many community

107

leaders have spent most of their adult lives seeing it as their role to provide free water and they feel confused by the change. Free systems may be of poor quality, they may be intermittent and they are frequently unsustainable, but the reality is that water is such a crucial part of people's lives that it is a potent political resource.

Another problem that undermines the willingness to pay is that payment schemes do not reflect the rural ways of life. These tend to be opportunistic and risk-minimizing, reacting to problems as they occur. An often heard remark sums this up. 'Why should tariffs be collected when nothing is wrong?' Users are generally indifferent to the future needs of a water supply system. They tend to consider the tariff collection as simply an imposition of the ESA and, where trust does not exist, a dubious one at that.

Willingness and, to a lesser extent, ability to pay, are two of the hottest topics in the water and sanitation sector. They are also central to the issue of cost recovery. Assuming, as we do, that payment for a water supply service is a central part of sustainable community management, we are still left with the problem of how to convince the community that this is right. The World Bank argument, that communities are willing to pay for water from a system because it is the only way they can get it and therefore demand is high, would be convincing if it were true. The reality, however, is that many people do get their water for free, and have done so in the past. It is not true to say that people are always willing to pay for a high-quality and safe water supply, because all around the world people are used to low quality, unsafe but free supplies, of whose dangers they may be largely ignorant.

Ninety per cent cost recovery:
Nhlungwane water project in South Africa

The water project consists of four reservoirs and 41 standpipes for 226 households. An additional four handpumps are maintained by the Department of Agriculture. The water committee holds monthly meetings and has relatively good financial records and excellent cost recovery (over 90 per cent). Committee members carry out a bi-weekly check of the pumps and water structures, and the community reports any problems to the committee or the operator. There is no meter to record water consumption rates. However, households (of three people) are allowed 75 litres of water per day on weekdays and 125 litres at the weekends. All standpipe taps are locked to prevent water wastage, and the responsibility for holding the key is rotated amongst the nearby households. As yet there are no illegal connections. That there is good cost recovery and positive attitudes may be related to the fact that water is scarce in the area and without the system there would not be enough water to survive. However, it is also evident that the committee is highly motivated, with a constitution that all local people follow.

The existence of multiple water sources is a problem for sustaining water supply systems. This was the case for the Department of Water Affairs and Forestry (DWAF) Rotterdam project in South Africa, where the existence of old handpumps and water from a nearby river undermined the implementation of a household network (Rall 2000). This is a complex question that calls into account whether there is clear demand for a system, and if not, whether there is at least genuine need. Where need exists, as reflected for instance in a high rate of water-borne disease morbidity, or because there is a genuine need for a periodic back-up in times of low quality, it should be possible to create demand through effective training or awareness raising. Where this is not the case, it is highly likely that the system is superfluous. The fact that people are not prepared to pay for water from a household network would simply seem to reflect a failure to adequately assess the need for this type of water supply. In Kenya: 'In areas where there are alternative sources of water the communities are not serious and will not really bother about the systems, but where there are no alternative sources, the communities try their best to make sure the project is sustained even with the little resources they have.'

Fitting the fee to the lifestyle

A fee for a water supply service is mostly in cash. But cash is scarce, especially in communities that depend on subsistence agriculture and exchange of goods. The research team in Pakistan had some bad experiences with fee collection in the remote communities in the Northern Areas. It proposed to examine alternative strategies, such as a fee through barter. The team also proposed to collect the fees in two instalments a year, linked with the marketing of crops and/or livestock instead of fixed monthly collections. More or less the same happened in Rangpur, in Nepal, where there was a regular collection of water tariffs. Since there was a limited fund, the community first decided to collect funds (two Rupees) on a monthly basis from each household. But this strategy did not work and the community decided to collect O&M funds on a seasonal basis twice a year and this worked out well. This money for the O&M fund was deposited in a separate bank account. A user payment card is still in use.

Willingness to pay, except in a few special cases, cannot therefore be taken for granted. Rather it must be created, by working with communities to raise their expectations of what can be delivered, to raise their awareness of improved health, and to raise their understanding that the service for which they are asked to pay will make an impact in their broader livelihoods. What is more, the concept of willingness to pay may need to be unbundled. First, there is the principle of willingness to pay, which is closely tied to ownership. If a community feels that it owns and is responsible for a simple system, then it is commonly willing to undertake repairs on an ad hoc basis.

Second there is the issue of willingness to pay regularly and on time. Developing this may take longer and involve more effort. Payment schedules must reflect rural income patterns (which seldom consist of a smooth income flow throughout the year). They must be backed by scrupulous bookkeeping and financial transparency, and – the red thread – will often need some outside support and supervision. One way to facilitate willingness to pay is to link payments to regular income-generating activities. This was the approach taken by a pilot project in Zimbabwe, where money from the production of vegetables was used to maintain the water supply systems. (Lovell 2000).

It is too easy to regard payment for a water service in isolation from other household needs for cash as well as, critically, from income flows and their timing. Money for water has to compete with many other household needs for money. Willingness and ability to pay will depend on household priorities and on the proximity of alternative sources. On an annual basis, payment for the water may represent a reasonable proportion of average annual income, but average income tends to arrive in a lumpy fashion both between and within years. Payment schedules have to be carefully devised or what may seem reasonable on an annual basis will appear extortionate when a payment falls due. How financial management and collection methods impact on willingness and ability to pay is discussed in the next sections. Here is just one example.

In Barrel Chiquito, in Guatemala, a low fee was fixed because people have limited economic resources. Each month they had to pay Q87 per person. Very little could be done with this amount. It allowed the committee to repair small problems in the water system, buy some cleaning materials and pay the water engineer. When there was a major breakdown there was not enough money for repairs. The committee had to go back to the users and ask for an extra contribution. This caused a high level of protest. In the meantime the system stopped functioning and people refused to pay even their monthly contributions.

'Ability to pay'

How can you tell the difference between willingness to pay and ability to pay? Is 'inability to pay' *claiming* to be poor and unable to pay? Or is it, *being* poor and unable to pay? The answer cannot be given in general terms. Not participating in a scheme or 'free-riding' often takes place using the excuse 'unable to pay'. It happens everywhere. The Kenya team, who experienced this in many projects, believes that the underlying issue is the attitude towards the whole process of implementing and managing a water supply system. This is linked to lack of self-esteem and especially lack of ownership. As long as people perceive water supply as a public good to be given away, that sense of ownership and responsibility for a water supply will be lacking, and this makes room for people to claim that they are poor and need assistance. When the PAR team first came to the communities, initial demands were invariably for new pumps or pipes or for support to extend the system. 'It took a lot of time to convince people in the communities that they should take up ownership of the system and that management was crucial to sustain the system.'

However, even increased ownership and empowerment does not automatically mean that people are able to pay. Willingness to pay is the driving 'sector narrative' of the World Bank/WSP. It is based on an assumption of the ability and willingness of the poorest to pay and a couching of the 'right' to pay in a language of empowerment (Sara and Katz 1997; World Bank Group Water Supply and Sanitation 2002). It may be convenient to believe that willingness to pay, based on a feeling of ownership and self-esteem, automatically translates into ability to pay, but there is an increasing body of evidence to suggest that this is not always the case. Poverty and inability to pay need to be explicitly addressed.

Willingness and ability to pay should therefore not be regarded in too theoretical a manner. They emerge and take shape in local contexts and the balance between the two changes, depending on the quality of the management of the system. Honest, proper and transparent management will increase willingness to pay, while sensitive scheduling together with flexibility in terms of payment, and linking water supplies to income-generating activities will all also address the ability of community members to pay.

Communities can address inability to pay issues

Communities themselves often address ability to pay, having the best insights into who should be able to pay in the community, and who cannot. They take the decisions on who should be exempted from payment, and such decisions take shape through negotiation and are based on the balance of power in communities. Accepting the inability of some people to pay, and offering exemptions, happens quite often. In many rural societies older people, people with disabilities or single-woman households are exempted from payment, and not only for water services.

NEWAH in Nepal has developed participatory tools to help communities to make decisions on different fee levels for different groups, and to decide on exemption from payments. In the absence of guidelines from governments, enabling communities to decide for themselves who should pay and who should be exempted is probably the best way. It is probably also true that a community sense of ownership and willingness to pay has to be created first, and a sound and transparent financial management introduced before you can address the issue of ability to pay. If financial management is bad and motivation and responsibility are low, the discussion on ability to pay will be polluted and cannot be focused in the right way.

Financial management capacities

Cost recovery is a complex issue. The capacities required to carry it out are also complex and place great demands on the management structure, and specifically on the water committee. Some of these capacities will be present in most communities, some exist only in communities with long histories of endeavour, and some will not exist at all. By 'capacities' we mean not only skills, experience and training, but also motivation, honesty and the right temperament. For the community to have the capacity to carry out financial management it needs the right people with the right skills, motivation and training in the right place, and it implies that they have the respect of the community and are able to communicate clearly with community members.

Whose money is it?

As she dipped her hand into her purse she wondered 'whose money is this. Is it mine or is it project money?'

Meet Maria Musembi, the treasurer of the Kiveetyo Kathyoli water project in Kenya. Seen as honest and hard-working by the community, the members of the water project entrusted her to keep and look after the project's money. Indeed, she was seen as unlikely to squander the money. But she also had her own money. Not so much, but still it kept mixing with that of the project since she kept it all in one safe place. Many a time she could swear that the project money was 'eating' her money because she found herself occasionally over-stretched and unable to meet her personal financial obligations. The small pieces of paper that she wrote for the money that she had received from the project members kept either getting washed along with her clothes or lost. One day matters came to a head. In a moment of great unhappiness she collected all the pieces of paper on which she had recorded the contributions received from the project members, walked to the chairman and handed them over declaring that she was completely fed up.

That was before NETWAS intervened and trained her on the role and responsibility of a treasurer. Today she is happy with her role and so are the members of the project. 'I now write a receipt for each and every coin that I receive and write a payment voucher for each expense that we incur. I ensure that the money is banked and that the cash book is updated. Today I can tell you whose money it is. Recently she was refunded KSh 3000 by the project, personal money she had spent on the project in the old days believing it to belong to the project.'

Look at the decisions that need to be made for cost recovery. Will all operational and maintenance costs be borne by the community or will major repairs be met by an agency or the government? What about costs for the replacement of the system? Will another agency or the government pay? None of the 22 communities in the PAR project paid capital costs. How do you explain to the community that they have to contribute to a replacement that may be needed in 15 to 20 years? These are complex questions. It takes trained economists years of university-level education to understand the concepts underlying issues such as interest rates, inflation, capital depreciation and discounting of future cash flows. They are also issues that cut to the heart of community management, for, given the complexity of making such calculations, it is in no way reasonable to expect a community to do so unaided and on its own. However, given the fact that many communities have to manage without such aid, there must at least be a proper match between a community's ability to pay and its ability to manage. There may be sufficient money in a project to pay for individual house connections but, without the support framework, it may be better for the community to remain at the level of a more simple shared borehole, where the management ability of the community is sufficient to ensure continuing operation over the design lifetime of the pump.

Experience from Latin America shows how a lack of effective budgeting skills can lead to unsustainable systems. In Belén, Guatemala, an initial fee was set by the ESA without training the community in budgeting or cost prediction. When the supply system began to malfunction it was found that the money raised was insufficient to cover the costs of repairs. However, when the fee was unilaterally raised, payments fell to 45 per cent of their expected levels. The research team trained the committee in cost analysis, which helped them to form a better budget and explain and justify fee levels to community members. Coupled with an overall improvement in system performance, this led to resumption of fee payment at the higher levels. In Barrel Chiquito, Guatemala, the community realized that the amount they were raising was not enough. Again, they improved their budgeting and after a period of explanation the community agreed to raise their contributions. Meanwhile, in Aguacatán, Guatemala, at times local committees did not manage the money properly. Record keeping was not the best and some committee members became corrupt. In La Sirena, Colombia, an administrative mess between various boards resulted in payment delays, creating a large group of delinquent payers, as well as unsuitable use of water and its waste. This situation prompted the board to prepare a user census and to try alternative ways to control the use of water, including installing water meters in the houses where community users were suspected of wasting a lot of water.

Budgeting is an important skill but, as the above examples show, all the skills and capacities dealt with in the previous section are essential – particularly communication. The committee needs to convince the community of the logic behind determining the fee and it needs to report on how the money was spent. If they need to adapt the fee they must be able to present the figures on which their proposals are based. Communication with the community has also been a problem in some of the Kenyan communities. Water committees are often one-man shows, often with the best of intentions, who see themselves as being accountable only to the project agency or to the local administration. They do not communicate with the users and their records are not transparent. This leads to mistrust and, in the end, refusal to pay.

Another problem in Kenya is the confusion of roles and tasks. In many cases the chairman does the work of the treasurer by collecting the money. The net effect is that payment records are not the responsibility of the proper office bearer and as a result are poorly kept, if kept at all. In bigger piped systems, where a lot of money is collected, office bearers – especially the chairperson and the treasurer – sometimes embezzle the money collected. Since the committees are not legal entities they cannot be sued and thus they get away with it, and the members end up being demoralized and refusing to pay for the water. There is now emphasis on training and empowering the communities to question whenever there is suspicion of embezzlement. Communities also need guidance on the kind of people that should lead them. Members of water user associations are now being elected and there is a link with the administration so that it can come in and assist when there are problems. Communication between committee and users, legal back-up for users, and mediation when there are problems are crucial processes towards achieving sound and sustainable financial management.

Water supply systems are dynamic. The user group may grow, new connections are made and the system may be extended to other parts of the community. Financial management needs to adapt to these new conditions. Many examples show that committees have great difficulties in doing so.

Good budgeting, good record keeping, transparency, and good communication with the community, the ability to adapt to changing conditions; such capacities are not automatically in place in communities. In many other situations these tasks are undertaken by independent, professional people. Now people without much education and without much experience are tackling them. The people with these key responsibilities are not independent of the community, but part of it, and they have their own personal interests. These may one day be confused with the interests of the whole of the community. Maria Musembi could swear that the project money was 'eating' her money because she found herself occasionally over-stretched, and in this case it turned out that she was correct. For someone less sincere than Maria it could be the other way around – his or her money 'eating' the project money. Without good budgeting and record keeping and without rules for reporting and communicating with the community, embezzlement lies around the corner, and it often ensnares people who started out honest and well motivated. The temptation is big if money is scarce and so necessary to survive. The only way to overcome confusion or embezzlement is through good financial management skills and systems, transparency, and where needed, our red thread – external support.

The system depends on trust

Maria Musembi does not have the right skills, but the community trusts her and that makes the system work. Everything revolves around trust in the committee members, their capacities and their honesty, and trust in the people who collect the money. However, trust is more difficult to gain than to lose.

In La Sirena, Colombia, women who were not members of the committee and who were therefore alienated from decision making, were more adamant about refusing to pay. Collecting was largely carried out by men, who did not have the trust of the women. One of the women says: 'The reason why people refuse to pay the monthly contribution is because those who are charged with collecting the money are not honest. They ask us to pay while they and their wives do not pay. They expect those whose husbands have no position to pay.' This woman insisted that until they have a system that is transparent, the conditions would not change. Similar stories come from other communities.

Doña Eugenia from Belén in Guatemala says: 'It's not known what was done with all the money that was received from the sale of the new taps. The committee doesn't give information about how much has been obtained from the sale of the new connections, nor about the investment of this money. Neither do they inform us about the total number of beneficiaries. It would be good if those in the committee informed us about everything that happens so that people don't go around spreading rumours.'

The support of outside audit

In the rush to implement community water projects, we often forget that one of the fundamentals of the entire financial system that underpins the modern world is that of the involvement of outside professionals, both for day-to-day accounts, and more importantly for verification. There is not a company in the world that must not open its books to an external auditor. Increasingly, this is the case even with small NGOs. Why expect communities to be different? The auditing of books by an outsider who is seen as fair and unbiased is one of the critical roles that support institutions can and should play. It keeps everyone up to the mark and ensures that errors cannot propagate themselves endlessly through the system. Involving an outside auditor was a key step in ensuring efficient cost recovery in Kiveetyo and in helping Maria Musembi to carry out her job. The team reports: 'The committee has in place a bookkeeping system that is updated at least on a monthly basis. Cash receipts are issued as and when the cash is received. This has ensured that the mixing of project cash with personal cash by the treasurer does not occur. They have an external agent undertake periodic financial management audits with the involvement of relevant government ministries. Charges for this are minimal. A bank account is in place and cash collected is banked intact. Internal controls were also observed where the chairman and secretary counter-checked the work of the treasurer. As a result of these measures, the revenue collection has improved tremendously.' Our red thread is all about the need for (and the all-too-frequent lack of) outside support to communities. Auditing is one such red thread issue.

Fees, collection and enforcement

As we've seen, setting a fee at the start of the project is difficult. Which costs should be included? Only those for operation and maintenance? Does this include payment for the caretaker? Should members of a water committee be paid as well?

Now we come to the question of collecting the fee and the type of fee, which in turn depends on the type of system. With kiosks (water points where water is sold directly on payment) as in Kenya, it is simple – people pay for the amount of water they collect. But what if different people share a water point, a pump or a tap? Often households pay the same monthly flat-rate fee. This may cause suspicion. Why should I pay the same as another household that uses more water?

Rates are sometimes collected once or twice a year to make the process simpler and less time-consuming. But the treasurer must have enough money in the account to pay for repairs during the year and to pay the caretaker. Paying the caretaker can also be quite complicated. In Lele, Nepal, the caretaker was initially paid a monthly amount to monitor performance, clean the system and do repairs. But some people complained that the caretaker was not doing enough and proposed to pay him a fixed amount per repair work.

Keep experimenting

In Lele, Nepal, an initial payment scheme tried to collect a fixed monthly amount for operation and maintenance. Although this was decided at a mass meeting, only 20 per cent of the people paid regularly, with 20 per cent refusing to pay at all because they thought the water supply system was provided by the government free of cost. Following an outsider-facilitated workshop, a second approach was tried based on traditional religious payment. Payment was to be in the form of corn (4 kg corn/year/household). People already make a similar payment to a Lama (Buddhist leader), and as such were felt to be familiar with the system. However, this did not work either, in this case because the time set by the committee for payment did not match with the auspicious (religiously appropriate) time for all the families. Committee members could not chase up payments frequently in the scattered village. The committee members realized that this decision was not as practical as they thought. They adopted a third approach, based on a one-off payment for each tap installed. This was deposited in the bank as a maintenance fund, and the interest was used for minor repairs of the system. While this was an improvement, it still failed to raise sufficient money. However, due to the increased capacity in the committee and community to solve their problems, the committee was able to try a final experiment, in which they held a community workshop and decided to collect NRs 5 per month for regular maintenance. The PAR team provided each household with a user card on which payments of the monthly charges are recorded by the treasurer.

Sometimes contributions are ad hoc. When there is a breakdown, the cost of repairs is calculated and shared among the users. This increases downtime, but can be effective since users experience the problem and are therefore more willing to pay for the repair.

In Cameroon, the MINMEE has set a tariff for simple community water supply systems. CARE Cameroon adopted the tariff but other agencies did not because they say the fee is too static, and the conditions in a community and the type of system should be taken into account. Certainly, if the collection and use of the fee is managed entirely by the community, this is a valid argument. On the other hand, where some part of the fee is remitted to an institutional support agency to offset the cost of more major repairs, it may reflect an acceptable form of cross-subsidy.

Enforcement – systems and people

A system of enforcement is needed to make people live by the rules. And once it has been adopted, people need to implement it. Both the system and the people need to be chosen with great care to ensure that they are seen as being legitimate. In the communities in Northern Pakistan a common problem was that the water committees were too passive in collecting the fee. In Hasis, committee members were expected to help the operator to make door-to-door collections, but they left him to do the job on his own. As he lacked the status necessary to make people pay, he soon became discouraged and stopped collecting. A different approach was tried in Pakora, where the members of the committee responsible for collecting the fees were selected on the basis of their representation of the different *muhallahs*. It was agreed that each member should cover fee collection in his or her different *muhallah* and this had satisfactory results. A similar approach was taken in Yampaphant, Nepal, where the water user committee had bitter experiences with previous collection methods. When a new financial system was introduced, they selected one co-ordinator for each communal tap and gave this person the responsibility of collecting water fees. Every user got his or her own user card that recorded fees paid. The combination of new financial methods and efficient collection led to a great improvement, to the extent that they were also able to appoint a watchman. Mr. Khil Prasad Lamichhane, chairman of the WUC, said: 'The user cards are very useful to keep the record up to date. The financial system has become more transparent and official.'

Fines can be a useful way to increase payment levels, as was found in Lele, Nepal, where the committee invented a fine and discount system to maintain the regularity of payments. If someone paid his or her fee between the 1st and 7th day of every Nepalese calendar month, then 50 paisa would be discounted. If they paid after these days then 25 paisa per day had to be paid as a fine. This made the users of the system enthusiastic. Payment records improved considerably.

In most of the 22 communities the establishment of a scale of fees and a system of collection took lots of experimentation and time to become sustainable. A crucial support in allowing this to happen was the outside mediation provided by the PAR project. With reference to our red thread, it is highly questionable whether the necessary period of trial and error will happen in communities where such extensive facilitation is not available.

Women do it better

The role of women in fee collection can be crucial. In Hoto, Pakistan, the committee faced great difficulties in collecting the fees from users. They approached the women's organization to tackle the problem. The women's organization visited all those households that were not paying and listened to them. They explained the importance of paying, why they were paying, what the money would be used for, what benefit they would receive if they paid, and what damage it would do to the water supply system if they didn't. In this way, the women's organization became successful in motivating families who were opposed to water tariff payments.

In a meeting in another Pakistani community, a lady about 40 years old, representing the women of her village said: 'Our men are not taking an interest in the project because we, the women, make water available in the home for their use. They don't feel our hardships in fetching water from distant sources. They are used to open defecation even during the day but we women cannot. If they are not paying the money for the project we are ready to raise it by selling some of our cattle.' Just after this meeting two women were reported to deposit their shares of PRs 1000 each and many asked the male community leaders to sell their cattle.

CHAPTER 10

Selecting and designing water systems and protecting the source

MUCH OF THIS book focuses on the problems that arise after a water system has been installed, once the community is left to manage it. But what about the design and installation of the system in the first place, and any future installation or upgrading? Part of the long-term management challenge is to make sure that the system can keep up with changing needs – that it can expand, as the number of people wanting a service grows, and that it can meet demand for higher-quality water or household connections. In addition, the community may be faced with major repairs, which require highly technical decisions about whether the system needs to be replaced. In the longer term, a community that takes over the management of its water system will want a large say in any new system that comes to replace it. This implies not only an advanced knowledge of water systems, but also of the geology of the area, the potential of locally available water sources, and the likely effect on any neighbouring water systems or communities. As with setting tariffs, these are difficult management and resource decisions even for accomplished and professional agencies, let alone for rural communities.

Designing and constructing appropriate systems

The trick to achieving the most appropriate design is to correctly analyse the existing (or possible future) capacity in the community, the level of external support available and the demands of the community, and to provide a system that is compatible with all three. This can have a dramatic impact on people's welfare and health. In Pakistan, household taps were provided as a direct result of community demand. This level of service, coupled with the messages disseminated through a health and hygiene programme, resulted in increased water use and healthier communities. 'The significant impact that has been made on diarrhoeal morbidity in the communities (i.e. a reduction of 50 per cent) is a direct result of consumer satisfaction with the product they have chosen and the messages women and children have chosen to adopt.'

While seemingly obvious, the issue of looking at available options before developing new infrastructure is important. Sometimes, rather than upgrading technology, the more sustainable option may be to 'downgrade' it. In Cameroon, people restored and maintained handpumps and wells that had been abandoned for years. Where possible, pumps were repaired, and those that had gone beyond repair were simply replaced with a rope and bucket system. Initially, the rope was pulled up by hand. Later they developed a pulley system that eased the water lifting. The pulley was locally made and works very well using very little energy.

But it is not all positive. In the past, agencies often parachuted systems in without consulting communities. In Batcham, Cameroon, after handpumps had been installed, the Government constructed a pumping system in the village during the Water Decade, through a company from Denmark called Scanwater. The system did not last for even a year because not one villager knew a thing about the technology. The choice of technology was so complicated that, even if the villagers had been trained to manage it, the system would still not be sustainable.

Another technological misfit can be found in Hasis, in Pakistan, where a suitable site to develop a gravity-fed system could not be found for half the community so they were simply left out of the system. Rather than attempting to find an option or mix of options that would ensure a water supply to the whole community the implementers went ahead and developed the sort of system they were used to.

A suitable system must respond to a mix of hardware and software issues. The design of a water supply system must not only reflect hydrological conditions and technical possibilities, it must reflect community demand and capacity to manage the type of system and the level of service. Making the right choice can take place only with good consultation between agency and community, and with good information about the consequences of certain choices.

Communities obviously have a role to play in system design. They must participate in the choice of the system and the level of service, not only to match demand with system design, but also because local knowledge is essential, and because taking a community's local knowledge seriously is important in building a sense of ownership. Mr Khil Prasad Lamichhane, chairman of the WUC in Yampaphant, Nepal, says: 'Technicians aren't all-knowing. They too can make a mistake, so local knowledge, experiences and skills should also be considered. The community has bitter experiences with technical problems created at the intake of the new source.'

However, communities are not all-knowing either. Their choice may be influenced by 'keeping up with the neighbours'. In Batcham, Cameroon, the physical conditions of the village were unsuitable for storing surface water, but the community had seen gravity systems in other areas and wanted one for themselves. This probably had more to do with wanting the individual house connections possible through a gravity system than with a realistic perspective on hydrological conditions. If such problems are to be avoided, engineers and communities have got to work together.

Management problems can be created by poor system design, by a mismatch between system O&M requirements and community capacities, or by the failure of the implementing agency to monitor what is happening. In Pakora, Pakistan, the community suffered from all three failures. In one of the *muhallahs*, the main water supply pipe was of a smaller diameter than the branch lines. This created pressure problems. In addition, the inlet chamber was not constructed in the proper place, because the engineers could not find a suitable location, and the tank deteriorated day by day. There was no proper sedimentation and filter system in the tank. The supervision of construction was the engineer's duty but he could not be monitored properly because his supervisors were not on the construction site regularly. The problems that poor system design, poor construction and poor monitoring caused in Pakora could be solved only by upgrading the system.

Complex problems can be broken down into less complex ones

Seven communities in Aguacatán, Guatemala, all use the same source: El Pericon. A 17 km long conduction pipe serves all seven communities with water. The system breaks down frequently because of landslides, caused by over-intensive agricultural cultivation on the slopes, or because people just break the pipes to drink water. The service gets interrupted frequently and this makes people unwilling to pay for it, which results in empty accounts and no money to repair the breakdowns. The caretaker complains: 'It takes us a lot of time to see where the problems in the conduction line are. Hours of walking and lots of dangers climbing up and down the mountain. People don't see that.' But the people from the Chex community reply: 'When we come down from the mountain to inform those on the committee about the damages, we don't find anybody. Most of the time we have to go back without anything having been fixed. This means that we have to walk ten kilometres to come down and ten to climb back to our community. Only the Central Committee has the tools to make repairs. So the only thing we can do is come down on the market day and look for the president or the treasurer there.'

It took heated discussion between representatives of the seven communities of Aguacatán to decide that it would be better to divide the operation and maintenance of the system. They divided the 17 km conduction line into seven parts, with each community being responsible for one part. The Central Committee then distributed padlocks and keys as well as tools to the seven communities.

A case where poor system design caused great management problems has already been mentioned: Nyakerato, Kenya. It shows lack of co-ordination between implementing agencies and insensitivity towards community dynamics. This story of confusion and conflict started with one group of families living on the western slopes of the hill requesting a spring protection which was converted into a small gravity-fed system. This system became known as Nyakerato A. With time, other families further away demanded a water service as well and, with the support of a donor agency, the gravity lines were extended. As time passed people living up on the hill where a gravity system was not feasible, were given a shallow well. This was called Nyakerato B. During this period, people living on the eastern slopes of the hill realized that they could benefit from the developments that were going on as well. They demanded and got a gravity line to serve the eastern slopes, which became Nyakerato C. Because of problems during construction, the gravity line in this area is much shorter and has fewer distribution lines than the system serving the western slopes. The Nyakerato community now gets water from a range of different sources: springs, shallow wells, protected springs and a gravity system. This has caused many problems between the different groups in the community and only by dividing the water system into three and giving each of them its own management responsibility, could some of the problems be solved. There is, however, still a lot of conflict over the different levels of service.

After 30 years of investment in rural water supply there should be considerable experience in constructing water supply systems, but there are still numerous reports of bad design and bad construction. Implementing agencies and construction companies are often free-riders whose designs and constructions are not supervised. They should be part of a framework where quality control is institutionalized. The Cameroon team reports: 'Quality control, however, still plays an important role in community management of water supplies. This could be in the area of defining clearly the procedures for establishing systems that meet the appropriate standards, such as protecting wells using lining and covers, location of toilets relative to sources, control use of catchment areas in a manner that avoids contamination, etc. Periodic monitoring of quality could also be set up to ensure that water provided does not become a public danger with time.'

Changing conditions in a community often put severe pressure on the systems as originally constructed and therefore also on their management. The following example from Campoalegre, in Colombia, where they have an extensive piped system, reveals all kinds of problems including illegal connections by people who migrated into the area and settled on unregistered plots. Illegal connections are a problem that many communities face, whether caused by existing inhabitants, by migration or by population growth. People may also demand a higher level of service. Responding to such dynamics is mostly too difficult for committees and caretakers. In particular, caretakers who are trained only once to operate and maintain a static system may become overburdened. Adapting to new requirements may be beyond them.

How can you plan additions to the system to accommodate new customers, or upgrade service levels? How do you match demand and supply and make sure that the resource is sustainable? How can you solve all the technical problems?

Many of these tasks are, and will remain, well beyond the abilities of all but the most advanced communities. Here again, we find our red thread. What happens after the system is installed? The community grows, services need to be upgraded, repairs need to be made. It is clearly the role of the committee to decide how these issues should be dealt with, but it is not their role to actually do the work. Just as calculating the internal rate of return on an investment should not be expected to be part of a communities' task, neither should calculating the dimensions of a system. Regardless of who actually does the job, whether it is an NGO, a government agency, or a private sector actor, the community and the caretaker must be supported in commissioning and overseeing the work. No programme of training, however participatory and inclusive, can prepare a community to make these sorts of decisions unaided.

Inspection of the piped system

Mr Arnulfo Morera, caretaker in Campoalegre, reports: 'We are here in "Quebrada los Ataudes". We shall go behind Mr Carlos' house where there is a problem with the de-sanding tank, which has no cover. There is also a problem with one of the pipes which has lost its support structure. From here we go on to Tranquilandia where we have another problem, because they take out an inch and a half of water which they use for a swimming pool and we haven't been able to get them to return the water. Then there is a part which goes up what we call a viaduct. Then we come to the mines. We have had to strengthen the system here, but we shall still have a problem, because when this breaks down we shall disturb these people. We go on to Montebello and here we have another problem, as there are a lot of leaks, so the water is not getting through as it used to do. What we call 'leaks' is actually unauthorized use of water by the people of Piamonte and Tranquilandia, who take off a large amount of water.'

Managing quantity and quality

A key area affecting the management of community water supplies is the resource base itself. How reliable is it? Is quality sufficiently high and, if not, what can be done? Is there enough water for all activities, or for domestic use only? Is there potential or existing conflict over water resources?

Water supply systems seldom arrive in a vacuum; normally, communities have been using and managing traditional sources. Water supply and resource management are necessary because the introduction of a system changes something and, as we have seen, water supply systems often have to compete with traditional sources. In Sigomere, Kenya, many people continued to use existing springs and wells, leading to a failure to maintain pumps on boreholes.

How water from different sources should be divided between different uses is an important managerial question that only a community can answer. How can sustainable drinking water supply be identified and protected, and how should the remaining water be allocated? What uses of water from a domestic supply system should be accepted and what should not? Should the water system include watering livestock, backyard vegetable growing, making bricks, running a laundry service, brewing beer? A system not only improves domestic water supply, but all kinds of other activities as well. In some communities, multiple uses from the supply system were accepted and encouraged; in other communities they were restricted or banned outright. Much depends on the quantity and the quality that a system can supply compared with the quantity and quality of other sources. Multiple uses can cause severe constraints in the management of a water supply system but, as we have seen, they can also offer sources of revenue to manage a system.

Another group of important questions relates to ownership and protection of the source. Who owns sources? What are the rights and obligations of the source owner? Can the owner be encouraged to allow access? How much of a protected area is necessary around sources, particularly surface ones? How can this area be protected, particularly when the source is on private land? How can allowances be made for changing water availability, through patterns of flood and drought?

Finally, upstream and downstream users interfere with each other. Upstream users take downstream users' resources. Sharing a resource for a water supply system can cause considerable management problems.

Managing the resource base, just like managing the system, calls for a mix of technical and managerial skills that may not be present. In Nkouondja, the caretaker commented that although farming in the catchment area is now controlled, neighbouring farm owners want the protected catchment area to be reduced to give them more farmland. The problem for the caretaker is to determine the area that is sufficient for catchment protection. Deciding the area around a spring or well that needs protection is complex, and depends on physical features such as topography, geology, soil type and rainfall. These features may be too difficult for a caretaker to assess.

Protecting the source – the first step

Managing or protecting the source and, these days, the catchment area as well, is the most common water resource-focused activity carried out in water and sanitation projects. In several of the Guatemalan communities, buying the 'source' was the first step in their community water supply projects.

However, in many other countries, even those where there is legislative support for source protection, enforcement is poor or non-existent. In Cameroon, for example, the law protects catchment areas for drinking water sources by declaring the land at the catchment to be of public interest. But the law is hard to enforce. Many sources are located on people's farmland and it has not been easy (or right) to evict landowners, especially when a 50–100 metre radius has to be taken as a protection area. Lack of enforceable legislation for catchment and source protection is also a problem in Campoalegre, Colombia. Juan Carlos Gonzalez, President of the Water System Administration Board of Campoalegre, says: 'The lack of control of the water sources is a serious problem. In the past we had water 24 hours a day supplied by seven water sources in the higher part of the stream. At the moment we have only two hours of water a day and we use three or four additional sources on the private property of Mr

Alcides Salamanca. Mr Alcides Salamanca is not interested in reforestation. The man wants to develop the property, not reforest it.' Doña Fabiola Gómez describes the problems with source protection in La Sirena, Colombia: 'Well, here we have the water intakes. This one is the one of the Melendez river, this one is the Valencia's one, this is the Epaminondas. Here we have the problem that they are sawing and cutting trees, which causes organic matter contamination. Here we have the filters but they are overloaded because they were designed for a given amount, and far too much water is coming down.'

Kiveetyo – multiple sources, multiple systems

The Athi Water Project was operated by the Kenya Department of Water. It served only a part of Kiveetyo. This supply became unreliable due to high costs of pumping and water treatment .The source was a surface water from the Athi River, which is heavily contaminated and carries high sediment loads.

Due to this unreliability, the community installed the gravity-fed Kiveetyo/Kathyioli Water Supply which, even though it has very low water yields, gives a steady flow of water which is rationed to the three main lines at Kiveetyo, Kathyioli and Mutitu in rotation during the day. At night, water is allowed to flow into the storage tanks of institutions, mainly the schools. The community intends to build a larger reservoir in order to store the night flow. Furthermore, plans are underway to harness more springs from up in the hills, a move which is likely to cause resentment from those communities living up in the hills who are unable to benefit from such a gravity system.

One notable feature is that, although the Athi Water Project and the Kiveetyo/Kathyioli Water Supply served some common areas, they are not interconnected. This is primarily due to the fact that the community fears that it will lose control of its gravity-fed system and will be forced to pay the Water Department, as those being served by the Athi Water Project have to.

Many communities do manage some form of source protection, and this can be efficient, particularly for surface water. In Nyen and Mbemi, Cameroon, the catchment area has been fenced, and trees are now growing round the area. All activities inside this fenced area have been forbidden. In Colombian communities, protection of the source and the catchment area has a high priority because water is getting more and more contaminated by small industries and agriculture.

Ensuring an adequate and sustainable supply

Failure of sources during the dry season, and particularly during drought is a persistent problem for those living in semi-arid regions. The Yanthooko Women's Group operates and owns one shallow well. Physical limitations hinder equitable distribution because, in Yanthooko, shallow wells are possible only along the dry river bed, and the water can thus not be distributed evenly across the whole village. During the dry period, water scarcity causes long queues. The Women's Group is still speculating on how to address low water yields during the dry season.

It is not only drought that forces communities to come up with solutions. Sometimes it is the competing uses of water. In Hoto, Pakistan, the water committee addressed the problem of sharing reduced resources by devising a system of rotation, a water schedule, which would take into account all the water needs of the villagers. The schedule allows the spring water to flow through the water supply system for four days a week. In this way, the 10 households are assured of an adequate water supply to charge their *gulks* (water pits). During the remaining three days, the water does not flow through the pipes, but is instead allowed to flow through the water channels, where it can be used for agriculture.

Protecting quality

Surface water sources in particular need a lot of attention to maintain quality, to protect them from contamination and, where this is unavoidable, to treat the water to make it fit for consumption. In general, prevention is better, cheaper and less managerially intensive than cure. In Pakora and Hoto in Pakistan, for example, the water channels are totally unprotected and easily become contaminated by agricultural, livestock and human activities. This microbiological contamination results in a high incidence of diarrhoeal diseases, particularly among children below five years of age during the summer months. Skin diseases are also common. Communities in Colombia, however, all have some sort of filtration and treatment works. With increasing population density and increasing pollution this is likely to become the norm.

Quality is one of the most important issues in relation to our red thread. Water quality is not easy to monitor. There are few, if any, low-cost, appropriate technology options available to ensure biological or chemical quality. While simple techniques such as bucket chlorination can combat bacteriological contamination, problems such as arsenic or fluoride are far more difficult. Because illness results only from long-term exposure, there is no short-term indicator of a problem. Once the problem is recognized, there are few effective remedies apart from developing a new source. Monitoring quality is yet another essential task for which communities need outside support.

CHAPTER 11

The enabling environment

COMMUNITY MANAGEMENT SHOULD not be a reason for agencies to escape their role. It is true that the communities take control and responsibility, but there are technical problems which still require the services of a trained technician – staff who should be at the service of villagers. Community management should include the ability of villagers to contact and request assistance from agency staff. In Cameroon, some communities even take the responsibility of paying the staff's transport fare.

This chapter will deal with five important aspects of the enabling environment: legislation, policies, implementation capacity, technical issues, and support systems. The enabling environment, or lack of it, is where our red thread comes to its end. This section should be about the policy initiatives that governments take to support decentralized services and community-managed water supplies. However, it is mainly about the lack of legislation, policy and support structures. It highlights the lack of a helping hand, the lack of a legal framework to support community management, the lack of adequate resource legislation, and the lack of financial mechanisms designed to help communities in financing, or managing their cash resources.

Let us first examine what it is we mean by an 'enabling environment'. Our red thread has picked out the key factors as we have come across them in the earlier sections: issues like legislation, financial resources, and outside mediation. A crucial part of the enabling environment is a support agency (or agencies), dedicated to helping and backstopping community managers. Such a support agency would play many of the roles notable by their absence in the 22 communities, and act as an outside facilitator to get over otherwise insurmountable problems linked to community dynamics. A support agency should be there to help design the system, to sort out the more complex technical problems, to provide a platform and facilitation for negotiating resource issues, to help supervise contractors carrying out capital work, and perhaps to help ensure a maintenance contract is carried out properly.

When these support agencies are there and work effectively, they are appreciated. As the team in Cameroon put it: 'It is not only about participation and involving community members. Such processes need the support of agencies whose role should be well defined. The process as we carried it out in Bokito Rural involved agencies, local village groups, and interested individuals. They all play an important role. Other parties involved were the Department of Community Development (CD) in Bafia and the CD head office in Yaoundé.'

The public sector

'Participation has limits and this process and its leaders cannot be expected to solve everything in the community. The state also has to assume its role and not leave everything to the people. Everyone should assume their own responsibility. We don't expect the state to do everything, but we don't expect everything to be handed on to the community,' says a member of the committee in Ceylán, Colombia.

In the final analysis it is the public sector that is responsible for creating the right enabling environment. The public sector has the mandate, tools and responsibilities to ensure that existing capacities, whether in communities, NGOs, government agencies or in private enterprises, can be brought together to serve communities. The public sector can define the policies and legislative frameworks in which all stakeholders can effectively operate to ensure sustainable community-managed water supplies.

The public sector ranges from national to (roughly) municipal/district level. Heterogeneity is a keyword, since in every country or region the structure and the set-up of the public sector varies substantially. The most important aspect in this variation is the degree of (de)centralization. Some governments oversee a structure in which all decisions concerning even the smallest, local issues are taken by the central government, and the lower government levels are there only to facilitate and execute central policy. Other governments have a decentralized system, in which regional, provincial or even local governments have decision-making powers of their own, and carry responsibility for their actions.

The box opposite outlines some of the challenges for the public sector as seen by the government of Cameroon.

Legislation

Legislation provides the initial framework within which community management takes place. It defines who owns or can own water supply systems and what rights and obligations go with the ownership. It should identify the roles and responsibilities of the main actors. It should also provide support for community-level rules and by-laws, such as those covering cost recovery.

The report of the National Reference Group meeting in Cameroon in August 2000 says: 'The legal framework and policy plays an important role in community management. The legal framework starts from the community's internal rules and regulations legalized by an administrative authority, and goes up to laws and policy guidelines regulating and guiding staff, as well as protecting the community management structures against recalcitrant members. The legal recognition of the water management committees is an issue that still needs to be addressed in Cameroon. It was observed that the legal recognition of this structure as a separate institution within communities might be problematic, especially in cases where an umbrella structure such as a village development committee exists. Members effectively agreed that there is a need for a legal

---

How the government of Cameroon sees the problems of community management

Initially the state executed, exploited and maintained water systems and their facilities through competent ministerial departments. When the economic crisis set in and a structural adjustment programme imposed by the IMF was implemented the state could no longer respect its maintenance obligations of the systems. It was therefore necessary to share the responsibilities with beneficiaries. The first management committees to manage Ministry of Mines, Water and Energy constructed systems were created in 1985.

Major problems relating to the monitoring and follow-up of systems:
- discontinuation of state services
- inadequate capacity of management committees vis-à-vis the size of the systems they manage
- lack of sanctions of recalcitrant users for failing to contribute for O&M
- frequent interventions by incompetent actors in the sector
- highly diversified technology creating maintenance difficulties in even the same zone
- absence of professionalism on the part of some partners of the state
- absence of a legal national policy guiding intervention in the sector.

Solutions already implemented include:
- regional harmonization of manual pumps to facilitate maintenance
- consolidation of a network of local technicians for repairs
- water resources law in the process of being promulgated
- old systems with sophisticated technology now being transformed and simplified with the intention of adapting them for management by users.

Much remains to be done:
- training and incorporation of young local entrepreneurs in the maintenance system
- future involvement of municipalities in supporting or assisting management committees in tasks that are above their capacities
- creation of an adequate institutional framework for the sector.

**From a presentation by Claude Bile-Bile of MINMEE,
National workshop on community management in Cameroon
29–30 March 2001**

---

framework for the management of community water supplies. This should be included in a policy for the rural water and sanitation sector, which is currently lacking in Cameroon.'

The legal status of water committees is often not clear, even where seemingly clear mechanisms for awarding such status exist, and this robs them of authority when they try to enforce their rules. The Kenyan team observes that in theory the legal status should not be in dispute, but says that the rules need tightening up. 'The problem is that by not having legal recognition, the committees cannot take legal action against those who do not pay for water, neither can consumers sue their committees for malpractice. The highest source of difficulty, which unfortunately should provide a conducive environment of community management of water projects, are the by-laws. In most cases they are silent or phrased in such a manner to allow loopholes.'

Securing the legal status of committees is a big step. Many issues that have never been addressed before need to be accounted for at this point, and the legislation often fails to do so. A NETWAS country case study about Uganda writes: 'The new water statute was enacted in 1995. The water statute, however, is silent on whether Water User Committees can sue or be sued. Neither does the water statute indicate whether Water User Committees have a collective responsibility or limited liability with regard to the funds they collect.'

This lack of legal status not only confuses relationships between committees and users, it can also be a constraint on external relationships. In Kenya most of the facilities are on private land and sometimes this creates problems of accessibility. The Water Act provides for the government to acquire land for public utility but even if the government did so there would still be questions of to whom to hand over the land, since the water committee is not a legal entity.

While legalisation is not enough on its own, it is a powerful weapon in the armoury of community managers. The Water System Administration Board of Campoalegre considered different options for solving a problem with illegal water use. Because they were registered and had legal back-up they could at least consider calling in the police. The committee had its water right registered by the *Corporación Autónoma Regional del Valle de Cauca* (an institution which has the duty of protecting, looking after and managing water resources at departmental level). When the community did not receive sufficient water due to 'theft' by new communities that were settling around Campoalegre, the board came up with various solutions. One was to change the pipeline design and use galvanized pipes, leaving the other communities without water. Another alternative was to negotiate with the other communities to legalize the situation, including the administration of the system, and to ask them to pay the monthly fee. A third alternative was to ask the Police Inspector to enforce the law and to make people respect the rights of the inhabitants of Campoalegre.

In Colombia, Act 142 on Public Utilities is a nationwide political and legal framework for the operation and administration of water supply systems. The research team believes that this is a start, but that the legal framework needs to relate more closely to the actual needs of community management to give it legitimacy. 'While this is an important step for community management, it is also true that the framework should be adjusted by consulting the local reality.

Only then will the support strategies be effective and promote local empowerment, and avoid management committees becoming entrepreneurial organizational models. The legal existence of a community organization alone does not assure its acceptance on the part of the community. Participatory processes are required to gain legitimacy as a condition for sustainability.'

Policies

Many countries are in a process, at least in theory, of changing the role of government from supplier to facilitator and regulator. In fact, as most people familiar with the sector know, the change is often externally driven and governments struggle with decentralization and with handing over responsibilities and power to district and local authorities. Many of the institutions on these levels do not have the capacity to take up the new roles. But the problems are not only in capacities. Often decentralization pays lip service to donors and multilateral organizations, but there is little real commitment to empowering institutions at lower levels with workable policies, regulations and guidelines. The recommendations in the box below were expressed by sector professionals in Cameroon, all of whom had long experience in working with community-based water supply management and had come to realize how big the gap is between the community level and the government.

Recommendations of the Cameroon national workshop on community management of rural water supplies in Yaoundé, 29–30 March 2001

Participants of this workshop,

Recognizing the importance of water for all living things,

Convinced by the importance of water for Cameroon's sustainable development,

Aware of the problems and difficulties in the management of rural water supplies,

Encouraged by the positive experiences of rural communities involved in the participatory management of rural water supplies,

Recognizing the important role that water will play in Cameroon's efforts in poverty reduction,

Convinced by the interest that the Cameroon Ministry of Mines, Water and Energy is demonstrating in the development of the rural water sector,

Hereby recommend to the Ministry of Mines, Water and Energy (MINMEE) the following:

That the Ministry of Mines, Water and Energy

1   Encourages the co-ordination and formalization of increased collaboration between all important stakeholders in the Cameroon rural water supply sector.
2   Facilitates the institutionalization of a National Reference Group (NRG) as a mechanism for the exchange of institutional and community-based experiences in the Cameroon rural water supply sector.
3   Finalizes and disseminates relevant texts of application to the National Water Law of 14th April 1998 to guide and support community management of rural water supplies.
4   Develops and implements a demand-driven national capacity-building strategy in the rural water sector in collaboration with key sector stakeholders.
5   Establishes appropriate mechanisms for the involvement of the private sector in community management of rural water supplies.
6   Facilitates updating and operationalization of the existing databanks for Cameroon's rural water sector.
7   Facilitates the dissemination of information that can be used to improve the training of stakeholders in the water sector and management of rural water supplies.
8   Facilitates effective financial management of water supply systems and services by Cameroon's local councils.
9   Encourages the identification and publication of best practices in the management of community rural water supplies.
10 Develops strategies to enable local communities to benefit from the HIPC initiative in the management of their water supply projects.
11 Takes these recommendations in account in the preparation of the Sectoral Strategy for Water Supply in Cameroon.

The change of government role from supplier to facilitator is a paradigm shift. It turns the world of the public sector upside down because it aims at empowering local-level institutions such as communities, while building and strengthening their capacities. Perhaps the biggest constraint in this paradigm shift is the shift in mentality of politicians and government bureaucrats. They fear losing the power that has provided them with the prestigious and privileged positions in which they have been working since independence. Sometimes bureaucrats just fear losing their jobs. However, as is often said, there will be no less work for government. Providing the policy and institutional frameworks for decentralized institutions and the private sector is a major responsibility for government and will not necessarily result in less work.

Community management builds from the bottom up, while decentralization typically comes from the top down. Where they meet is somewhere in the middle, typically around the level of district or municipality government. Both community management and decentralization will still take a long time to mature, but they cannot do without each other. In a number of countries where decentralization of the water sector is taking place governments seem to have realized this and have explicitly chosen community management as the preferred option for rural water supply and are investing great amounts of money in capacity-building at lower levels. This is the case in Uganda, Ghana, South Africa, Tanzania and India.

Poorly implemented decentralization often creates an institutional vacuum. This is the case in Colombia. 'Decentralisation processes have led to the disappearance of national agencies responsible for the development of water and sanitation programmes from the rural areas. While decentralisation has allowed community-based organisations to be more autonomous, it has also caused the disappearance of external assistance from the local government, which has failed to establish mechanisms to provide support to rural areas either because of the lack of financial and technical resources, or because the financial resources are being invested only in the main parts of the municipalities.' (Garcia 2001: 29). As a response to this institutional gap, 27 communities recently founded the Association of Community Based Organisations Providing Water Supply and Sanitation Services in South West Colombia. The aim was to make a contribution that would:

- strengthen the decentralization process
- improve the quality of water supply and sanitation services in rural areas and small towns
- achieve sustainable management
- generate economies of scale for training, spare part acquisition, project development, etc.
- become a communication bridge between communities and local, state and national institutions
- influence national policies on public utility services
- develop an organizational model that could (after review) be implemented in other countries where similar conditions exist. (Garcia 2001)

Not only does decentralization often fail to support community management, it sometimes appears to oppose it. In Colombia the institutions that were established as part of decentralization sometimes find themselves in conflict with the long-standing community-based organizations that grew from the bottom up. In Ceylán, a system of autonomous administration has been in existence since 1989. The people of Ceylán have refused to dismantle their community-based organization which is still managing their community water system.

Capacity of support agencies

Assuming that there is some sort of support agency, or that a support network is to be provided by local government, the next crucial question is that of capacity within such a support structure. Are staff sufficiently skilled and sufficiently motivated? Are they clear as to their new role? Do they feel comfortable with it, especially where it may have changed radically over only a few years? Will they be proactive in their dealings with the community?

If the support agency is not clear about its own role, and if it does not communicate that role effectively to the communities, then there will be a fracture in this flow of support at the very point where it becomes critical. Often people in communities simply do not know anything about the institutions at decentralized level or the public institutions and, when they do come into contact with them, they approach the devolved bureaucrats with timidity and too much respect.

The research team in Nepal asked Mr. Rajendra and other committee members to go to the District Water Supply Office (DWSO) and request assistance. The committee members were reluctant. They rolled their eyes at the suggestion as if to doubt their ability to make such an approach. They plucked up their courage and set off for the DWSO. However, they knew so little about it that they went to the wrong place and ended up at the Nepal Water Supply Corporation. They went back to the research team somewhat shamefaced and poked fun at themselves and their own lack of knowledge. But behind the laughter was a serious point: As Nani Babu said: 'We don't even know who the DWSO is, how we can ask them for support?' The research team gave the delegation directions to the DWSO office and called the District Engineer to request his support. Since then the Lele committee has visited the DWSO office frequently for support and consultation. The DWSO, for example, gave them a letter of recommendation to support their registration of the committee as a legal entity. After Mr. Rajendra met with the District Engineer of the DWSO Lalitpur, he felt encouraged. The District Engineer assured him of further support for the management of the water supply system of Lele, which was really important for Mr. Rajendra's morale.

This lack of information about decentralized support for communities is bound to lead to timidity and a failure of the two levels to develop close links and work together, unless the decentralized bodies are very proactive in seeking to build links with the community. ESAs such as NEWAH in Nepal play an important role in facilitating the transition and in helping to develop new attitudes.

The Cameroon team identifies the same difficulty in building an effective relationship between support institutions and communities, and describes this relationship as a bottleneck. 'There are repairs that are above the capacity of the users. These require the service of agency staff. The villagers find it difficult to get to these agencies, which are often in the cities or bigger towns. Even when they make efforts to communicate, the response is often slow. Thus, highly motivated staff need to be trained to assist communities.'

The team also identified the kind of response that can win the respect of village communities. 'The Provillage project of DED (Deutsche Entwicklungsdienst) developed a good system whereby a trained technician is assigned to an area to handle maintenance problems that are above the capacities of community people. These technicians are given motorcycles so they can move about easily and are supported financially by the project, but the villagers also compensate them for this service. This will gradually build the spirit of payment for services rendered so that after the project the technician can continue to function and the communities continue to pay for his/her service.'

The Government often acts to decentralize at the macro level without knowing what the real impact is at the micro level. Unless the support agencies are skilled and motivated, the enormous effort and expense of decentralization can be wasted. In Uganda, these questions are being asked. A country case study written by NETWAS staff about Uganda reports: 'The government of Uganda is following a policy that decentralizes power and decision-making to the lowest practical local government level. Responsibility for the delivery of basic services now lies at the District and Town Council levels. The government is allocating an increasing amount of funding to Districts via conditional and unconditional grants. The financial year 1999–2000 saw a huge increase in conditional grants, mostly from donor funding and HIPC (Highly Indebted Poor Country) debt relief, going to districts for water supply and sanitation through the Poverty Action Fund. ... In spite of the commitment by the government to community-managed water supply projects, existing institutional arrangements and human resources at district level to support community systems are insufficient. Intensive capacity-building at the district level is required to implement the intended government policy.'

This country case study on Uganda reports on a problem that will resonate with anyone with experience in community management. 'The project extension staff have allowances as long as the donors are around, but as soon as the donor has pulled out and there are no allowances their morale goes down and they don't continue their work. Yet they are very important to the communities for the continued support. It is thus important that the project should develop a system to make sure that extension staff continue working, or there should be a mechanism at district level to motivate the extension staff after the donors have withdrawn.'

Technical issues: spare parts and standardization

One vital aspect of implementation capacity is for support agencies to be capable of preventing and overcoming confusion over standardization and spare parts. These issues, despite being old, raise their heads again and again.

The Cameroon research team describes a nightmare scenario that is all too real for the people involved. 'There are numerous different types of manual pumps used in the country. These include Vergnet (French made), Briau

(Cameroon made), Volanta (Dutch), Wavin (Dutch) and other Belgian and Bangladeshi designs. The absence of guidelines or policy-setting standards has created a vacuum in which a donor can choose any type of manual pump. Most of the time, the villagers do not have any choice. In the Northern zone, where the manual pump is the main technology for improved systems, staff of the Ministry of Mines, Water and Power (MINMEE) and of the Department of Community Development (CD) of the Ministry of Agriculture have very different opinions about the pumps. MINMEE staff prefer the Vergnet, which is French while CD staff prefer the Briau. CD staff argue that spare parts for Vergnet are very expensive for community people. MINMEE staff advocate the French efforts to train local mechanics and set up spare part stores. The result of this difference of opinion is that different manual pumps are installed in the same area, sometimes just on the other side of the road.'

Lack of co-operation often results in disagreement on the type of handpumps to be purchased. You do not have to go as far as Zimbabwe, where only one type of locally manufactured pump is allowed, to realize the benefits of a degree of standardization (Moriarty and Lovell 2000). At the very least, all capital equipment should have a reasonably well-entrenched system for the delivery of spare parts. This is essentially a policy issue, but one that needs to be solidly rooted in market reality and which is demand-responsive so that communities are not denied access to something they may need.

A general problem with the spare parts is that the quality is poor. Most locally manufactured parts become unreliable, although they are cheaper. For example, in Cameroon a tap manufactured locally and sold in local markets costs about CFAfr4000, but will last for only six months. An imported tap from Switzerland costs CFAfr12000, but lasts for more than four years. Helvetas experimented with this tap in Nyen and Mbemi, and the villagers believe that it is better and cheaper in the long term than the locally made one. The problem is availability, because Helvetas sells the Swiss taps only to its own projects. Such problems can be resolved only by a firm policy and an effective support agency which is part of, or closely linked with, a state organization.

Who is the support agency?

We have talked a lot about the support agency, and have developed at least some idea of what it is. But who should take up the roles assigned to this conceptual entity? Community-level support systems can be provided by a number of different organizations and institutions, such as local government, local line ministries, NGOs, CBOs, or dedicated national community water and sanitation support agencies (such as South Africa's Mvula Trust or Nepal's NEWAH). Regardless of who they are, to meet the demands of our red thread they must be at least semi-permanent. An NGO engaged in a three-year district-level project does not fit the bill, however good its participatory practice.

Findings from the 22 communities show that where community management is accepted by the local administration, a productive and mutually reinforcing partnership can develop. This happened in Sigomere in Kenya: 'It was observed that the committee works very closely with the local administration and the social services department. There is daily interaction with these nearby institutions. The local sub-chief is a co-opted member of the management committee. These institutions have been instrumental in the growth and stability of the project, as they have provided forums in which the conflicts and management problems have been resolved in an amicable and inclusive fashion. The local administration oversees the smooth running of the elections of the committee and also helps to moderate any major issues.'

In Cameroon, communities feel very threatened when support from the local administration appears to weaken. 'The Department of Community Development (CD) was conceived with this type of support. However, since the arrival of the economic crisis, motivation, finances, transportation and other working assets have significantly declined. The staff themselves are old and few, to the extent that providing services for communities has become very difficult. Whatever the reason, this backup support is necessary and should be re-established. Formerly caretakers were paid by the state; if such initiatives could be revived, the better.'

In Kenya, community evaluation identified a direct correlation between project success and support from line ministries and other local government arms. "This helps the project not only to deal with the technical issues but also with the social issues that have brought many a project to its knees.'

Policies, legislation, support agencies and guidelines and capacities for support – the enabling environment – should all be developed hand in hand. The policies are often there, but legislation to make these policies effective, or the statutes to apply policies at local level, are missing. Without capacity-building at decentralized levels, particularly at the district/municipality level where decentralization meets community management, and without transferring funds from national to decentralized levels, favourable policies and legislation will not help. The change from provider to facilitator is a paradigm shift and difficult to achieve. However, governments and donors can build on the experiences and the successes of community-managed systems in their countries. If they listen well, they will find guidance on how to structure institutional support in their own communities.

CHAPTER 12

Why do systems fail?

W HY IS IT so hard to sustain community-managed water supplies, and why
do communities have to struggle so much? All through Part 2 we have
been looking at the underlying reasons for failure and we have, through our red
thread, tried to pick out in particular a lack of long-term support in a number of
critical areas as being in large part to blame. Now we want to look one layer
deeper, to underlying concepts and assumptions.

The mismatch between rural communities and water projects

'When the system was completed we were happy. We thought that the system
would remain in the same condition for our whole lives. We never thought this
(failure of the system) could happen. We were never told by the implementing
agency that it could happen. The implementing agency just told us "now it is
yours", you must look after the system yourself.' Nani Babu Silwal, Chairperson,
Lele Water Users' Committee, Nepal.

Engineers and social scientists pin the blame on each other

Much of the debate in the water and sanitation sector has been between 'engineers' and 'social scientists', with the latter accusing the former of obstinacy and
lack of insight, and the former accusing the latter of a lack of any grounding in
the real world. It is true that for a long time managers and decision makers in
the water sector have had a technical background, often civil engineering. Not
only have they come from a technical background, they have come from a particularly narrow one, which has notably failed to move with the times. While in
industry and manufacturing worldwide the concept of a multidisciplinary
approach has been embraced and internalized, this has not (with a few notable
exceptions) happened in the closed world of rural water supply. Project
managers continue to resist change and to have problems with acknowledging
the impact of social conditions on water projects (Bos 2001). This is, of course,
in no small part because a social or sociological approach to water projects
complicates matters for technicians.

However, the fault is not only with technicians. The social sciences, and
particularly the academic branches, have been spectacularly unsuccessful at turning their ever more detailed (and costly) 'understanding' of communities and
community dynamics into useful tools. The inventors of PRA (participatory
rapid appraisal) complain about how it has been 'polluted' by actually being used.

Much of the debate in the water and sanitation sector is trivial academic back-biting. In the meantime communities continue to suffer from lack of sustainable water supplies, and ever-increasing hordes of social scientists coming to 'empower' them.

Community management, as a management option for rural water supplies, forces practitioners working in the water sector to get to know and deal with these complex mixes of social, technical, and financial realities and to attempt to deal with them. If communities are to be acknowledged as the managers of water, then we have to know who these communities are, what skills they have, and how they should be involved and supported. Management is not just technical, social or financial; it is all three, and it is impossible to focus on one aspect at the expense of the others. Management seeks to resolve a range of issues such as: Who operates a supply system? Who maintains it? Where do they get spare parts? What are the cost implications of different technical options? Who pays for the service? How should the community be organized to secure long-term reliability of a water supply? What rules and regulations are needed in the community? Who enforces the rules? If sector policies and international declarations say that the community itself should decide on these issues, and that they themselves should manage their water supplies, then these questions must be answered.

Water supply systems and management often fail in the turbulence of community dynamics; in the lack of cohesion, gender inequity, and the lack of capacities. Community dynamics often clash with and reject the alien bodies that are imported water supply technologies. Water supply projects, parachuted into a community, put new strains on the existing dynamics; the inequities that already exist between different tribes and clans in the community, between low and high caste, between the powerful and the marginal, between religions, between men and women. The dynamics already exist and will not be 'solved' with the implementation of a water supply system. To think that a bunch of pipes, pumps and tubes could change community dynamics is naïve. But so is blaming communities, or thinking that there is something to be solved. The dynamics of communities are what has allowed them to survive in the past and often help them to carry on doing so, although old ways of doing things and unresolved social discord can become a severe handicap in a rapidly changing world. The struggle with water supply systems is not the community's fault; it is caused by the mismatch between these dynamics and the newly imported technology and systems. Which raises the question: Why is the mismatch between community dynamics and water projects so profound?

Water supply projects – community realities cut into pieces

The project approach itself is increasingly seen as one of the villains of the piece in terms of the failure to achieve sustainable water supply systems. Development projects tend to homogenize target groups. They equalize them and pretend that conditions are the same everywhere. They have standard procedures, regardless of the dynamics of the communities where they are implemented, because community dynamics are too difficult and time-consuming to handle. Projects are also typically implemented in an institutional vacuum. Because 'government' has 'failed', project organizers go direct to the community, where they work for three years putting in infrastructure, and, if they are advanced, engaging in institution-building and management training. Then they hand over the system and disappear. The community is on its own.

Participatory methods can help to reveal these community dynamics, at least on the level of diagnosis and analysis. However, all too often, and particularly once the benevolent eye of the project is no longer focused in this direction, decision making at community level reverts to the normal situation where those with more power determine what will happen. Participation at the level of decision making and management is difficult and it takes a lot of time and patience to mediate the disputes that arise in such participatory processes. Participatory approaches are therefore not enough. 'Community-based or community-level development has, for example, helped and empowered people, improved services, enhanced self-confidence, harnessed energies for the collective good, influenced policy directions and led to more appropriate research. But it cannot be expected to be the only or even major vehicle for social change' (Guijt and Shah 1998:8).

Another well-documented limitation of 'projects' is that they impose sector boundaries that bear little relation to the complex web of the livelihoods of rural people. There are agricultural projects, health projects, economic projects and water projects. In the water sector there are additional boundaries as some water supply projects focus on domestic water and health issues and others focus on water resources and productive uses. As we have seen, rural people seldom view their reality from the point of view of one sector. Most crucially for water supply projects, they seldom acknowledge a difference between water for domestic uses and water for productive uses.

Water supply systems – alien bodies in the community.

Modern water supply technologies and their associated institutions – be they handpumps or complex gravity systems – are almost always alien to communities (Minnigh and Moeliono 2001). They are frequently (though far from always) more complex than traditional systems, and are invariable different. Neither is the technology neutral. It is not a water supply black box that can be simply plugged into existing situations. Rather, it brings with it a whole range of management, financial, and social implications. When the system is implemented, so are all the surrounding social and institutional elements. Unfortunately, the assumptions about social and institutional conditions that underlie these technologies do not necessarily match the reality of communities into which they are placed.

To give some concrete examples: the simplest built-in assumption with any technology is that the spare parts and skills needed to maintain it are available. In many countries there are now good supply structures for spare parts, but this is far from true everywhere. Management of the system is another assumption for successful implementation of water supply systems. The technology must be managed to ensure that it remains useful and sustainable. Without proper management the technology will break down. Another assumption imported with the piece of technology is that costs must be recovered to maintain the technology. Fees must be set and collected, books must be kept, transparency of financial management must be adopted. You also need a capable water committee that takes decisions about the system and administers the system, and you need rules and procedures for the election and proper functioning of the committee. These management tasks and capacities are often new in rural communities.

A core assumption with most domestic water supply technologies is that they will be used for domestic use alone. Taps are designed for drinking, not for irrigation. Whether a multi-use system would look very different to a single-use system is difficult to say – no one has tried to design one.

Both the technology and the in-built value assumptions are alien to rural realities. It is not only the hardware – the pipes – that are imported. The software – assumptions – are also strange to community people, and they become even more alien if they are not properly supported because, for example, there is no spare part supply system, or there are no guidelines and no support for management. However good their intentions, Northern donors import their assumptions about 'rational' decision making, effective management, democratic management, equity and specialization with the technology. They import these things into realities that may be irrational, undemocratic and holistic (generalist). That is why community management is often a struggle, not only to keep up with maintaining hardware but above all to keep up with the software.

When projects operate in isolation, either spatial or institutional, and when governments do not subscribe to the value assumptions such as democratic management, equal access, cost recovery, participation and equity, communities are left with the alien technology and its alien assumptions. This often results in an even bigger struggle to maintain the hardware and live up to the standards of the imported software.

Often, no one is really to blame; not the community and its diversity, nor the project implementers, nor the concept developers. But the mismatch between the parties can be dealt with only by people who have invested the time in gaining local knowledge and understanding, and who then take their time in removing the most negative consequences of community dynamics and project implementation. As Minnigh and Moeliono say: 'The incorporation of an alien body and its concepts is a matter of time extending beyond the lifetime of a project, determined by local conditions, including priorities, political and power relationships' (Minnigh and Moeliono 2001:23).

Communities cannot do it by themselves

Implementing a water supply system and managing this system up to the level of a water service for the community not only takes time – it needs to be supported. Solutions cannot come solely from the community. There is a clear role for a support structure at the 'intermediate levels' such as the district, municipality or ward (that exist between the national bodies and the community) to deal with the limitations of communities in management, to support communities, and to act as an outside facilitator. In fact the role of the 'outsider' is probably the single most overlooked concept in community management. Numerous studies have tried to identify why community management has gone wrong; why after three years of training and participation, as soon as the 'project' moves on the system collapses. Most of these focus on community dynamics. None that we are aware of focus on the project worker, the outsider, the honest broker, the trusted friend. Yet, all around us we see on the international and national arena, the critical role that outsiders play in conflict resolution. Why then are rural communities supposed to be different?

The community and the trusted friend cannot operate in isolation. They need policies and regulations to guide them and they need legislation to stay on the right track. They need capacity-building to do better, not once, but continuously, because conditions change. They need resources to make it possible. Then, in time, the bodies will become less alien.

These support structures can be within government, or outside it, or in combination with public and private actors. They must be permanent, and they must be multi-disciplinary, encompassing technical and social expertise, and also expertise in the development and application of policies for rural community water supply management. The support structure that is the consequence of this approach is a structure where actors with different interests and different capacities all have their role to play. The right fit must be found in local, district or national contexts.

PART 3
THE WAY FORWARD

THIS THIRD PART of the book moves the focus from the individual community and/or system to the provision of services to entire populations. Through a synthesis of the findings and an analysis of community experiences we describe a coherent vision of the future of community management and, more importantly, how it can achieve increased coverage in rural water supply.

Community management is presented here as a valid and appropriate management model for rural water supply. However, to turn community management into a management model requires another approach, not from the perspective of an individual community, or an individual project, but from the perspective of a rural water supply service. Such a service does not aim to implement and construct only some water supply systems in only some communities. It aims to design and implement the overarching framework of institutional support to keep those systems functioning, so that they adapt to demographic change and to changes in customer demand. Only with such a framework in place can coverage be increased responsibly and sustainably. Without it, project systems in rural communities will be doomed to fall apart.

Here the pattern in our red thread argument takes shape. The complex interplay within and between community and external factors is mapped. We demonstrate how the wrong sort of external support can leave a community worse off than it was before the intervention. We argue that government and local government cannot simply be cut out of the picture because we do not like the way they function. Indeed we identify the intermediate district or area level support as a crucial purveyor of red thread. We identify the critical components of community management and distinguish between doing all the work, and having at least some of the control of a water system. We end with a call for a change in direction – certainly on the part of governments and district and local institutions, but also crucially on the part of donors, external agencies and international NGOs. If community management is to become the success story that many believe it can be, then the era of 'water projects' must evolve into something better, so that donors fund what communities, local and national governments have decided they want and can successfully support and sustain.

CHAPTER 13

Mapping the key factors of community management

The complexity of sustainable management

At its simplest, we consider successful community management to be the provision of a fully sustainable service that provides an equitable water supply to a community. As we explained in the introduction, by 'sustainable' we mean that once a community has been provided with a given level of service it should never have to revert to a structurally lower level of water in terms of quantity or quality. We also mean that it can sustain a system that will be maintained not only during its natural lifetime, but will also eventually be replaced or upgraded. By 'equitable' we mean that no section of the community is left with their minimum needs unmet.

This definition or benchmark should be true for any successful water supply service, whoever is responsible for implementing it. In response to those who may feel that we set an unrealistically high benchmark we pose the question of why a system that breaks down after 'only' five or even ten years should be considered sustainable. It is unacceptable to implement systems with no idea of what happens at the end of their design life.

It is clear from Part 2 that communities often come close to achieving this degree of success for short periods, but that there are also frequent failures, and that systems often do not survive in the longer term. Success requires a complex series of factors to be favourable, while failure can be precipitated by just one factor going wrong.

This complexity can be captured to some extent in a causal diagram that maps interrelated issues. Figure 13.1 shows the relationship between the desired outcome – widespread, equitable, sustainable community management – and various key factors. The arrows between factors show the flow of cause and effect. Those factors within the shaded area relate directly to the community and its capacity. Those factors outside the shaded area are outside the community and outside its control.

Figure 13.1 suggests that widespread, equitable, sustainable community management is directly dependent on a mix of water resource availability, total finances, management capacities of the community and appropriate service levels and technology. Outside the community it is also directly dependent on the efficiency/capacity of intermediate level actors (government, NGO and private). All these factors must be addressed if the desired outcome is to be achieved. Furthermore, it is the combination of causal factors that is important – the factors have meaning only in relation to each other. For example,

145

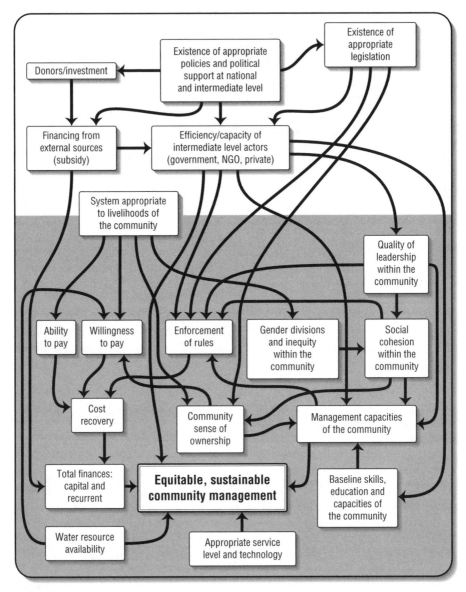

Figure 13.1 Causal diagram of the main factors affecting the achievement of widespread, equitable, sustainable community management

community management capacity is meaningful only in relation to the complexity of the system. What is adequate capacity for a simple system may founder when a complex system is installed. The diagram does not speak of absolutes, but rather of balances.

Each factor is influenced by, and influences, others. The diagram is therefore a conceptual representation of the main issues that we identified in Part 2. And although the diagram is complex, with multiple linkages between different factors, it is in fact a simplified representation of the reality within communities. Understanding and accepting the degree of complexity is key to understanding why a single intervention affecting a single factor can never lead to improved management. An analysis across the entire range of factors is needed to identify an appropriate balance.

The factors outside the community have been greatly simplified in this diagram. The enabling environment is represented very generally, while efficiency and capacity of intermediate-level actors represents a whole bundle of organizations, and a range of skills and capacities. This single factor could be unpacked to display a whole range of new factors, including technical backup, facilitation, spare part availability, private sector capacity, etc. Most of the external factors are not shown as impacting directly on sustainability, but rather as affecting aspects such as service level, financing and management capacity. The impact of these external factors appears in this diagram, and perhaps to the casual observer also in real life, to be less direct than do the factors related to community capacity. This may be one reason why failures of water systems are more often put down to failures of community capacity than to failures in support.

There is no correct state for any individual factor on its own. Sustainable community management is achieved only by the correct mix of factors. It is meaningless to talk about the 'management capacities of the community' in isolation from the technology or service level. It is equally pointless to judge the level of finances without looking at the service level. Good management capacities and appropriate technical solutions can compensate for poor water resource availability or low finances. However, where three or four factors are all poor, or unsuited to each other, overall failure will occur. Understanding this issue is at the heart of the search for flexible community management.

Management capacities of the community

In a narrow sense, it may appear that the management capacities of the community are made up of such things as bookkeeping, report writing, monitoring and evaluation, and day-to-day operation and maintenance. However, as can be seen in the diagram, the management capacities of the community are in turn based on a combination of many other factors, such as sense of ownership, gender divisions and inequity, baseline skills and education, social cohesion and leadership.

The factors most often focused on underlying management capacity inside communities are leadership, skills and capacities and 'sense of ownership'. Most commonly left out, and therefore most likely to cause problems later on, are gender divisions, inequity, and social cohesion, which in turn are affected by underlying equity issues. These aspects are difficult to deal with. However, failure to deal with them creates significant problems in achieving community management, and impacts directly on what is understood by the term 'community'.

A community with serious conflict between classes, castes, ethnic or religious groups will have little chance of successfully managing anything. Much has been written on 'the myth of community' (see, for example, Guijt and Shah 1998). However, perhaps the key assumption is that 'community' is a valid description for a particular group of people. If they do not represent a community, then community management is unlikely to work, particularly because active participation by all sectors of the community is absolutely essential. Opting out by any important group of users will inevitably lead to conflict and eventual failure. Perhaps the most obvious example is the role of caste. In some Asian communities, lower caste people have to be given their own systems, as they are barred from sharing systems with higher caste members of the community. From the point of view of system design, this offers a clear example of a community division so deep that what from the outside looks like one community is, to those living on the inside, two or more divided communities.

Sense of ownership

A sense of ownership is clearly crucial to achieving efficient management, and this is often cited as one of the key differences between community and traditionally managed systems. Ownership is shown in the diagram as being affected by social cohesion, which is itself a factor of gender, other forms of equity and the quality of community leadership. But a sense of community ownership also depends on factors outside the community's control. For example, the system selected (usually by outsiders) must be appropriate to 'livelihoods' in the community. We define livelihoods to include productive uses of water, such as irrigation for crops, and domestic uses such as drinking, cooking and hygiene which enable people to stay well and to work. This aspect of overall system appropriateness is separated out to make more explicit the link with overall management and financial success. If a system is designed to take account of people's actual and desired use of water it will be more likely to engender a sense of ownership. The design of systems to take into account the different uses to which men and women put water can also significantly alter gender divisions.

The other crucial external factor affecting ownership is the existence of appropriate legislation. This reflects the findings from Part 2 that a legally recognized title (or at least clarity of legal ownership) is essential to allowing communities to accept ownership. As we saw, illegal connections and lack of clarity over how water should be used made community management more complicated in, among other places, Belén (Guatemala), Campoalegre (Colombia) and Yampaphant (Nepal).

Quality of leadership

Leadership issues are frequently seen in projects as a key part of community capacity-building. Management requires leadership, whether 'democratic', 'traditional' or a mix of the two, and there must be clear and broad acceptance from all major groups of its legitimacy. Leadership can refer either to leadership of the community as a whole, or to leadership of a water committee: the two will be strongly linked and the quality of the latter will largely reflect that of the former. Where divisive leadership exists, stable community institutions become extremely difficult to achieve and this makes long-term management problematic. Training in leadership skills can be a very effective way to develop community capacity. However, where leadership conflicts lead to severe conflict within a community – for example between 'traditional' and 'modern' leadership groups – this may prove to be an insurmountable hurdle.

Baseline skills, education and capacity of the community

Skills and education are crucial to the management capacity of a community. They should also help to determine the correct management model or institutional option required, and the balance between what a community can do for itself and its need for outside support. Institutional and technical options must be geared to the capacity of the community. A complicated system of reporting, minute taking and accounting is not going to be suitable for a community where 90 per cent of the inhabitants are illiterate. Great care must be taken that the institutional option adopted will not by its level of complexity lead to a situation where control is effectively vested in a small, educated elite. The baseline skills of the community – and particularly the skills of those selected to manage a water supply – is one key area where external facilitators can have a substantial impact. Management capacity can be substantially improved by training and capacity-building. The community and those supporting them should also pay attention to the need for skills and capacities in the pool of people from whom replacements will be drawn. Will similar training be available for the next cohort of community leaders?

Financing

Management capacity and financing are two issues closest to the hearts of most managers and planners of community management projects. More than technology choice, and far more than water resources, they represent the heart of most ongoing discussions on community management, particularly those revolving around demand responsive approaches (DRA). Financing can be found either within the community through cost recovery, or externally to the community in the form of subsidies or grants. For a system to be sustainable, the finances must be covered and it must be clear at the inception of a system where both operational and replacement costs are to come from. A common situation on the ground is that capital costs come mainly from a donor (national or external), and operation and maintenance from the community. Where eventual replacement is to come from is left vague, but generally the assumption is that when it becomes necessary a new donor will be found. This may be a valid assumption for pilot systems, but is this going to happen when the community management model is expanded to take in whole regions with large populations?

The community management diagram (Figure 13.1) underlines this dual track approach to finance by separating out financing from external sources and cost recovery. Financing from external sources comes from outside the community, and is discussed in the next chapter. Cost recovery, however, is a key factor within the community, and developing the necessary machinery and skills to achieve it is a crucial part of any community-managed system. Cost recovery is directly affected by a combination of willingness and ability to pay, as well as by a sense of community ownership and by enforcement of rules. In addition, it is strongly, but indirectly, affected by the appropriateness of the system in terms of addressing people's different uses for water within their overall livelihood strategies.

Willingness and ability to pay

Taken together, willingness and ability to pay can be seen as representing economic demand. They are separated here to make the point that there is a crucial difference between theoretical willingness (as identified in contingent valuation methodology 'willingness to pay' surveys) and the actual ability to find cash when the bill comes due. The gap between the two has been reported by, for example, Rall, who found worrying signs that, despite a professed willingness to pay for improved water availability, the actual end result of charging for water in South Africa was a dramatic drop in consumption, and hence in income for operation and maintenance (Rall 2000). Where water is in short supply, willingness to pay may be taken as a given. Where water is abundant this may not be the case, and greater awareness-raising around health issues related to water quality may be necessary.

The ability of the poorest people to pay is crucial. One of the main ways in which ability to pay can be dealt with in community management approaches is by designing into the overall efficiency of the system income-generating uses of water (represented in the diagram by the link from systems appropriate to livelihoods in the community to ability to pay). We saw in Part 2 how remote communities in northern Pakistan collected fees twice a year linked to the marketing of crops and livestock, while in Zimbabwe money from the production of vegetables was used to maintain the water supply system.

Enforcement of rules

The other key element of cost recovery is the effectiveness of enforcement of payment rules. Communities are not monolithic entities; they contain fissures and fault lines, and every society has its 'free riders'. People do not pay their bills, or refuse to allow metering, and in the absence of strong institutions and frameworks they get away with it, at least until the system fails. Enforcement of rules and a sense of ownership are two critical factors linking community management capacities and cost recovery. Providing a framework and mechanisms for enforcement is a critical role for external actors in community management.

Enforcement of rules, as befits its role as a key link, is influenced by many factors. External factors include the efficiency and capacity of intermediate-level actors, and the existence of appropriate legislation. At community level, management capacities, social cohesion and the quality of leadership are influencing factors. As has been seen, the community's ability to enforce rules depends on strong support from outside agencies. In particular, the ability to bring defaulters before some form of authority with the power to enforce payment is crucial.

Systems appropriate to livelihoods of the community

This factor represents something of a new departure for the water and sanitation sector, which traditionally has its roots in the provision of 'domestic' or 'drinking' water services, with the main justification found in improved health. 'Livelihoods' is a term that covers all the aspects of how people make a living, and includes health considerations as well as such things as the use of water for market gardens. The factor is grouped with the financial factors because of its crucial role in linking the supply of water with the ability and willingness to pay. It influences willingness to pay, sense of ownership and gender relations through the health and other non-cash benefits of an improved water supply. It is perhaps most crucial to cost recovery in terms of improving ability to pay, and in changing a community's perception of water as a key factor in economic activities in rural areas. By explicitly designing water supplies to take account of economic activities, money can be raised for system maintenance (Moriarty, 2002).

Appropriate service level and technology

When designing a system that will be managed by the community, the technology and service level should match the needs of the community, its management capacities, the likely level of long-term sustainable financing, and the water resource being used. A crucial assumption is that such a technological option exists. If it does not, then it has either to be developed or adapted from existing technologies. The mismatch between technology and the other three critical factors lies at the heart of many failures of community management.

Water resources

Perhaps the greatest unspoken assumption of community management is that there is an adequate water resource available. Yet the overall management of a water resource (as opposed to a drinking water supply) is not usually seen as a legitimate area for a community management. As the PAR experiences clearly show, failure to manage overall water resources effectively lies at the root of much failure of community-managed systems, as, for example, when different communities compete to exploit the same inadequate resource. This issue falls largely outside the scope of this book. Nevertheless, it is clear that for a community water supply system to be sustainable the resource must be sustainable and that, as a result, this is a crucial issue for inclusion in future community management programmes.

Summary

We can see that community management breaks down into a list of key factors, which must all be addressed and made to fit with geographic, institutional, political and economic settings if a community management is to be successful. It is rarely a single factor that decisively affects the success or failure of community-managed systems, but rather a number of factors acting together. Weakness in one factor may be compensated by strength in another. So, in Colombia, for example, lack of stable government and enforceable laws is balanced by a long tradition of community management over a range of activities. The resulting skills and abilities, in addition to relatively high income levels, allow community management of complex systems to flourish.

We strongly believe that the complexity of the choices being made requires some form of formalized decision support strategy, based on an assessment of these factors in relation to all the communities within a region. Such a strategy or tool should help those working on rural water supply to make decisions such as when, how, and how many resources are needed to implement and support efficient community-managed water supply systems. In the PAR research project, and in many community management 'pilot projects', relatively large resources can be, and are being, put into solving social issues, developing community capacity and so on. However, as community management becomes mainstream, the delivery of unlimited resources to 'problem' communities will become less and less feasible. Deciding on the basis of relatively quick and cheap methodologies whether to go ahead with implementing a project in a community will be important.

Any community management approach must give communities, right at the start of the project, a clear picture of the implications of agreeing to manage their own systems. This may include offering a choice of service levels and technologies. It must include a clear list of undertakings in terms of time, money, and labour that the option(s) entail. These choices must be presented in a manner appropriate to the level of education and ability of the community. In general, they should be tailored to the 'lowest common denominator' – that is, if a community is 90 per cent illiterate, options should not rely on complex records or bookkeeping. Without adequate human resources (in the form of education

152

and skills) a given institutional model may be wholly inappropriate. Without adequate financial resources (internal or external) operation and maintenance is impossible.

Improving management capacities through training is clearly going to be part of any mainstream community management project, and must be given the necessary time and resources. However, trying to heal a deeply divided or traumatized community is not a routine task, and may be better left to people or organizations specialized in working in such situations. Equally, identifying intractable problems relating to ownership or resource availability at an early stage in project development will be essential to cost-effective implementation.

CHAPTER 14

Factors external to the community

T HE PREVIOUS CHAPTER focused on the community-level factors that influence the success or failure of community management. This is where most emphasis has been placed in the majority of existing community-managed systems. However, Figure 13.1 also showed a number of factors that, taken together, can be loosely referred to as the enabling environment for community management. This chapter explores the outline and content of such an enabling environment.

Towards sustainability – introducing the time factor

Figure 14.1 lacks reference to time. Nothing indicates at what stage in the process of managing a system the diagram is located, whether in the initial (and capital-intensive) implementation phase, in the operational phase or eventually in the (also capital-intensive) renewal/expansion phase. Ignoring time allows this single diagram to unpick the key factors of community management, but it means that there is also an additional layer of complexity that is not shown, as each key phase of system management represents different mixes of institutions, problems, and people.

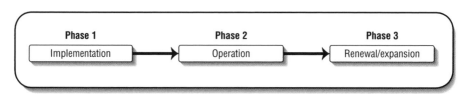

Figure 14.1 Phases of system life

The interaction between a community and a system can change over time. The factors represented in the causal diagram (Figure 13.1) can all exist in a number of different states at any given time. So, for instance, leadership quality can be good, bad or indifferent at a given time in a given community. The impact of a community management implementation project or programme will typically try to alter or improve these states to achieve both successful implementation and sustainability. If, during implementation, it is judged necessary to alter the state of certain factors (for instance improving community capacity through training) it is equally necessary for that change to be made permanent. A simple rule for those primarily involved in the implementation phase should be that no capacity-building is undertaken unless a means for renewing and maintaining the capacity has been identified.

Figure 14.2, and the two that follow, help to illustrate this point using a highly simplified version of the causal diagram, focusing on the mix between technology, management capacities and financing. Management capacity has in turn had its causal network simplified to reflect initially only the quality of leadership and the baseline skills of the community. It will be noted that each of these factors has been given a range of simple states, with the simplest of all being that the outcome – equitable, sustainable management – either happens or does not.

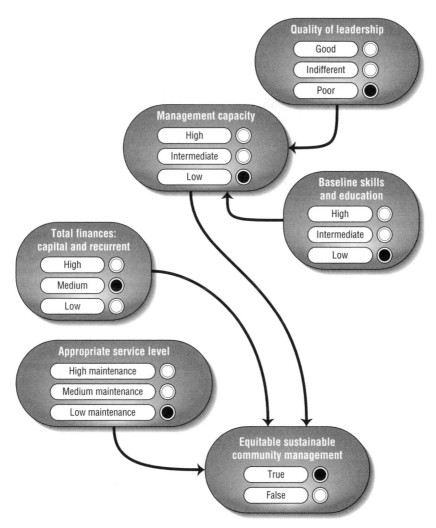

Figure 14.2 Prior to project intervention

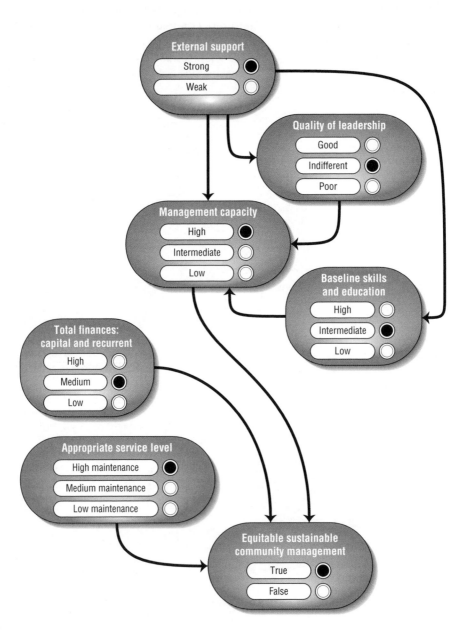

Figure 14.3 During project implementation

Figure 14.2 shows the baseline state of a hypothetical community. Baseline skills and leadership quality are both 'poor', with the result that management capacities are 'low'. However, perhaps because the community is relatively wealthy, or because water is in short supply and hence demand high, total finances are moderate. The result is that equitable and sustainable management can be achieved, as long as the technology is simple and requires low maintenance. This illustration could well describe the situation of a prosperous rural community of peasants with little formal education who successfully manage an open well that they have provided for themselves. It is again important to underline that the terms used to describe the states are relative, and imply no value judgements (with the exception of good and poor leadership). 'Low management capacity' is perfectly adequate for 'low maintenance' or 'traditional' technologies.

Figure 14.3 shows the same community towards the end of the implementation phase of a community management project. Training and capacity-building have raised the capacity of the community to an intermediate level, and they have also improved leadership. With the support of an external agency, this combination of community skills and external support now leads to high management capacity which, combined with the existing finances, means that a system of medium complexity and maintenance level can be sustained, such as a piped gravity-flow network with house connections and stand posts. The external agency, pleased with its job of capacity-building, has now installed such a system with the full co-operation of the community.

Figure 14.4 shows the situation five years after the project has finished and the external support agency has moved on to other communities. The community has managed to maintain its skill base but unfortunately the old leadership problems have resurfaced. Perhaps more importantly, the ESA is no longer involved in the day-to-day running of the project, with the result that management capacities have gone from good to intermediate. This is still an improvement on the original 'low', but a reduction in terms of where they were during project implementation. However, the combination of medium finances and intermediate management capacity means that the system is no longer sustainable. A technology requiring medium maintenance might be sustained, but that is not what was installed. The system is a failure, not because the initial capacity building was inefficient, or because the technology was inherently too difficult, but because the technology choice was based on a state of affairs (involvement of an ESA) that now no longer exists, and upon the hypothesis (that the community once provided with enhanced capacity could maintain it indefinitely) that has proved to be untrue.

This is a highly simplified example. However, it illustrates two crucial points about community management that have been made throughout this book. First that for community management to be successful, systems (technical and institutional) must be designed to suit a complex array of factors. Second, that any effort to sustain improvements in the capacities of a community requires

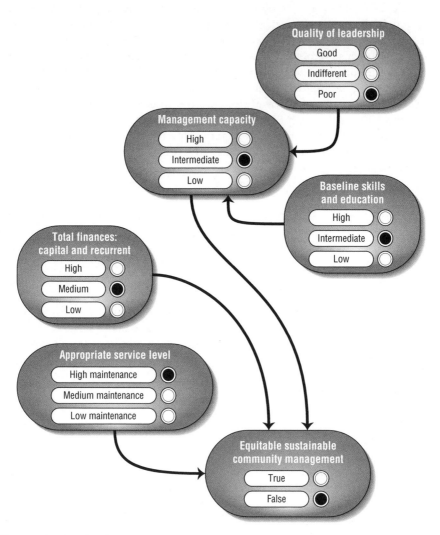

Figure 14.4 Post implementation

long-term external support. Communities cannot maintain enhanced capacity on their own indefinitely. The gap between the skills needed to manage simple traditional systems and even the simplest of 'modern' technologies is a large one. These modern technologies rely on a complex network of supporting services and parts, and the role of external support is critical.

It is increasingly clear that, apart from the simplest of traditional systems, there is always a need for some form of long-term support and backstopping for community management. Once a water source becomes more complicated than an open well or a protected spring, there will be breakdowns and mechanical failures that the community cannot manage without some technical skills or technical support. As systems become more complex, a crucial element of institutional support will also be required. Without this level of backstopping, community management will inevitably fail once the temporary support structure provided by the 'project' is withdrawn.

An enabling environment

Figure 14.5 is simply the top part of Figure 13.1 – focusing only on those elements that are outside of the community. It contains only five factors. However, although few, these external factors are vital.

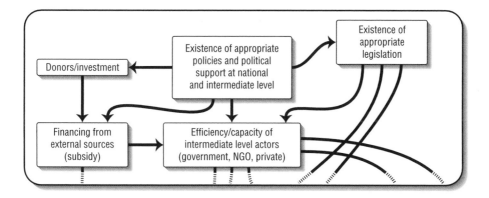

Figure 14.5 Core factors providing an enabling environment for community management

In terms of providing day-to-day support to the community, the most important factor is efficiency/capacity of intermediate level actors. This factor bundles together all the various institutions and individuals who could be involved in providing direct support to a community in any or all of the three phases. In different phases, and in different countries, a (non-exhaustive) list of these agencies would include local (district[1]) government, local NGOs and CBOs, international NGOs, the private sector (formal and informal, contractors and consultants), local offices of national line ministries, training organizations, banks and other financiers, and donor projects. Before considering this central and, in our 'red thread' analysis, most commonly overlooked factor, we shall briefly consider the other key factors.

---

1 'district' is used here to refer to the primary unit of local government. In various countries it is referred to by different terms – district or municipality being most common. Typically it deals with populations of order of magnitude of hundreds of thousands, although in India this stretches to millions.

Policy environment

A supportive policy environment is essential to community management, not least because clear policies should lead to effective and supportive legislation. A thoroughly developed policy that actively promotes community management is essential for both intermediate-level support agencies and communities to gain the support they need to make community management work. Policy encourages line ministries to transfer power to communities, it supports local government in listening to communities and, of course, it opens flows of resources – financial and other – to communities.

A critical issue in many countries is to persuade donors to stop funding piece-meal projects and to start pooling their resources with those of governments to achieve maximum impact. A strong policy that makes it clear that government is serious about supporting decentralized community management can be a power-ful inducement to donors to change their funding approach.

It is a feature of community management as a stop-gap measure that it often takes place in the absence of such a framework, with the result that the systems developed are often ignored by the organs of the state. In the absence of any policy and, as a result of a general failure of government to undertake its duties, such approaches can only assure service in the short term. For intermediate-level actors to take up longer-term roles and responsibilities, a clear supporting and enabling policy is essential.

Effective legislation

Effective legislation is a crucial element in providing the outlines of the enabling environment. Only primary legislation can allow for clear ownership of systems, a fully legally enforceable system of cost recovery and the development of appro-priate contracts. These, and other legal elements, are essential to turning community management from an ad hoc approach, practised where government has failed or abdicated its responsibility, to a fully-fledged management option for water supply. Everything discussed about intermediate-level support should be seen as implying an assumption of effective and appropriate supporting legal frameworks.

Financing from external sources

One particularly important aspect of policy relates to deciding the level of financing external to the community that is available for community manage-ment. While, clearly, the overall wealth of a nation will influence what can be spent, this is not the determining factor, as we believe that the issue essentially relates to priorities rather than to absolute amounts. Given an effective policy environment that prioritizes rural water supply, external funding can be found. This is reflected not only in the connection between policy and financing, but also in that between policy and donor investment. And the connection is a two-way street. Poor countries with good policies can expect substantial support from donors. Donor support and investment can equally enable the development of appropriate policy and good legislation. To achieve scaling-up, external funding must come through government, regardless of whether it originates from donors or a country's own resources. Direct donor project funding can never lead to sustainability.

These key elements from outside the community provide the framework in which the intermediate-level actors who directly support the community can work. As community management becomes increasingly widely accepted, there is a growing number of examples of such policy environments to choose from. Countries that are currently implementing people-centred or community-based approaches to large-scale rural water supply provision include South Africa, India, Ghana, Uganda and Tanzania.

Intermediate-level support – the missing link

While national-level policies and legislative frameworks are clearly crucial to enabling and supporting community management, it is equally clear that in our decentralizing world it is not the national-level actors who will be involved in day-to-day interactions with communities. The people who do that are those who occupy the intermediate level – that vast fuzzy region that lies between national and local. The intermediate-level includes all those organizations that in some way or other interact directly with a community in one of the three phases of system implementation, operation and renewal. Definitions vary between countries and regions, but typically the intermediate-level actors include:

State	– decentralized offices of line ministries, local government
Private sector	– formal and informal consultants, contractors, service providers
NGOs	– local grassroots organizations, local branches of national bodies, and in some cases project-level teams from international NGOs
Donors	– projects
Others	– independent regulators, CBOs, professional associations, local universities, banks, local courts, regional or local training organizations.

Given our emphasis on longevity and sustainability, it is clear that the most important intermediate-level actors will be local-level state actors, local-level private sector, and local (grassroots) NGOs and CBOs. Because of the temporary nature of projects run by international NGOs and donors, their interaction will usually take place in the implementation phase.

Table 14.1 shows a matrix setting out the principal activities necessary to support communities during the three phases of a system's life cycle as set out in Figure 14.1. The matrix also identifies the main actors involved in providing this support. The private sector represents a range from contractors and consultants who may undertake individual tasks for either state or community, to service providers who in some models of community management undertake the management of the entire system under the direction of a community board.

Activity	Line ministry	Local government	NGO/ CBO	Private	Regulator
Overall process		*			
Phases 1 and 3 – Implementation and Renewal/expansion					
System design	*			*	
Construction				*	
Technical capacity-building	*		*	*	
Management capacity-building			*	*	
Financial capacity-building			*	*	
Contract development	*	*			
Phase 2 – Operation					
Technical capacity maintenance	*		*	*	
Management skills maintenance			*	*	
Financial skills maintenance			*	*	
Facilitation/negotiation			*	*	
System operation and maintenance (where this is contracted out by the community)			*	*	
Spare parts supply				*	
Monitoring		*			*
Financial support – auditing		*			*
Contract enforcement		*			*

Table 14.1 Key intermediate-level actors and activities in support of community-managed water systems

The stars in Table 14.1 show those actors we believe to be most suited to particular activities. There is clearly no 'correct' answer to who does what, and this will vary from place to place. The point is that, for community management to be successful, each and every activity identified must be clearly allocated to one or other actor, all of whom should be clear about what is involved in carrying them out, and all of whom should have both the capacity and mandate to do so. Equally, for community management to be scaled up in terms of either coverage or increased sustainability, then the roles and activities suggested in Table 14.1 must be assigned to competent, local, viable actors.

In our view, local government is in all cases the preferred actor to drive the process, given a range of problems with the legitimacy and reach of NGOs. This is not to say that local government is always legitimate, but that where it is legitimate it is the institution most suited by mandate (and ideally by capacity) to carry out the role of primary supporter to communities. However, as can be seen from the table, local government cannot carry out all the activities listed, and is best suited to even fewer. Local government's role therefore lies most clearly in bringing together the various actors and in overseeing their effective collaboration and co-operation, as well as in providing overall leadership and direction.

A range of skills is required from a variety of actors. Just as the factors affecting community management could not be addressed as single unconnected issues, neither can the actors and their skills be dealt with in isolation from each other. All must act together to provide the essential network of efficient and capable support at the intermediate level. Different combinations of actors and skills can provide different levels of support tailored to a particular mix of factors and states within factors; when this mix is right, systems become sustainable. Different levels of community capacity require different combinations of skills from external supporters to allow different technical solutions to their quest for sustainable water.

Whatever the particular mix of actors, they must have, or must develop, sufficient capacity to undertake and accomplish their roles. The greatest danger of the current approach to community management is the tendency, in the absence of strong intermediate-level institutions (particularly local government), to work around them in order to 'get the job done'. This fundamentally misunderstands 'the job'. The job is not to construct or rehabilitate a system, but to achieve a service that is sustainable in the long term – a much more complex task.

Not a full circle – the role of the community

We emphasize intermediate-level support for communities, based on the research findings that communities cannot ensure sustainability on their own. In some models, such as those from Colombia, where operation and maintenance is fully professional, communities may not need to be involved in day-to-day operation and maintenance at all, limiting their role purely to decision making and strategic management. This does not mean that we are arguing for a return

to the old days when governments implemented water supply systems for recipient communities.

Community management in developing countries came into being for a reason: the failure of government to implement or sustain effective water systems. However, the evidence of Part 2 makes it clear that communities cannot take over the whole burden. The question therefore ceases to be one of either community or government, but rather one of identifying and matching the capacity and potential of communities to manage, with the capacity and potential of government agencies to support. Capacities have to be matched against each other and linked to an appropriate water supply system to ensure long-term sustainability. The capacity of the community is the starting point, and support structures, systems, financial systems and everything else must be tailored to it. By clarifying the difference between governance and operation, we seek to make the role of the community clearer. The community must be in charge of a host of factors to do with demand responsiveness, ownership, appropriateness and cost recovery. However, being in charge does not mean being left unsupported.

Advocating the strengthening of intermediate-level actors, and the re-involvement of state organizations in community management is not going full circle. We are not saying that community management has failed, and that a return to government implementation is the answer. What we do say is that, if community management is to become *the* approach to water supply for rural communities, it needs to take place within a framework and a support structure. Government is often the most efficient (and legitimate) location for that structure. In particular, to address the needs of those 1.5 billion people who have yet to benefit from any adequate water supply, it will be necessary to build streamlined approaches into national strategies to allow community management to become a generic management approach rather than a reaction to local failure.

CHAPTER 15

From system to service – scaling up

THIS CHAPTER IDENTIFIES the key actions needed to successfully scale up community management. It also clarifies two important issues. First, what are the key elements that distinguish community-managed systems from other models for service provision? Second, under what circumstances is it the best or most appropriate management option?

The heart of community managment

What is the core of community management – the elements that must be there for us to say that a system is being managed by the community? Based on the discussion in the previous chapters, we would suggest that the following four elements can be identified to some extent in community-managed systems.

- collective community *control* of the system
- collective community *operation and maintenance* of the system
- collective community *ownership* of the water supply system
- collective community *contribution* to costs (operating and capital).

Control, operation and maintenance

There is an important distinction to be made between control and operation, although the two are often assumed to be synonymous, and in practice carried out by the same people. Put simply, control means the ability to make strategic decisions about how a system is designed, implemented, and managed: to select service levels, set tariffs and, if desired, employ someone else to look after operation and maintenance. Most often, control is implemented through management committees or boards. Operation is the day-to-day maintenance of the system and can be carried out either by the community itself – especially in simpler systems – or by paid professionals.

We believe that the essence of community management lies in control rather than operation and maintenance, because control covers the decision-making powers that put a community truly in charge. Therefore, a system where a private sector operator carries out the operational management, under the control of a committee selected by the community, is a community-managed system; one where an outside agency pays the community to undertake certain routine maintenance activities, while retaining strategic decision-making powers itself, is not.

Ownership

Ownership is at the root of successful community management. It is also one of the vaguest and most overused buzzwords in the sector, perhaps second only to 'demand' – for which ownership is often seen as a vital ingredient. Frequently, what it refers to is a 'sense of ownership' brought about by contributions to planning, construction or capital costs. It is frequently reduced to a box to be ticked once a community has contributed 5 per cent or 50 per cent to capital costs, or contributed their labour ('sweat equity') to system construction. They have paid for it, so now they are supposed to feel that they own it, even if nobody has given them any legal rights over the system. An important finding of the PAR research is that legal ownership is crucial. Some of the 22 communities in the PAR project suffered greatly from conflict when different communities competed for the same source and ownership was disputed. In most countries, the community has not been given sufficient legal status to own the source or the system, and cannot therefore protect it. The point of a sense of ownership is that community members behave as if they do own it, and people who own things (particularly poor people) do their best to protect them. If communities have no legal status or legal ownership, their 'sense of ownership' will be a sham and will soon evaporate.

Contribution to costs

Cost recovery is one of the most debated topics in the sector. We argue that a cash contribution to capital and operating costs is not an essential feature of community management. It is possible to imagine a system where a donor finances implementation and where grants and subsidies cover operation and maintenance costs, but where the community still owns and controls the system. Something like this is being realized in South Africa, which is implementing a 'free basic water' policy through community-managed systems (DWAF, 2001). However, this is the exception. In practice, in most developing countries the community meets at least the operational costs. Ensuring that communities are capable of collecting, managing and using revenues is an important part of ensuring sustainability.

Whoever pays, it is critical that *all* costs, implementation, operation and maintenance, and eventual replacement are clearly identified, and that responsibility for meeting them is clearly assigned. The exact mix between community and external sources will vary according to the context. What is less clear is whether an initial contribution to capital costs – as is now insisted on by the World Bank and other donors – plays any role in increasing ownership, or whether it serves as yet one more barrier to trying to reach the poorest.

Control is the key

Each of these four elements must be addressed to achieve successful community management, but we would argue that it is control and ownership that are the defining characteristics of a community-managed system. In particular, if the community has control, then it can be said to be managing its system. Can such control happen without ownership? There is no absolute answer. It will be very difficult to control something where the ownership is not clear. If the ownership is clear, but resides outside the community (for instance with government), it will be possible to exercise real control over some decisions, but only with difficulty over others. For instance, the community may have the power to decide on limits for water use even where it does not own the system. It would, however, be impossible to use plant and machinery as collateral for raising money on the open market if ownership rests outside the community. We would argue that legal ownership should rest with the community, but we acknowledge that, where there is a strong ethos of public (government) ownership, or where government has yet to develop sufficient trust in communities and their management abilities, this is likely to be politically impossible.

When is community management appropriate?

Given all the problems discussed in Part 2, why is community management a feasible option, and under what conditions is it the most suitable option or management model? We have seen how the version of community management practised by the rural water supply and sanitation sector in developing countries traces its roots to the perceived failure of governments to implement, and more importantly to sustain, water supply systems. Those in the sector who have a utilitarian approach ('whatever works best for the community') see community management as the only realistic option to provide some level of service. However, they often also see community management as a stopgap measure to be abandoned once government reforms itself, and can undertake its 'proper' function again. Those coming from a rights-based direction see community management as a means of empowering communities. The provision of functioning water supplies can come to be almost peripheral to the wider aim of making communities stronger, more cohesive and more able to demand their rights. The two schools of thought come together in the widespread adoption of participatory and 'people-centred' approaches to rural water supply.

Both schools of thought share a dislike and/or distrust of government. An important outcome has been an approach focused almost exclusively at community level, ignoring or bypassing government in the race to effectively and efficiently expand coverage or empower communities. This is unfortunate because, despite successes in empowering communities, the reality remains that community management approaches have not been noticeably better at sustaining systems than what went before. Yet one of the main justifications for investing in the costly software side of community management – the training of committees, pump mechanics, caretakers and so on – is increased sustainability.

The issue of flexibility in community management-based approaches is crucial, but often ignored in the 'one size fits all' – handpump or nothing –

approach practised in much of the developing world. Rural people use water in a wide variety of ways (domestic, productive, spiritual), and systems that are designed to provide a level of service commensurate with those needs are much more likely to succeed in being owned and paid for by communities. Only community-managed approaches have the flexibility to provide millions of communities around the world with tailor-made water supply solutions.

The answer to the question 'why use community management?' is, 'because it is the best option under certain circumstances'. The question then becomes 'under what circumstances should community management be recommended?'

Figure 15.1 provides one framework for answering the question. It is a simple conceptual representation of how community management (or management *by* the community) fits in with other management models not based on community control (management *for* the community). The triangles symbolize the relative workload and, more importantly, control. In either model, communities need support from the intermediate level, and service providers need to be responsive to the demands and needs of the community/customers.

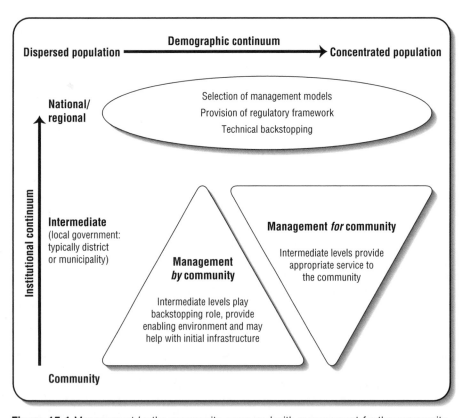

Figure 15.1 Management *by* the community compared with management *for* the community

Figure 15.1 suggests that one factor influencing the choice between community management and other models is demography. Where populations are dispersed or inaccessible, a community-based solution will be more effective; where populations are concentrated, a service provision model is indicated. In both cases, the community (or users) should have a role to play. However, other possible axes could be used, such as a poor to wealthy continuum, where poor communities are more likely to manage their own water supply and rich communities are more likely simply to buy into an existing system.

The reasons for using community management are therefore:

- because there is no alternative for economic, geographic or demographic reasons
- because empowerment of communities is a good thing
- because there is no other way to provide the necessary flexibility.

The diagram suggests that community management is most appropriate to dispersed rural communities, and poorer communities. Yet clearly, the minimalist version of community management practised in many developing countries is not sustainable, as it leaves communities unsupported and loads them with unrealistic expectations.

Scaling up community management

Given our hypothesis that community management is worthwhile, what are the main challenges to scaling up this approach to meet the needs of people in developing countries who have no access to either safe drinking water supplies or adequate sanitation facilities?

The first step is to start to look beyond the community. For community management to move from implementing a system to maintaining a service requires attention to the enabling environment within which the community exists. We include in this the laws, policies, institutions and actors that support and build on a community's own capacities.

Scaling up coverage is pointless unless sustainability is improved at the same time. Coverage issues are mainly related to implementation ability: the capacity to get concrete poured and management committees trained more quickly and effectively. But simply implementing more projects that fail after a few years is not an answer. Sustainability issues are related to the ability to backstop the new community capacities indefinitely, to replace people who leave their positions or die, to bring legal accountability to financial management by auditing water committees, to facilitate agreements and resolve conflicts. Scaling up community management requires different actors with different capacities for the different phases of system development.

While good policy and legislation are, of course, essential, these are relatively easy to develop when compared to the huge task of improving the capacity of intermediate-level actors to implement and sustain water systems. A successful community-management approach therefore looks beyond the community, to address the needs of those whose role it will be to support the community in the future. Systems must be designed not only with community capacity in mind, but also to improve the capacity of intermediate-level support. Currently, there is a glaring gap in capacity at the intermediate level and we would argue that filling that gap – by training and capacity-building but also by changing attitudes and work practices – is the most pressing need in terms of scaling up community management.

Finally, scaling up also requires different approaches to implementation, especially a move away from projects. Projects seem effective in terms of providing systems on the ground, but are almost inevitably hopeless at setting the basis for increased coverage or in ensuring sustainability. Sustainable community management requires strategies and planning at district (regional, provincial) level and partnerships between different actors. This is a particularly important issue for international NGOs and donors, who often see government as the enemy and an obstacle to efficient implementation. Sustainability is made virtually impossible by such approaches, and the long term presence of international NGOs is no substitute for trying to develop local capacity.

CHAPTER 16

Investing in support

A call for action

OUR AIM IN writing this book is to identify the critical lack of ongoing support for communities that are left to manage their own water systems. What are the implications of our 'red thread' for international and national policy as well as for the major actors in the water and sanitation sector? We have written as if there has been no recognition of the need for change in community support, mainly because this is generally an accurate picture of the specific experiences in the six countries of the PAR project. However, this is not always the case, and a number of countries have tackled the challenge of institutionalizing and scaling up community management. These include Zambia with its system of WASHEs (Sutton 1998), Ghana (Yelbert 1999) and Uganda (Arebahona 2000). South Africa is making a conceptually elegant attempt to bring together the first world management approaches developed under its former apartheid regime and the high levels of coverage appropriate for developing countries in much of its rural areas. The rural water supply sector reform programme in India, while still at a 'pilot' stage, is aiming at a massive injection of cash and training into scaling up community management. In each of these countries, governments, donors, NGOs, CBOs and communities are involved in an ongoing process of re-evaluating their roles, responsibilities and activities. Any attempt at global scaling up must build on their experiences, which will give valuable information on the activities needed, and the right people and organizations to undertake them.

We end our book with a call for action. This change of direction must come in the first place from donors and from governments of developing countries, and to a lesser extent the international and local NGOs that implement community-managed systems. The international donor community played an important role in bringing about the changes in thinking on water supply and sanitation in the 1970s and 1980s. Not only did they change thinking, they also played a large role in implementing (financing) and facilitating projects promoting a community management approach. Donors, together with their country-based NGOs, carried out many pilot projects which have often been completely outside government management structures. This was especially true in the early 1990s, when community management remained a new concept of which many governments were profoundly suspicious.

Pilot projects appeared to be legitimate at the time, but this approach must change. It should no longer be acceptable for donors to implement projects in isolation of national structures and planning. The argument of 'efficiency' falls apart if the unspoken assumptions about improved sustainability prove to be unrealistic. However poor the capacity of government, it is a clear finding of this work that community-managed systems cannot be sustainable in the absence of external support. This support, except in truly exceptional circumstances such as war, must, to be legitimate, take place within a government-provided framework.

One of the great fallacies of community management projects is that, if left alone by interfering politicians, social and technical project staff can pass over enough skills to the community in a three-year project to allow them to manage their systems in perpetuity. The stories in Part 2 challenge this. Of course, it can be argued that if the training were to be better the outcome would be more successful. However, we believe that the internal dynamics in any but the most fossilized of communities will ensure that a management system designed around complex alien technology will fail without external support.

Governments must also mend their ways. They must accept community management as a legitimate form of system management, and must provide the necessary legislative and policy environment to support it. Equally, they must enable those who provide support – NGOs, local government, private sector, decentralized line ministries – the necessary space, and where appropriate, resources to play their role.

Multi-lateral donors are often in the strongest position to spearhead such changes in thinking, because of the legitimacy that their broad-based membership gives them. On the advocacy side, international resource centres, and water-based networks such as the Water Supply and Sanitation Collaborative Council (WSSCC) and the Global Water Partnership (GWP) have a potentially important role to play in spreading the message about community management. They have a particularly important role to play in explaining to donors the adjustments that they need to make in their own funding and planning if they are to a contribute to the success of community management.

This book has not been shy about wearing its heart on its sleeve. Based on studies from six countries about community management at the level of the community, it has spotlighted the lack of support available to communities trying to manage their own systems. The key advocacy message is for the need to stop treating community management as the last option and neglected orphan of management options, but to accept it as a fully-fledged, logical and appropriate model for a given set of circumstances. And having acknowledged it as such, to begin to address systematically the institutional development and capacity-building to create the enabling environment in which community management can take place.

The principal need therefore is for the development of capacity; the capacity of governments to develop and implement effective policy and legislation, and the capacity of local government and water supply ministries to identify and implement cost-effective support structures that build on management capacities within communities. This support must address not only ways to make technically complex repairs, but also to facilitate and enable the community institutions necessary for effective management to flourish. To achieve this, NGOs and donors need to work more closely with governments. International NGOs must realize that an essential part of their mission is to involve and help local government assume its role, so that once the implementation phase is over communities and their water systems do not simply enter a period of slow decline awaiting the next rehabilitation project.

Research is needed to develop the capacity-building tools and institutional models required by governments and agencies. Such research should not focus on new models or pilots, but consist of a hard-headed evaluation of what is already being done, particularly of the successes and failures of scaling up as practised in South Africa, Tanzania, Ghana, Uganda, and India. On the basis of such an evaluation of existing experience, new models and training materials can be developed. Case studies, based on critical analysis, can be documented, and exposure visits and meetings organized. Promising approaches can be tried in other countries and settings, with a strong element of adaptive management. This will encourage a switch from a 'blueprint' approach to a flexible approach that allows governments, NGOs, donors and communities to learn from experience.

Community management is one of the strongest models for helping to achieve the aims of Vision 21 in terms of sustainable, equitable, and environmentally responsible provision of domestic water needs. It should not be allowed to fail for want of the necessary institutional support.

Community features

Community	Population to nearest 100)	Main occupation	Status of water supply system	Main management problems
Kenya				
Sigomere	5000	Subsistence agriculture	Traditional water sources Non-functioning piped scheme Shallow wells with handpumps Borehole equipped with electric, submersible pump and piped reticulation	Different committees managing different systems Fraudulent money handling
Kiveetyo	2500	Subsistence agriculture	Traditional low-yield water sources Gravity-fed Athi Water Project Gravity-fed Kiveetyo/ Kathyioli Water Supply System	Community does not pay O&M costs Water committee feels responsible to implementing agency, not to community Problems with owner of land around water intake
Nyakerato	1000	Subsistence agriculture	Gravity scheme with several extensions over time Shallow well	Conflict and clan rivalry Lack of clarity on land ownership Illegal connections
Yanthooko	33000	Subsistence agriculture	Traditional water sources Shallow well with handpump Supply supplemented by household rainwater harvesting systems	Poor record keeping Lack of communication No constitution – lack of rules Closed society, excluding new members
Colombia				
La Sirena	4000	Informal economic activities	Originally locally built water intakes with hoses, upgraded to a gravity-piped system with treatment plant in the 1980s	Intra-community rivalry for control
Ceylán	3000	Coffee and plantain plantations	Water tank and gravity system made of bamboo pipes subsequently modernized and now including a drinking water treatment plant	Struggles for control of community-based organizations

Community	Population to nearest 100)	Main occupation	Status of water supply system	Main management problems
Campoalegre	1700	Stone crushing factory and poultry farming	Gravity-fed water supply system with a treatment plant	Great numbers of illegal connections due to population growth and migration Conflicts over loss of water volume
Guatemala				
Aguacatán	3600	Subsistence agriculture and wage labour in commercial agriculture	Traditional sources Home-made wells replaced in 1986 by gravity water system with one source serving seven communities	Severe conflicts between the seven communities Technical and administrative challenges related to committee motivation
Barrel Chiquito	1900	Subsistence agriculture and wage labour in commercial agriculture	Traditional sources Sponsored water and latrine project completed in 1991	Lack of maintenance Fees do not cover costs Lack of attention to water project due to too many responsibilities for the pro-improvement committee
Belén	2000	Subsistence agriculture and wage labour in commercial agriculture	Traditional sources Gravity-piped system with house connections inaugurated in 1983 for then population of 516	Too many connections sold without considering source capacity Non-consultative decision making of committee members Angry members stopped paying fees
Cameroon				
Bokito Rural	1500	Subsistence and cash crop agriculture Small-scale livestock production	Traditional sources 1984: a community-dug well 1985: borehole with a manual pump 1990: water storage tank with an engine-driven pump and tap stands of poor construction	Lack of funds to reconstruct the water storage tank, engine driven pump and tap stand system
Nkouondja	2500	Subsistence and highly commercialized agriculture	Traditional sources supplemented by a gravity system with 21 standpipes	Centralized decision making No transparency in financial matters Lack of willingness of users to pay Unreliable supply in dry seasons

Community	Population to nearest 100)	Main occupation	Status of water supply system	Main management problems
Batcham	57 000	Subsistence and cash crop agriculture and small livestock production	Traditional sources Borehole with engine pumping system constructed in 1988 but soon broken down Seven manual pumps placed at community dug wells	Lack of ability to repair the existing engine pumping system Spare parts not locally available High level of dependence upon outside support
Nyen and Mbemi	3000 and 2000 respectively	Subsistence and cash crop agriculture	Traditional sources supplemented by gravity system drawing from 5 catchment areas with underground storage tank and a number of stand pipes	Maintenance of system in decline after government stopped paying care-taker Centralized management style Conflicts between Nyen and Mbemi communities
Pakistan				
Ghaziabad	300	Subsistence and livestock farming	Initially an irrigation channel Gravity-fed systems with water tanks for storage and yard taps inaugurated in 1993	Low system pressure Poor water quality due to uncovered storage tanks Poor families unable to pay fees
Hoto	1200	Subsistence agriculture and livestock farming	Traditional sources Gravity-fed system with storage tanks and yard taps constructed in 1985	Water in poorly constructed storage tanks contaminated No caretaker, with president conducting maintenance Few community members paid O&M fee System fell into disrepair
Pakora (Bala – upper and Paeen – lower)	1700	Subsistence agriculture and livestock farming	Irrigation channels and traditional sources Gravity-fed system with water storage tanks and yard taps constructed in 1992	No training Poor construction of water storage tank Low rate of fee payment Disappointed caretaker No regular meetings
Hasis (Bala – upper and Paeen – lower)	1000	Subsistence agriculture and livestock farming	Irrigation channels and traditional sources Gravity-fed system with water storage tank and household taps and tap stands	Part of Hasis not connected Lack of dialogue between stakeholders Quarrels between caretaker and users No dedicated water committee No training

Community	Population to nearest 100)	Main occupation	Status of water supply system	Main management problems
Nepal				
Yampaphant	500	Subsistence agriculture and dairy production	Traditional sources Gravity-fed system with tap stands constructed in 1992 and pit latrines	Water source insufficient for system constructed Increasing refusal to pay fees Water users committee inactive Trained maintenance worker left village
Lele	400	Wage labour in agriculture and stone quarrying	Traditional sources Open flow gravity-fed system with tap stands constructed in 1993	Water users committee inactive Trained maintenance workers inactive Technical problems stemming from system design General conflict in community
Rangpur	1900	Subsistence agriculture and wage labour in agriculture	Traditional wells and rivers 72 boreholes with handpumps installed between 1992 and 1994	Inactive committees Not enough money to cover costs Suspicion among users about funds Lack of skills to carry out major repairs Political fighting for control
Gajedi	1600	Subsistence agriculture and wage labour in agriculture	Traditional wells One handpump and one tubewell installed around 1990 24 tubewells subsequently installed in 1992	Insufficient water yields and sand discharge from handpumps Irregular committee meetings Poor performance of maintenance worker Committee not registered Poor accounting and bookkeeping practices

APPENDIX 2

Country indicators

Category Indicator	Period	Cameroon	Colombia	Guatemala	Kenya	Nepal	Pakistan
Basic population data							
Total population (millions)	2000	14.9	42.1	11.4	30.7	23.0	141.3
Annual population	1975–						
growth rate (%)	2000	2.7	2.0	2.6	3.3	2.2	2.8
Predicted annual population	2000–						
growth rate (%)	2015	2.0	1.5	2.4	1.8	2.2	2.5
Basic economic data							
GDP PPP[1] (US$ billion)	2000	25.3	264.3	43.5	30.8	30.6	266.2
GDP per capita annual							
growth rate (%)	1990–2000	-0.8	1.1	1.4	-0.5	2.4	1.2
Population living below US$1							
income a day PPP[1] (%)	1983–2000[2]	33.4	19.7	10.0	26.5	37.7	31.0
Population living below							
national poverty line[3] (%)	1987–2002	40.0	17.7	57.9	42.0	42.0	34.0
Human Development Index[4]							
HDI[4] rank (out of 173)	2000	135	68	120	134	142	138
HDI[4] value	2000	0.512	0.772	0.631	0.513	0.490	0.499
HDI[4] value	1990	0.513	0.724	0.579	0.533	0.416	0.442
Life expectancy at birth (years)	2000	50.0	71.2	64.8	50.8	58.6	60.0
Adult literacy rate[5] (%)	2000	75.8	91.7	68.6	82.4	41.8	43.2
Educational enrolment ratio[6] (%)	1999[7]	43	73	49	51	60	40
GDP per capita PPP[1] (US$)	2000	1703	6248	3821	1022	1327	1928
Corruption Perceptions Index[8]							
CPI[8] score	2002	2.2	3.6	2.5	1.9	N/A	2.6
CPI[8] rank (out of 102)	2002	89	57	81	96	N/A	77
CPI[8] rank (out of 85)	1998	85	79	59	74	N/A	71

1 PPP (Purchasing Power Parity) is an adjustment that accounts for price differences across countries, allowing international comparisons of real output and incomes. PPP US$1 has the same purchasing power in mentioned economy as US$1 has in the USA.
2 Data refer to the most recent year available during the period specified.
3 National poverty line: the poverty line deemed appropriate for a country by its authorities.
4 Human Development Index (HDI): a composite index measuring average achievement in 'a long and healthy life' (indicator: life expectancy at birth), 'knowledge' (adult literacy rate and educational enrolment ratio) and 'a decent standard of living' (GDP PPP per capita). A higher index refers to a higher level of development, the maximum score being 1.
5 Percentage of people aged 15 years and over that can read and write.
6 Educational enrolment ratio: the number of students enrolled in primary, secondary and tertiary education as a percentage of the population of official educational age.
7 Preliminary UNESCO estimates.
8 Corruption Perceptions Index (CPI) ranks the degree to which corruption is perceived to exist among public officials and politicians. Corruption is defined as abuse of public office for private gain. The CPI is a composite index drawing on different polls and surveys from independent institutions carried out among business people and country analysts, including surveys of residents, both local and expatriate. A higher value and rank refers to less perceived corruption. Comparisons of indexes year-on-year are complicated by differences in available data.

SOURCES: (All data except CPI) UNDP (2002), *Human Development Report 2002: Deepening democracy in a fragmented world.* Oxford University Press, or http://www.undp.org/hdr2002/back.pdf; (CPI) Transparency International (1999), *Annual Report 1999*; Transparency International (2002), *Transparency International Corruption Perceptions Index 2002.* Transparency International, Berlin, or www.transparency.org.

APPENDIX 3

Exchange rates in US dollars

The table gives the exchange rates in US dollars of the currencies of the countries that participated in the PAR project, in February 1998 and February 2002.

Currency	Value in US dollars in February 1998	Value in US dollars in February 2002
100 Nepalese Rupee (NRs)	US$ 1.638	US$ 1.298
100 Pakistan Rupee (PRs)	US$ 2.272	US$ 1.659
100 Kenyan Shilling (KSh)	US$ 1.674	US$ 1.279
100 Cameroon CFA Franc (CFAfr)	US$ 0.163	US$ 0.132
100 Colombian Peso (Col. Peso)	US$ 0.074	US$ 0.044
100 Guatemalan Quetzal (Q)	US$ 15.995	US$ 12.5
100 South African Rand (SAR)	US$ 20.290	US$ 8.691

Source: *ABN AMRO Business Supporter 98–02,* p. 11 and *ABN AMRO Business Supporter 02–02*, p. 11

APPENDIX 4

PAR project documents used in Part 2

Kenya

Ikumi, P. (2001). *Community Management of Rural Improved Water Supplies – Country Case Studies: Kenya, Tanzania and Uganda.* Nairobi, Kenya, NETWAS.

NETWAS (1997). *Draft Report Participatory Action Research Synthesis Workshop, April 29 – May 4, 1997.* Nairobi, Kenya, NETWAS.

NETWAS and IRC (2001). *Kiveetyo: Putting ownership where it belongs.*
http://www.irc.nl/manage/manuals/cases/kiveetyo.html (October 23, 2002).

NETWAS and IRC (2001). *Nyakerato: One community, three water supply systems.*
http://www.irc.nl/manage/manuals/cases/nyakerato.html (October 23, 2002).

NETWAS and IRC (2001). *Sigomere: Getting organised.*
http://www.irc.nl/manage/manuals/cases/sigomere.html (October 23, 2002).

NETWAS and IRC (2001). *The Story of Yanthooko: Women taking the lead.*
http://www.irc.nl/manage/manuals/cases/yanthooko.html (October 23, 2002).

NETWAS (2001). *Report of a Workshop on Community Empowerment and Management Transfer in Rural Water Supply.* Nairobi, Kenya, NETWAS.

NETWAS (2001). *Report of the Exhibition and Workshop on Community Management: 'Lessons from the Grassroots'.* Nairobi, Kenya, NETWAS.

Oenga, I.O. (1995). 'The Role of Communities in the Management of Improved Rural Water Supplies Project: Participatory Action Research'. Conference Paper presented at: ITN Africa Conference, 5–8 December 1995, Harare, Zimbabwe. Nairobi, Kenya, NETWAS.

Oenga, I.O. (1997). 'Understanding the Role of Communities in the Management of Improved Rural Water Supplies: Participatory Action Research'. In: *Proceedings of 23rd WEDC Conference (1997), Water and Sanitation for All: Partnerships and Innovations.* Durban, South Africa.

Oenga, I.O. and Ikumi, P. (1998). *Sigomere: The voice of the community is heard, the case study.* Nairobi, Kenya, NETWAS.

Oenga, I.O. and Ikumi, P. (1998). *Kiveetyo.* Nairobi, Kenya, NETWAS.

Oenga, I.O. and Ikumi, P. (1998). *Kenya: The Nyakerato case study.* Nairobi, Kenya, NETWAS.

Oenga, I.O. and Ikumi, P. (1998). *Yanthooko Case Study.* Nairobi, Kenya, NETWAS.

Oenga, I.O. (2000). *Education for Developing Community Research and Training in East Africa.* Nairobi, Kenya, NETWAS.

Cameroon

Amouyé, N, Poubom, C. and Tayong, A. (1996). *Identification of Innovations and Indigenous Knowledge in Nyen-Mbemi, Batcham and Nkouondja.* Buea, Cameroon, PAID.

Amouyé, N, Poubom, C. and Tayong, A. (1996). *Identification of Potential Solutions with Communities.* Buea, Cameroon, PAID.

Amouyé, N, Poubom, C. and Tayong, A. (1996). *Problems Analysis and Prioritisation at Nyen-Mbemi, Batcham and Nkouondja.* Buea, Cameroon, PAID.

IRC and WSMC (2001) *Batcham: Stimulating community initiative.*
http://www.irc.nl/manage/manuals/cases/batcham.html (October 23, 2002).

IRC and WSMC (2001). *Bokito Rural: When resistance is changed into commitment.*
http://www.irc.nl/manage/manuals/cases/bokito.html (October 23, 2002).

IRC and WSMC (2001). *Nkouondja, Cameroon: A committed village leader.*
http://www.irc.nl/manage/manuals/cases/nkouondja.html (October 23, 2002).

Nchari, A.N. and Amouyé, N. (1994). 'Experiences in Community Water Management in Cameroon'. Paper presented at: The Planning and Training Research Workshop on the Role of Communities on the Management of Improved Rural Water Supplies in Developing Countries, held in The Netherlands, 17 October – 24 November 1994. Buea, Cameroon, PAID.

Tayong, A.M. and Jaff, B. (1999). *National Reference Group (NRG) Meeting Report: Participatory Action Research (PAR) on community-managed rural water supplies in developing countries.* Buea, Cameroon, PAID.

Tayong, A.M. and Jaff, B. (2001). *Report of a National Workshop on Community Management of Rural Water Supplies in Cameroon.* Buea, Cameroon, WSMC.

Tayong, A.M. (2001). *Report on the Systematisation Strategy*. Buea, Cameroon, WSMC.
Tayong, A.M. (2001). *State of the Art of Community Management of Water Supplies in Cameroon*. Buea, Cameroon, WSMC.

Colombia
Bastidas, S.P.F. (2001). *Asociación de Organizaciones Comunitarias Prestadoras de los Servicios de Agua y Saneamiento de sur Occidente Colombiano: Sistematización de la Experiencia*. Cali, Colombia, CINARA–Universidad del Valle.
CINARA (1994). *Proyecto El Rol de las Comunidades en La Administración de Sistemas de Abastecimiento de Agua Rural: Revisión Bibliografía*. Cali, Colombia, CINARA – Universidad del Valle.
CINARA (1995). *Taller Presentación de Proyecto a La Sirena*. Cali, Colombia, CINARA – Universidad del Valle.
CINARA (1995). *Taller de Presentación del Proyecto: Localidad de Ceylán, Municipio de Bugalagrande – Valle del Cauca*. Cali, Colombia, CINARA – Universidad del Valle.
CINARA (1995). *Taller de Capacitación en Diagnostico Participativo La Sirena*. Cali, Colombia, CINARA – Universidad del Valle.
CINARA (1996). *El Desarrollo del Proyecto en Colombia: Balance de los Dos Primeros Años*. Cali, Colombia, CINARA–Universidad del Valle.
CINARA (1996). *Diagnostico Comunitario de Ceylán (Bugalagrande) Valle Del Cauca*. Cali, Colombia, CINARA – Universidad del Valle.
CINARA (1996). *Taller de Capacitación en Diagnostico Participativo Campoalegre*. Cali, Colombia, CINARA – Universidad del Valle.
CINARA (1996). *Taller de Intercambio Comunitario Recuperación del Proceso con los Equipos de Investigadores Comunitarios (E.I.C.)*. Cali, Colombia, CINARA – Universidad del Valle.
CINARA (2001). *Estudios de Caso en Gestión Comunitaria*. Cali, Colombia, CINARA–Universidad del Valle.
CINARA and IRC (2001). *Campoalegre: Local watershed management to ensure a sufficient water supply*. http://www.irc.nl/manage/manuals/cases/campoalegre.html (October 23, 2002).
CINARA and IRC (2001). *La Sirena: Women taking leading positions*. http://www.irc.nl/manage/manuals/cases/sirena.html (October 23, 2002).
CINARA and IRC (2001). *Ceylán: Overcoming political interference*. http://www.irc.nl/manage/manuals/cases/ceylan.html (October 23, 2002).
CINARA and IRC (2002). *Gestión Comunitaria*. http://www.irc.nl/manage/cinara/ (October 23, 2002).
García, M.V. (2001). *La Gestión Comunitaria de Sistemas de Abastecimiento de Agua en Colombia en Poblaciones Menores de 12.000 Habitantes: La persistencia de lo local en un mundo globalizado*. Cali, Colombia, CINARA – Universidad del Valle.
Gomez, C.B. and Rojas, A.P. (1998). *La Sirena: Una Historia Entre Aguas*. Cali, Colombia, CINARA – Universidad del Valle. Completed in The Hague, The Netherlands.
Gomez, C.B. and Rojas, A.P. (1998). *Ceylán: The Challenges of Community Organisation*. Cali, Colombia, CINARA – Universidad del Valle.
Gomez, C.B. and Rojas, A.P. (1998). *Campoalegre: Quenching Thirst*. Cali, Colombia, CINARA – Universidad del Valle.
Pérez, M.A.R. (2001). *Análisis Comparativo entre la Gestión Comunitaria y Otras Formas de Gestión de Servicios de Agua y Saneamiento en Pequeñas Localidades en Colombia*. Cali, Colombia, CINARA–Universidad del Valle.

Nepal
Hari, M.S. (1998) *The Role of Communities in the Management of Improved Rural Water Supply Systems, Learning by observation: Case studies of the Gajedi Ward No. 2 in Rupandehi District, the Gajedi Ward No. 4 in Rupandehi District, the Yampaphant, Tanahu District, the Rangpur Ward No. 1, 7 and 8 Rautahat District, Nepal*. Kathmandu, Nepal, NEWAH, PAR Project.
Madhav B. (1998). *Participatory Action Research on the Role of Communities in the Management of Improved Rural Water Supplies. Sustainable Development through Community Management. The Case Study of Gajedi*. Kathmandu, Nepal, NEWAH, PAR Project.
NEWAH (2001). *The Gajedi Community – Nepal*. http://www.irc.nl/manage/manuals/cases/gajedi.html (October 23, 2002).
NEWAH (2001). *Lele Community in Nepal: Trying out different water tariff collection systems*. http://www.irc.nl/manage/manuals/cases/lele.html (October 23, 2002).

181

NEWAH (2001). *Rangpur: The long path to a reliable water supply service.*
 http://www.irc.nl/manage/manuals/cases/rangpur.html (October 23, 2002).
NEWAH (2001). The *Yampaphant Community: Overcoming problems with a previous water supply system.*
 http://www.irc.nl/manage/manuals/cases/yampa.html (October 23, 2002).
NEWAH (2001). *Country Study Report Nepal Community Water Supply and Management Situation.* Madhav
 Bhattarai Communication Section Nepal Water for Health. Kathmandu, Nepal, NEWAH.
NEWAH (1995). *Report on Intra-Project Exchange Cum Observation Visits of Lele and Yampaphant Water
 Supply System Projects.* Kathmandu, Nepal, NEWAH.
NEWAH (1995). *Project Exchange Visit Cum Observation Visits of Gajedi and Rangpur Water Supply System
 Projects.* Kathmandu, Nepal, NEWAH.
NEWAH (1995). *The Role of the Communities in the Management of Improved Rural Water Supplies. Nepal
 Country report.* Kathmandu, Nepal, NEWAH.
Paudyal, L. (1998). *Participatory Action Research on the Role of the Communities in the Management of Improved
 Rural Water Supplies: Struggle for sustainable development in Yampaphant, Tanahu.* Participatory Action
 Research Project, Kathmandu, Nepal, NEWAH.
Paudyal, L. and Khadka, R. (1998) *Report of Community Workshop Lele, Lalitpur.* Kathmandu, Nepal,
 NEWAH.

Pakistan

Aga Khan Health Service Northern Areas and Chitral. (1997). *Summary of Mid-term Review Pakistan.*
 Participatory Action Research, Water Sanitation Hygiene and Health Studies Project.
Ahmad, T. and Alibhai, K. (2000). 'Health and hygiene education programmes: Northern
 Pakistan'. In: *26th WEDC Conference Water, Sanitation and Hygiene: Challenges for the Millennium.* Dhaka,
 Bangladesh.
Ahmed, J. and Alibhai, K. (2000). 'Community management of RWSS in Northern Pakistan.
 Evolution of Women's Involvement in Water and Sanitation Projects in Northern Pakistan'. In:
 26th WEDC Conference Water, Sanitation and Hygiene: Challenges for the Millennium. Dhaka, Bangladesh.
Halverson, S.J. and Aziz N. (1998). *Hoto, Pakistan: A Village on The Road to Change.* Gilgit, Pakistan,
 Water and Sanitation Extension Programme, WASEP.
Halverson, S.J. (1998). *The Role of Communities in the Management of Improved Rural Water Supplies in
 Developing Countries. 'Winding Up' Workshop in Preparation for The Final Documentation of Process and Results.*
 Gilgit, Pakistan, WASEP.
Hussain, M., Khan, S. and Alibhai, K. (2000). 'Water tariffs: a challenging issue for WASEP
 implementation'. In: *26th WEDC Conference Water, Sanitation and Hygiene: Challenges for the Millennium.*
 Dhaka, Bangladesh.
Pervaiz, A.N. and Hussain A. (1994). *A Situation Analysis of Rural Water Supply and Sanitation in Pakistan.*
 Prepared for The Planning and Training Workshop at IRC International Water and Sanitation
 Centre, The Hague, The Netherlands.
Saleem, M, Hussain A. and Dilferoze (1994). *A case study of Village of Madinatul Karim, Gilgit, Pakistan.*
 Prepared for The Planning and Training Workshop, IRC International Water and Sanitation
 Centre, The Hague, The Netherlands.
WASEP and IRC (2001). *Ghaziabad: The importance of a local leader.*
 http://www.irc.nl/manage/manuals/cases/ghaziabad.html (October 23, 2002)
WASEP and IRC (2001). *Hasis: A traditional system of fining.*
 http://www.irc.nl/manage/manuals/cases/hasis.html (October 23, 2002)
WASEP and IRC (2001). *Hoto: A village on the road to change.*
 http://www.irc.nl/manage/manuals/cases/hoto.html (October 23, 2002)
WASEP and IRC (2001). *Pakora: How to manage an originally unwanted water supply system.*
 http://www.irc.nl/manage/manuals/cases/pakora.html (October 23, 2002)
WASEP (2001). *Water and Sanitation Extension Programme of the Aga Khan Planning and Building Service
 Pakistan.* www.irc.nl/manage/wasep (October 23, 2002)
WASEP (1998). *Consequences of a Gifted Water Supply Scheme. Case Study #4.* Participatory Action
 Research on the Role of Communities in the Management of Improved Rural Water Supplies.
 Gilgit, Pakistan, WASEP.
WASEP (2002) *Impact of Participatory Action Research in Hasis: The community of clans.*
Water and sanitation extension programme the Aga Khan planning and building service for
 Pakistan. Gilgit, Pakistan, WASEP.
WASEP (2000) *Drinking Water Status in Northern Pakistan.* Pakistan, WASEP.

Guatemala

Agua del Pueblo (1996). *Informe Proceso de la Fase no. 2 Investigación Participativa de Campo.* Guatemala, Agua del Pueblo.

Agua del Pueblo (1996). *Memoria del Taller Sobre Diagnostico Participativo y Técnicas para la Participación Comunitaria.* Guatemala, Agua del Pueblo.

IRC and SER (2001). *The Aguacatán Case Study: How seven rural communities manage their water supply.* http://www.irc.nl/manage/manuals/cases/aguacatancs.html (October 23, 2002).

IRC and SER (2001). *Barrel Chiquito: Dealing with financial matters – from loans to water fees.* http://www.irc.nl/manage/manuals/cases/chiquito.html (October 23, 2002).

IRC and SER (2001). *Belén: How to change ineffective management.* http://www.irc.nl/manage/manuals/cases/belen.html (October 23, 2002).

SER, Equipo IAP Guatemala (1998). *Como la Comunidad Maneja el Abastecimiento de Agua; Caso Aguacatán, Huehuetenango, Guatemala.* Quetzaltenango, Guatemala, SER, and Delft, The Netherlands, IRC International Water and Sanitation Centre.

SER, Equipo IAP Guatemala (1998). *Experiencia de Gestión Comunitaria en la Comunidad de Belén, El Palmar, Quetzaltenango, Guatemala.* Quetzaltenango, Guatemala, SER.

SER, Equipo IAP Guatemala (1998). *Experiencia de Gestión Comunitaria en la Comunidad de Barrel Chiquito, San Cristóbal Cucho, San Marcos, Guatemala.* Quetzaltenango, Guatemala, SER.

SER, Equipo IAP Guatemala (1998). *Experiencia de Gestión Comunitaria en la Comunidad de Aguacatán, Huehuetenango, Guatemala.* Quetzaltenango, Guatemala, SER.

SER, Equipo IAP Guatemala (2000). *Como Siete Comunidades Rurales Mejoran su Capacidad para la Gestión del Agua (caso Aguacatán).* Quetzaltenango, Guatemala, SER.

SER, Equipo IAP Guatemala (2001). *Las Mujeres Dirigiendo un Sistema de Abastecimiento de Agua (estudio de caso de la comunidad de Barrel Chiquito).* Quetzaltenango, Guatemala, SER.

SER, Equipo IAP Guatemala (2001). *Paso a Paso: Las mujeres empujando la gestión comunitaria del abasto de agua rural (cantón Belén).* Quetzaltenango, Guatemala, SER.

South Africa

Mvula Trust (2002). *Community Sanitation: A selection of stories from the IRC Lessons Learnt Project 2000 / 2001.* South Africa, The Mvula Trust and The Department of Water Affairs and Forestry, and Delft, The Netherlands, IRC International Water and Sanitation Centre. http://www.mvula.co.za/ur/fieldstories/Community%20Sanitation_IRC%20LL%20stories.pdf (October 23, 2002).

Mvula Trust (2002). *Community Water Supply: A selection of stories from the IRC Lessons Learnt Project 2000 / 2001.* South Africa, The Mvula Trust and The Department of Water Affairs and Forestry, and Delft, The Netherlands, IRC International Water and Sanitation Centre. http://www.mvula.co.za/ur/fieldstories/Community%20Water%20Supply_IRC%20LL%20 stories.pdf (October 23, 2002).

Mvula Trust (2002). *Water and Sanitation: The Mvula Trust Policies and Sector Challenges: A Selection of stories from the IRC Lessons Learnt Project 2000 / 2001.* South Africa, The Mvula Trust and The Department of Water Affairs and Forestry, and Delft, The Netherlands, IRC International Water and Sanitation Centre. http://www.mvula.co.za/ur/fieldstories/Policies%20and%20challenges_IRC%20LL%20stories.pdf (October 23, 2002).

Other relevant documents from and on the PAR project

Gomez, C.B. and Rojas, A.P. (1997). *La IAP Un Enfoque Para El Fortalecimiento de la Gestión Comunitaria de los Servicios Públicos: Tres Casos Ilustrativos – Experiencia en Colombia.* Cali, Colombia, CINARA – Universidad del Valle.

International Institute for Environment and Development (IIED) (1999). *Community Water Management.* PLA notes, no. 35, Participatory Learning and Action. Sustainable Agriculture and Rural Livelihoods Programme, London, UK, IIED.

IRC International Water and Sanitation Centre (1997). *Water Supplies Managed by Rural Communities: Country reports and case studies from Cameroon, Colombia, Guatemala, Kenya, Nepal, and Pakistan.* The Hague, The Netherlands, IRC International Water and Sanitation Centre (IRC project and programme paper 5-E).

IRC International Water and Sanitation Centre (2000). *Community Management: The Way Forward, Workshop Report.* Rockanje, The Netherlands, IRC International Water and Sanitation Centre.

IRC International Water and Sanitation Centre (2002).'From System to Service: Scaling up community management'. In: *Report on Proceedings of the 'From System to Service' mini-conference*. Held at The Hague, The Netherlands, December 2001. Delft, The Netherlands, IRC International Water and Sanitation Centre.

IRC International Water and Sanitation Centre (2002). *Beyond Community Management of Rural Water Supply: Proceedings and resource material of an e-conference*. Delft, The Netherlands, IRC International Water and Sanitation Centre. http://www.irc.nl/manage/debate/econf.html (October 23, 2002).

Lammerink, M.P, Bolt, E. and Bury, P. (1998). 'Putting Community Management in Place: Four years of experience with improving water management in rural communities'. In: *Community Managers for Tomorrow*. Document no. 1. The Hague, The Netherlands, IRC International Water and Sanitation Centre.

Lammerink, M.P, Bolt, E. and Bury, P. (1998). 'The Participatory Action Development Approach: Supporting community water management'. In: *Community Managers for Tomorrow*. Document no.3. The Hague, The Netherlands, IRC International Water and Sanitation Centre.

Lange, E. de (Ed.) (1998). 'Learning in the field: how 22 communities improved their water management'. In: *Community Mangers for Tomorrow*. Document no. 2. The Hague, The Netherlands, IRC International Water and Sanitation Centre.

Publications that came out of the PAR project

Bitting, C.D. (2001). *Water Management with a Difference.* Video. Yaounde, Cameroon, WSMC and Delft, The Netherlands, IRC International Water and Sanitation Centre.

Bolt, E. and Fonseca, C. (2001). *Keep it Working: A field manual to support community management of rural water supplies.* Delft, The Netherlands, IRC International Water and Sanitation Centre. (Technical Paper series no. 36).

Bolt, E. and Fonseca, C. (2002). *How to Support Community Management of Water Supplies: Guidelines for managers.* Delft, The Netherlands, IRC International Water and Sanitation Centre. (Technical Paper series no. 37).

Cepeda, C. (2001). *La Gestion del Agua.* Video. Cali, Colombia, CINARA and Delft, The Netherlands, IRC International Water and Sanitation Centre.

Joshi, S. (2001). *Pani, Water.* Video. Kathmandu, Nepal, NEWAH and Delft, The Netherlands, IRC International Water and Sanitation Centre.

Porres, A. (2001). *El Costo del Agua.* Video. Quetzaltenango, Guatemala, SER and Delft, The Netherlands, IRC International Water and Sanitation Centre.

Schouten, T. (2001). *The Seventh Video on Community Water Supply Management.* Video. Delft, The Netherlands, IRC International Water and Sanitation Centre.

Sumar, S. (2001). *Search for Water: Clean water is a basic right.* Video. Gilgit, Pakistan, WASEP and Delft, The Netherlands, IRC International Water and Sanitation Centre.

Wandago, A. (2001). *Our Water, Our Management.* Video. Nairobi, Kenya, NETWAS and Delft, The Netherlands, IRC International Water and Sanitation Centre.

References

Ahmed, J. and Lagendijk, M.M. (1996). *Water and Sanitation Inventory of 986 Villages of Northern Areas in Pakistan.* Issue paper no.8, Water, Sanitation and Hygiene and Health Studies Project, Aga Khan Health Service, Northern Areas and Chitral, Pakistan.

Andersen, R. (1989). *Rural Water Supply and Sanitation in Sub-Saharan Africa: A strategy brief.* Washington DC, USA, World Bank.

Appleton, B. (1994). *Water: A Priority for Life: A quarter of a century of caring for water supply and sanitation.* The Hague, The Netherlands, IRC International Water and Sanitation Centre.

Arebahona, I. (2000). 'Community Based Management System (CBMS) for rural water supply in Uganda: An integral component to development'. In: *Water and Sanitation News*, vol.7, no.1. Nairobi, Kenya, NETWAS.

Barrientos, C. (1988). 'Saneamiento Alternativo por Autogestión Comunitaria: Guatemala'. In: Guibbert, J. (1988). *Saneamiento Alternativo o Alternativas de Saneamiento: Actas del 1er seminario latinoamericano sobre saneamiento alternativo, Medellín, Colombia, Julio 24–29 de 1987.* Bogotá, Colombia, ENDA América Latina. pp.389–406.

Black, M. (1998). *Learning What Works: A 20 year retrospective view on international water and sanitation cooperation, 1978–1998.* Washington, DC, USA, UNDP–World Bank Water and Sanitation Programme.

Bos, A. (2001). *The Role of Engineers in the Demand Responsive Approach: A study from South Africa.* Loughborough, UK, WEDC.

Brikké, F. (2000). *Interview with François Brikké, 24 May 2000.* Delft, The Netherlands, IRC International Water and Sanitation Centre.

Chambers, R. (1983). *Rural Development: Putting the last first,* Harlow, UK, Longman.

Chang, K.K. (1969). *Intensive Village Health Improvement in Taiwan, Republic of China.* Ottawa, Canada, International Development Research Centre (IDRC).

DWAF (2001). *Free Basic Water Implementation Strategy.* Department of Water Affairs and Forestry, Pretoria, South Africa. Available from http://www.dwaf.gov.za/FreeBasicWater/Defaulthome.htm

Earth Summit (2002). *Roadmap to 2002.* Web site with link to Nordic Fresh Water Initiative (1991). http://www.earthsummit2002.org/roadmap/freshwat.htm (February 24, 2002).

Evans, P. and Appleton, B. (1993). *Community Management Today: The role of communities in the management of improved water supply systems.* The Hague, The Netherlands, IRC International Water and Sanitation Centre.

Galvis, C. Gerardo et al. (1997). 'Searching for sustainable solutions'. In: Visscher, J.T. (ed) (1997). *Technology Transfer in the Water Supply and Sanitation Sector: A learning experience from Colombia.* The Hague, The Netherlands, IRC International Water and Sanitation Centre and Cali, Colombia, CINARA. (IRC Technical Paper Series; no.32-E).

Garcia Vargas, M. (2001). 'Association of Community Based Organisations – Colombia'. In: *Report on Proceedings of the 'From System to Service' Mini-conference.* Held at The Hague, December 2001. Delft, The Netherlands, IRC International Water and Sanitation Centre. pp.27–32.

Gomez, C.B. and Rojas, A.P. (1997). *La IAP Un Enfoque para el Fortalecimiento de la Gestión Comunitaria de los Servicios Públicos: Tres casos ilustrativos – experiencia en Colombia.* Cali, Colombia, CINARA – Universidad del Valle.

Guijt, I. and Shah, M.K. (1998). 'Waking up to power, conflict and process'. In: Guijt, I. and Shah, M.K. (eds) (1998). *The Myth of Community: Gender issues in participatory development.* London, UK, ITDG Publishing.

GWSC, Ghana Water and Sewerage Corporation (1989). *Bolgatanga Community Water Supply and Sanitation Management Project: Progress report July – 1989 – December.* Accra, Ghana.

Hukka, J.J. (1998). *Institutions, Organisation and Viable Water Services: A capacity development model for drinking water provision and production.* Tampere, Finland, Tampere University of Technology.

ICWE, (1992). *The Dublin Statement on Water and Sustainable Development,* International Conference on Water and the Environment, ICWE.

Inpes-Bogota (1975). *Manual de Procedimientos en Promoción Comunitaria para el Programa Nacional de Saneamiento Básico Rural.* Bogotá, Colombia, Instituto Nacional para Programas Especiales de Salud.

IRC International Water and Sanitation Centre (1988). *Community Participation and Women's Involvement in*

185

Water Supply and Sanitation Projects: A compendium paper. The Hague, The Netherlands, IRC International Water and Sanitation Centre (IRC Occasional Paper Series no.12).

IRC International Water and Sanitation Centre (2001). *Community Water Supply Management: Stories from the field*. http://www.irc.nl/manage/stories (October 21, 2002).

Knecht, T. (1989). *Eine Untersuchung der Nachhaltigkeit von Wasserversorgungsprojekten auf der Basis von 'Community Development'*. Zurich, Switzerland, Zurich University.

Korten, D.C. (1986). *Community Management: Asian experience and perspectives*. West Hartford, CN, USA, Kumarian Press.

Lammerink, M.P., Bolt, E. and Bury, P. (1998). 'The Participatory Action Development Approach: Supporting community water management'. In: *Community Managers for Tomorrow*. Document no.3. The Hague, The Netherlands, IRC International Water and Sanitation Centre.

Lovell, C. (2000). *Productive Water Points in Dryland Areas: Guidelines on integrated planning for rural water supply*. London, UK, ITDG Publishing.

Minnigh, P. and Moeliono, M. (2001). 'Rural Water Supply Systems, An Alien Body for the Public Good: Case Study of Indonesia 1999–2000'. In: *Waterlines*, vol.19, no.3, pp.22–25. London, UK, ITDG Publishing.

Moriarty, P.B. and Lovell, C.J. (2000). 'Simplest is not always best – physical and climatic constraints to community water supply in Zimbabwe'. In: *Waterlines*, vol.19, no.2, pp.9–12. London, UK, ITDG Publishing.

Moriarty, Patrick (2002). 'Sustainable Livelihoods Approaches: An explanation'. In: *Waterlines*, vol.20, no.3, pp.4–6. London, UK, ITDG Publishing.

Narayan-Parker, D. (1989). *Indonesia: Evaluating community management: A case study*. New York, USA, PROWWESS, United Nations Development Programme.

Nchari, A.N. and Amouyé, N. (1994). 'Experiences in Community Water Management in Cameroon'. Paper presented at The Planning and Training Research Workshop on the Role of Communities on the Management of Improved Rural Water Supplies in Developing Countries, held in The Netherlands, 17 October–24 November 1994. Buea, Cameroon, PAID.

Njuguna, V., Ikumi, P. and Oenga, I.O. (2000). *Report for the Follow-up Community Evaluation of the Participatory Action Research Programme in Kenya*. Nairobi, Kenya. NETWAS.

Oenga, I.O. and Ikumi, P. (1997). *The Role of Communities in the Management of Improved Rural Water Supplies*. Nairobi, Kenya, NETWAS.

Otte, C. and Budhathoki, R. (2002). *Draft RCD Nepal Country Profile*. Kathmandu, Nepal, NEWAH.

Parwoto (1986). *A Model for Community Based Management Projects: A guideline for establishing a sectoral project at local level*. Jakarta, Indonesia, Ministry of Public Works, Agency for Research and Development, Institute of Human Settlements.

Rai, R. and Subba, H. (1997). 'Drinking water system management in rural Nepal'. In: *Water Supplies Managed by Rural Communities: Country report and case studies from Cameroon, Colombia, Guatemala, Kenya, Nepal and Pakistan*. The Hague, The Netherlands, IRC International Water and Sanitation Centre.

Rall, M. (2000). 'Cost Recovery at all Costs?' In: *Maru A Pula: Newsletter of the Mvula Trust*, no.16, March 2000. pp.1–3.

Razeto, J. (1988). 'Participación y gestión local: Chile'. In: Guibbert, J. (1988). *Saneamiento Alternativo o Alternativas de Saneamiento: Actas del 1er seminario latinoamericano sobre saneamiento alternativo, Medellín, Colombia, Julio 24–29 de 1987*. Bogotá, Colombia, ENDA América Latina. pp.443–451.

Republic of South Africa (1997). *The Water Services Act, Act 108 of 1997*, The Department of Water Affairs & Forestry. Government Gazette 18522, Government Printer, Pretoria. 108. 2001.

Roark, P., Buzzard, S. and Yacoob, M. (1989). *Towards Community Management: A guide to integrating behavioral sciences and engineering technology in water and sanitation projects*. Arlington, VA, USA, Water and Sanitation for Health Project (WASH).

Saladin, M. (2002). Wittenbach: Where a club for a few evolved into a co-operative for all. In: Wehrle, K. (Ed.) (2002). *Community Water Supply in Switzerland: Series of case studies*. St. Gallen, Switzerland, SKAT Foundation.

Sara, J. and Katz, T. (1997). *Making Rural Water Supply Sustainable: Report on the impact of project rules*. Washington DC, USA, UNDP–World Bank Water and Sanitation Program.

Schumacher, E.F. (1973). *Small is Beautiful: Economics as if people mattered*. New York, USA, Harper & Row.

SER, Equipo IAP Guatemala (2001). *Reporte de Abastecimiento de Agua Gestión Comunitaria: El caso de Guatemala*. Quetzaltenango, Guatemala, SER.

Shordt, K. (2000). *Action Monitoring for Effectiveness: aMe: Improving water, hygiene and environmental sanitation programmes: part I*. Delft, The Netherlands, IRC International Water and Sanitation Centre. (IRC Technical Paper Series: no.35).

Smits, S. (2001). *Perfil de Colombia, Su Sector Hídrico y CINARA*. Delft, The Netherlands, IRC International Water and Sanitation Centre.

Suchman, E.A. (1967). *Evaluative Research: Principles and practice in public service of social action programs*. New York, USA, Russell Sage Foundation.

Sutton, S., SWL Consultants – London, Mwansa, O.C. and Irish Aid – Dublin (1998). *Review of Irish Aid Support to the Water Sector in Zambia*. Lusaka, Zambia, Irish Aid.

Tayong, A.M. (2001). *State of the Art of Community Management of Water Supplies in Cameroon*. Buea, Cameroon, WSMC.

UNDP (1990). 'Global consultation on safe water and sanitation for the 1990s', New Delhi, India, September 10–14, 1990. Background paper. New York, USA, Secretariat for the Global Consultation on Safe Water and Sanitation for the 1990s.

UNICEF Pakistan (2001). *Water, Environment and Sanitation Programme: Update of situation analysis*. Pakistan, UNICEF.

United Nations ACC Sub-Committee on Water Resources (2001). *Water: A key resource for sustainable development: report of the Secretary-General*. New York, USA, United Nations Economic and Social Council. http://www.johannesburgsummit.org/web_pages/ prepcom1documents/sgrepwater.doc (October 22, 2002).

Visscher, J.T. and Lammerink, M.P. (1998). 'Putting Community Management in Place'. Paper presented at the International Symposium on Suitable Water Management and Technologies for Small Settlements. Delft, The Netherlands, IRC International Water and Sanitation Centre.

WASEP (2000) *Drinking Water Status in Northern Pakistan*. Gilgit, Pakistan, WASEP.

Water and Energy Commission Secretariat (WECS) (2001). *Draft Water Resource Strategy Nepal*. Kathmandu, Nepal, His Majesty's Government of Nepal.

Water Supply and Sanitation Collaborative Council (WSSCC) (1996). 'Third Global Forum: People and water – partners for life'. Biennial forum of the Water Supply and Sanitation Collaborative Council, Barbados, 30 October–3 November 1995, meeting report. Geneva, Switzerland, Water Supply and Sanitation Collaborative Council.

Water Supply and Sanitation Collaborative Council (1997). *Code of Ethics on Hygiene, Sanitation and Water Supply Services*. Geneva, Switzerland, Water Supply and Sanitation Collaborative Council. http://www.wsscc.org/load.cfm?edit_id=167 (October 29, 2002).

Water Supply and Sanitation Collaborative Council (2000a). *Vision 21: A shared vision for hygiene, sanitation and water supply and a framework for action*. Geneva, Switzerland, Water Supply and Sanitation Collaborative Council.

Water Supply and Sanitation Collaborative Council (2000b). *Iguaçu Action Programme*. Fifth Global Forum, Foz do Iguaçu, Brazil, 24–29 November 2000. http://www.wsscc.org/load.cfm?edit_id=78 and http://www.jiscmail.ac.uk/files/WSSCC/IAP_Core_Document.doc (October 23, 2002).

Whiteside, G. and Shrestha, V. (2000). *A Short Review of Nepal's Rural Drinking Water Sector*. Vol.3, Appendices. London, UK, Department for International Development.

WHO, UNICEF and WSSCC (2001). *Global Water Supply and Sanitation Assessment 2000 Report*. Geneva, Switzerland, WHO and WSSCC, and New York, UNICEF. http://www.who.int/water_sanitation_health/Globassessment/Global6-2.htm (October 23, 2002).

Wijk-Sijbesma, C.A. van (1979). *Participation and Education in Community Water Supply and Sanitation Programmes: A selected and annotated bibliography*. Voorburg, The Netherlands, IRC International Water and Sanitation Centre.

Wijk-Sijbesma, C.A. van (1981). *Participation and Education in Community Water Supply and Sanitation Programmes: A literature review*. The Hague, The Netherlands, IRC International Water and Sanitation Centre.

World Bank Group Water Supply and Sanitation (2002). Rural Water Supply and Sanitation: Links to information on Demand Responsive Approach (DRA). http://www.worldbank.org/html/fpd/water/rural.html (February 24, 2002).

Yelbert, J.E. (1999). 'Community management practices in Ghana'. In: WEDC (1999), *Integrated Development for Water Supply and Sanitation: Proceedings of the 25th WEDC conference*. Addis Ababa, Ethiopia.

187

Index

Note: A full list of acronyms appears on pages xiv-xvi at the front of the book.